BEYOND THE THRESHOLD

The measurement and analysis of social exclusion

Edited by Graham Room

The POLICY
PRESS

First published in Great Britain in 1995 by

The Policy Press
University of Bristol
Rodney Lodge
Grange Road
Bristol BS8 4EA

Telephone (0117) 973 8797
Fax (0117) 973 7308
E-mail: tpp@bris.ac.uk
Website: http://www.bris.ac.uk/Publications/TPP

First published 1995
Reprinted 1997

British Library Cataloguing in Publication Data
A catalogue record for this book is available from the British Library

ISBN 1 86134 003 6

Cover design by Qube, Bristol. Cover illustration by Andy Roberts, supplied by Tony Stone Images.

The Policy Press works to counter discrimination on grounds of gender, race, disability, age and sexuality.

Printed in Great Britain by Hobbs the Printers Ltd, Southampton.

CONTENTS

PREFACE

This book began life as a seminar sponsored by the Directorate-General V of the European Commission (EC) and the United Kingdom Department of Social Security (DSS). I am grateful to them for their encouragement in preparing these papers for publication and to the authors for undertaking the necessary revisions.

Viv Harper undertook the substantial burden of secretarial work involved in the text and I most grateful to her.

Graham Room
Bath
August 1995

LIST OF CONTRIBUTORS

Isa Aldeghi is Research Fellow at the Centre de Recherche pour L'Etude et L'Observation des Conditions de Vie in Paris, where she is a member of the department of social policy evaluation. Her recent work includes studies on unemployment, minimum income recipients and the development of poverty and housing indicators.

Jos Berghman is Professor at the DSS and Dean of the Faculty of Social Sciences at Tilburg University (The Netherlands). His main research interests are comparative and European social security and poverty policies.

Michael Bradford is Senior Lecturer in Geography and Dean of Students in the Arts Faculty at Manchester University. His research is focused on the analysis of the delivery of public goods and services. He has published extensively in the field of education.

Petra Buhr is Assistant Professor at Bremen University's Life Course and Welfare State Research Unit. She works on family as well as social policy and on poverty issues.

Peter Golding is Professor of Sociology at Loughborough University. His current research interests include the social impact of new communication technologies, and the links between the media and social policy.

Hans Kristensen is Deputy Director of the Danish Building Research Institute and Head of Research in the Division of Housing and Urban Planning. His main research interest lies in the problems of social exclusion and integration in urban and housing areas.

Stephan Leibfried is a co-director of the Bremen Centre for Social Policy Research. He has worked on poverty issues. Presently he is working on European social policy and on the interface of globalisation and national welfare states.

Frank Moulaert is Professor of Economics at the University of Lille I. His research interests are in regional development and urban planning. His recent publications deal with the link between economic globalisation and local development.

Serge Paugam is a member of the Observatoire Sociologique du Changement (operating under the auspices of CNRS/FNSP) and of the Laboratoire de Sociologie Quantitative (of the INSEE). His research deals with poverty and the effects of social policies, in particular in the countries of Europe.

Brian Robson is Pro-Vice-Chancellor at Manchester University and Director of Manchester University's Centre for Urban Policy Studies. His research is on aspects of urban policy, both in academic work on urban social areas and in applied work on the evaluation of urban policy.

Graham Room is Professor of European Social Policy at Bath University. He was formerly coordinator of the European Observatory on Policies to Combat Social Exclusion and coordinated the evaluation of the second European poverty programme. He is editor of the *Journal of European Social Policy*.

Rachel Tye was a research associate in the Centre for Urban Policy Studies at Manchester University and, since 1995, has been a researcher for Manchester City's Department of Planning.

Robert Walker is Director of the Centre for Research in Social Policy and Professor of Social Policy Research, Loughborough University of Technology. He has written widely on poverty, social assistance and the evaluation of public policies.

Brendan J. Whelan has been Head of the Survey Unit at the Economic and Social Research Institute (ESRI), Dublin, since 1978. His main interests are in the areas of survey methodology and in the application of survey techniques to studies of labour market functioning, poverty and income distribution and social policy.

Christopher T. Whelan is a sociologist at the ESRI, Dublin. He has published a number of papers dealing with the conceptualisation and measurement of poverty, the psychological consequences of unemployment and poverty and the relative value of class and underclass persectives. He is also joint author with Brian Nolan of *Resources, deprivation and poverty* (forthcoming from Clarendon Press).

Francesca Zajczyk is Professor of Methodologies and Techniques of Social Research at the Department of Sociology of the University of Milan. Her main fields of interest are poverty (with particular attention to methodological aspects) and the conception of time.

LIST OF FIGURES AND TABLES

Figures

Tables

LIST OF ABBREVIATIONS

BSHG	Federal Social Assistance Law
CBS	Central Bureau of Statistics
CDU	Christian Democratic Union
CERC	Centre d'Etudes des Revenus et des Couts
CNRS	Centre National de la Recherche Scientifique
CREDOC	Centre de Recherche pour l'Etude et l'Observation des Conditions de Vie
DoE	Department of the Environment
DSS	Department of Social Security
ED	Enumeration District
EEC	European Economic Community
EMU	Economic and Monetary Union
ESF	European Social Fund
ESRI	Economic and Social Research Institute
ESSPROS	European System of Integrated Social Protection Statistics
EU	European Union
Europass	European Research on Poverty and Social Security
GHQ	General Health Questionnaire
IFRESI	Institut Fédératif de Recherche sur les Economies et Sociétés Industrielles
INSEE	Institut National de la Statistique et des Etudes Economu
ISTAT	Istituto Centrale di Statistica
LIC	Low Income Commission
LIS	Luxembourg Income Study
LSA	Longitudinal Survey of Social Assistance Files
NUTS	Nomenclature des unités territoriales statistiques
REPLIC	Répertoire de Localisation Infra-Communale
RMI	Revenu Minimum d'Insertion
SDS	Social Deprivation Scale
SEP	Socio-Economic Panel
SRB	Single Regeneration Budget

one

POVERTY AND SOCIAL EXCLUSION: THE NEW EUROPEAN AGENDA FOR POLICY AND RESEARCH

Graham Room

Introduction

Recent years have seen increasing concern about the growth of poverty and social exclusion within Europe. In western Europe this has been associated with the resurgence of high unemployment; in central and eastern Europe the problems of the transition to a market economy are now raising similar concerns.

This growing concern has been evident in debates at the level of the European Union (EU). The anti-poverty programmes that the European Commission has been sponsoring have included action projects, research studies and efforts at statistical harmonisation. However, concern about social exclusion has now spilled outside the narrow realm of the social security section of the Directorate-General V (DGV) (Employment, Industrial Relations and Social Affairs). Social exclusion is written into the Maastricht Treaty and into the objectives of the Structural Funds. The Directorate-General XII (DGXII) (Science, Research and Development) includes social exclusion within its Fourth Framework Research Programme. Alongside these initiatives by the EU institutions, the Council of Europe has recently been commissioning studies of social exclusion focused on the wider range of European countries that make up its membership, and informed by its specific interest in human rights (Duffy, 1995). European research on social exclusion seems destined to expand quite markedly during the next few years.

Nevertheless, this growing range of initiatives is built on the series of poverty programmes that have been in progress since the mid-1970s. It may therefore be worth recalling the history of these programmes, as background to the argument in the rest of this chapter.

The poverty research of the European Union: a brief history

The first European anti-poverty programme (1975-80) included nine national reports on poverty and anti-poverty policy (European Commission, 1981). In some ways, these reports were the most significant element of that first programme, for in several countries (Italy, for example) the publication of the report spurred a new national debate. Alongside these national studies, people such as Peter Willmott were responsible for cross-national studies on particular aspects of poverty – in Willmott's case, unemployment, social security and poverty in France, Germany and the United Kingdom (Mitton et al, 1983). The first of a series of reports on the perceptions of poverty held by citizens in different European Commission countries in the mid-1970s was also sponsored by the first poverty programme (European Commission, 1977).

The second anti-poverty programme (1986-89) marked one step back and one step forward as far as research was concerned. With the European Parliament calling for action and not words, the European Commission planned the programme with no research element as such. Nevertheless, as part of our evaluation of the action programme (Room et al, 1993) we commissioned studies of national policies echoing the national reports of the first programme. As part of this same evaluation we engaged Michael O'Higgins and Stephen Jenkins to produce their estimate of the total number of poor in the Community: a figure of 44 million for the mid-1980s. The step forward was that the statistical office of the European Commission, Eurostat, was engaged to work on the long-term improvement of poverty indicators. As part of this, Eurostat set in motion discussions with the national statistical offices concerning the use of household budget surveys for producing comparable data on low income groups.

The third programme (1990-94) saw the reinstatement of a series of cross-national studies. Also of some significance has been the so-called 'Observatory' on policies to combat social exclusion (Room et al, 1991; 1992; Robbins et al, 1994). This Observatory, involving a network of research institutes, complements the other Observatories that the European Commission has established in the social policy field, dealing, for example, with family policy, policies in relation to elderly people and social security policies.

Accompanying these developments have been improvements in the data available for cross-national comparisons. Eurostat is, as already indicated, playing a growing role in orchestrating the harmonisation of national social statistics (for example, in relation to household budget surveys); and the European Commission has launched a European Community Household Panel Survey that could provide a powerful instrument for enquiries into the movement of households into and out of poverty (Eurostat, 1993). Probably no less significant than these initiatives by the European Commission has been the work of the Luxembourg Income Study (LIS). This project, by gathering together and rendering comparable more than 40 large microdata sets, from more than 17 countries, provides an international standard for cross-national studies of household incomes and of their relationship to social security and taxation policies (de Tombeur and Ladewig, 1994).

Within this succession of programmes there has been a varied vocabulary of disadvantage. 'Poverty' was at the heart of the Council Decisions that launched the first and second programmes and an explicit definition was provided that was loosely indebted to Peter Townsend. The third programme, in contrast, was concerned with the integration of the 'least privileged' – we are all privileged but some are less privileged than others. By the time the programme was actually launched, 'social exclusion' became the fashionable terminology. It is debatable as to how far these shifts reflect any more than the
• hostility of some governments to the language of poverty, and the enthusiasm of others to use the language of social exclusion. Many of the shifts in substance that have taken place in European research on disadvantage would probably have taken

place, whether the language of social exclusion or poverty had prevailed; and these shifts are in any case sometimes over-stated. Nevertheless, there has been at least some change of substance and it is to these that we now turn.

Poverty and social welfare: the wider debates

In surveying the history of European studies of poverty one is struck by an apparent anomaly. This is the disjunction between the poverty literature on the one hand and, on the other, the debates that have been raging over the different types of 'welfare regime' that characterise different industrial societies. In recent years we have seen the resurgence of an important body of literature concerned with the types of welfare system to be found in different European countries (Esping-Andersen and Korpi, 1984; Esping-Andersen, 1990). The focus is on the nation state, even if occasionally these writers ask what type of welfare regime may be emerging at the supranational level of the EU. National welfare regimes are distinguished according to the generosity of the welfare benefits that they provide, their coverage of different sections of the population and, most important, the extent to which these welfare benefits 'tame' the labour market, protecting the individual worker against its insecurities.

No student of social policy has been able to ignore these debates as they have developed over recent years. Yet, what is striking about much of the recent cross-national literature on poverty is its almost complete insulation from these debates. Leibfried and his colleagues have been almost alone in seeking to bridge this gap (Leibfried and Pierson, 1992). Leibfried has been looking at the place of anti-poverty policy within different welfare regimes: extending from the residual policies of the Anglo-Saxon world to the efforts of conservative and social democratic regimes to protect the worker from the insecurities of the market. Leibfried goes on to ask which of these different anti-poverty regimes is likely to characterise the emerging social policy of the EU. His answer is pessimistic. He expects that the EU in its anti-poverty policy, will be similar to the United States – the poor will be dealt with principally at local and national levels, while any new rights of European social citizenship are the preserve of more privileged sectors of the 'core' population (rights of workers, rather than rights to work or to earn a decent wage).

However, a major reconfiguration of the European poverty discussion may now be under way, offering the prospect of more substantial conceptual links with the literature on welfare regimes (see also Silver, 1994; Yepez del Castillo, 1994). This can best be explained by digressing briefly, in order to recall the history of the poverty studies that have been sponsored by the European Commission. When, in the late 1970s, the European Commission first launched studies of national poverty policies and poor populations, French researchers in particular proved to be most uncomfortable about using the Anglo-Saxon tradition of poverty lines (European Commission, 1981). During the 1990s, in contrast, under the inspiration of Delors and the French political debate, the European Commission is developing studies and programmes around the theme of 'social exclusion'. For example, in 1990, as already mentioned, the European Commission set up a network (Observatory), to monitor national trends and policies in the field of social exclusion. Apart from the French, however, most researchers involved in these European Commission studies, having been schooled in the Anglo-Saxon tradition, found it difficult to know how to operationalise 'social exclusion' as a point of reference for the analysis of policies and how to anchor it within any well-established intellectual tradition (Room et al, 1992).

This mutual incomprehension highlighted the very different theoretical paradigms that these two traditions seem to involve for analysing poverty and social exclusion. The notion of poverty is primarily focused upon distributional issues: the lack of resources at the disposal of an individual or a household. In contrast, notions such as social exclusion focus primarily on relational issues, in other words, inadequate social participation, lack of social integration and lack of power.

These two sets of concepts can be related to the different intellectual traditions from which they derive. Research into poverty, in its modern scientific form, is primarily an Anglo-Saxon (more specifically a British) product of the nineteenth century (Rowntree, 1901; Townsend, 1979). It is closely associated with the liberal vision of society, under which society was seen by the relevant intellectual and political elites as a mass of atomised individuals engaged in competition within the market place. The goal of social policy was to ensure that each person had sufficient resources to be able to survive in this competitive arena. It must be acknowledged, of course, that Peter Townsend, as the most prominent contemporary heir of this tradition, judges the sufficiency of the resources at the disposal of an individual or households by whether or not the person is able to 'participate' in the activities customary in their society. He thus makes an effort to break out of the limitations of the Anglo-Saxon legacy and also to include relational elements. Nevertheless, with his focus on the resources that individuals need to have at their command, distributional issues are still at the heart of his definition (Townsend, 1979).

In contrast, notions of social exclusion are part of a continental – and perhaps more particularly a French – tradition of social analysis. Society is seen by intellectual and political elites as a status hierarchy or as a number of collectivities, bound together by sets of mutual rights and obligations that are rooted in some broader moral order. Social exclusion is the process of becoming detached from this moral order (Castels, 1990). If it is the liberal vision of society that inspires the Anglo-Saxon concern with poverty, it is the conservative vision of society (using that term in Esping-Andersen's sense) that inspires the continental concern with social exclusion. Or, insofar as the principal moral rights and obligations that shape social relations are those of an egalitarian citizenship, rather than traditional hierarchies, it is (again using the term in Esping-Andersen's sense) the social democratic vision that shapes the debate on social exclusion.

It is in relation to these social rights of citizenship that one recent attempt to synthesise the two conceptual traditions can be viewed. The afore-mentioned European Observatory on Policies to Combat Social Exclusion (established by the European Commission in 1990), roots its analysis of social exclusion in these social rights (Room et al, 1991; 1992). Within the countries of the EU it is generally taken for granted that each citizen has the right to a certain basic standard of living and to participate in the major social and occupational institutions of the society. This right may or may not be expressed in legal terms; it may or may not be rooted in custom and tradition; and it may be precise or only vague in its formulation. Some statements of rights (including the European Commission's Social Charter) are no more than a declaration of policy that it is hoped will be put into effect some day. Nevertheless, such social rights are regularly reaffirmed in policy statements at national and Community levels (see, for example, European Commission, 1990a).

Social exclusion can be analysed in terms of the denial (or • non-realisation) of these social rights: in other words, in terms of the extent to which the individual is bound into membership of this moral and political community. Here, one obvious point of reference in the social scientific literature is Marshall's essay on citizenship and social class (Marshall, 1950), demonstrating, incidentally, that this is no simple debate between an Anglo-Saxon liberal tradition and its continental opponent. However, this is not the end of the matter. Where citizens are unable to secure their social rights, they will tend to suffer processes of generalised and persisting disadvantage and their social and occupational participation will be undermined. It is therefore also necessary to examine patterns and processes of generalised disadvantage in terms of education, training, employment, housing, financial resources, etc – in short, disparities in the • distribution of life chances. This may then also require us to investigate the ways in which inadequate resources and the denial of access to social rights may, if they persist long term, separate one subgroup of the population from the normal living patterns of the mainstream of society (Robbins, 1990).

Integrating the two conceptual traditions distinguished above, the Observatory thus sought to investigate social exclusion in both relational and distributional terms. To evaluate, on the one hand, the extent to which some groups of the population are denied access to the principal social and occupational milieux and to the welfare institutions that embody modern notions of social citizenship; to examine, on the other hand, the patterns of multidimensional disadvantage to which these groups are then vulnerable, especially insofar as these persist over time. It is as a successor to this effort at integration that the papers that are brought together in this book can be seen.

The new policy context of social exclusion research

The foregoing discussion has suggested that the conceptual terrain on which European poverty studies are now operating has changed significantly in recent years, and it is now becoming more connected with wider discussions of social welfare in Europe. The research agenda is, of course, reshaped not only by immanent developments within the research community, but also by policy shifts in the world of political action.

These developments include the Delors White Paper, concerned with growth, competitiveness and employment and the Flynn White Paper, concerned with social policy (European Commission, 1993b; 1994a). Both give a central place to combating unemployment and promoting reinsertion into work, as the most important single element in efforts to combat social exclusion. On the other hand, some of their proposals – concerned, for example, with increased flexibility and reduced social charges – could increase the levels of precarious employment and the risks of exclusion that more vulnerable groups of workers are facing. At the same time, under the convergent disciplines of Economic and Monetary Union (EMU), a number of member states are taking steps to cut back on social expenditure, in ways that are likely to increase levels of poverty and risks of social exclusion (Miller, 1993). These processes of European integration therefore hold threats, as well, no doubt, as opportunities, for efforts to combat disadvantage, and it will be important to ensure that the new generation of research studies that are launched during the coming years take these threats as one of their major points of reference.

It is against this double background of conceptual reconfiguration and policy change that the papers included in this book must be judged. They were originally presented at a major seminar convened at the University of Bath, under the sponsorship of the European Commission and the UK Department of Social Security (DSS) in 1994. The seminar had three principal concerns:

• the conceptualisation of social exclusion

- the measurement of social exclusion (in particular, using already available data sources)

- the definition of indicators for monitoring the effectiveness of policies for combating social exclusion.

The paper by Berghman assesses the conceptualisations of social exclusion evident in the various research activities sponsored by the European Commission in recent years. Subsequent contributions are concerned with the multidimensionality of social exclusion (Whelan and Whelan, Paugam), its dynamics (Zajczyk, Walker, Leibfried) and its spatial dimension (Kristensen, Aldeghi, Moulaert, Robson). Golding addresses the implications of public attitudes for the choice of indicators. All deal (albeit to varying degrees) with conceptualisation, measurement and policy indicators.

The final chapter brings together their findings and identifies some of the implications for policy indicators, for statistical measurement and for the conceptualisation of social exclusion.

two

SOCIAL EXCLUSION IN EUROPE: POLICY CONTEXT AND ANALYTICAL FRAMEWORK

Jos Berghman

Introduction

Any attempt to locate social exclusion from a social policy point of view must use a European frame of reference. For the policy-making context, in which social exclusion has been put, the agenda was not the traditional national one that was dominant in the old discussions of poverty and social deprivation, but rather the European policy level. Moreover, the various programmes, networks and initiatives that were subsequently set up at the European level constitute the framework in which the first attempts took shape to operationalise, analyse and monitor social exclusion. The first section of this contribution will therefore deal with the European policy context in which the fight against social exclusion came to figure. The second section will discuss the conceptual framework in which the concept of social exclusion should be located. The third section will focus on the ways in which its assessment and monitoring have been elaborated thus far and will venture some suggestions as to what the next steps should be.

Yet, before embarking on these issues it may be necessary to dwell somewhat on the way in which the concept of social exclusion was launched. It is, after all, a rather new concept – although it might have been used earlier as one of the many concepts that have been ventured as possible synonyms for poverty, its systematic use is of rather recent date (for an overview of concepts with some reference to poverty, see Bouget and Nogues, 1993). Towards the end of the second European poverty programme the European Commission published a document in 1988 in which reference was made to 'social exclusion'. One year later the concept was referred to in the preamble to the European Social Charter stating that "in the spirit of solidarity it is important to combat social exclusion" (European Commission, 1990b). In the same year the Council of Ministers adopted a resolution on "combatting social exclusion" (Council of the European Communities, 1989). The Council could do little more than request member states to combat social exclusion among their own citizens by improving their own policies. Yet it also called on the European Commission "to study, together with the Member States, the measures they are taking to combat social exclusion" and to report back (Commins, 1993, p 3ff). Following on from this, the European Observatory on Policies to Combat Social Exclusion was established and this has published three synthesis reports based on reports by 12 national experts (Room et al, 1991; 1992; Robbins et al, 1994). Meanwhile, the European Community Programme to Foster Economic and Social Integration of the Least Privileged Groups, the so-called third European Commission poverty programme or 'Poverty 3', had been launched. It originally covered 27 model and 12 innovative action projects for the period 1989-94 that would focus on multidimensional actions to foster economic and social integration involving (in some form of partnership) all relevant economic and social agents.

The members of the Observatory and the action researchers who were active in self-evaluating and steering the activities of the Poverty 3 projects were among the first to be confronted with the social exclusion concept. (An attempt to bring together and systematise the insights of the action researchers of the Poverty 3 programme was made by a working group: see Bruto da Costa et al, 1994.) The discussion that follows seeks to capitalise on the preliminary conclusions that they reached when attempting to establish a grasp on the concept (see also Robbins, 1993).

The context

Social exclusion is an issue that is part of broader social policies
and debates. Yet, at the national and even more so at the
European level, important developments can be pointed to that
are of relevance for the concept and policies of social exclusion.

At the European level, the social objectives and com-
petences have traditionally been quite restricted. Although
Article 2 of the Treaty of Rome mentioned the improvement of
living conditions as a basic objective of the European Economic
Community (EEC), the way this objective was further
operationalised and backed by possible competencies for the
European Commission-institutions gave proof of a rather
passive attitude. Articles 117 and following, suppose that the
improvement and harmonisation of living and working
conditions, and of social protection in the broader sense, will
follow almost automatically from the common market.

Yet, confronted with new social challenges, such as
increased life expectancy, changes in the structure of the family,
instability of the labour market and persistently high levels of
unemployment, and being aware of possible social dislocations
engendered by a more developed single market, the European
Community was challenged to take a more active approach.
The Maastricht Treaty on European Union (EU) included "a
high level of employment and of social protection" as explicit
objectives of the EU (Council of the European Communities,
1992b, Article 2). As far as EU activities were concerned, a
policy in the social sphere, comprising a European Social Fund
(ESF), the strengthening of economic and social cohesion and a
contribution to the attainment of a high level of health
protection were added to the list of Article 3 of the Treaty.
Finally, the Protocol on Social Policy and the Agreement that
was based on it (concluded among the member states other than
the United Kingdom), envisaged further objectives and
initiatives in the social field. Article 1 of this Agreement
explicitly mentions lasting high employment and the combating
of exclusion as objectives of the Community and the member
states. In the same vein, Article 2 states that the Community
shall support and complement the activities of the member
states in, among others, the field of integration of persons
excluded from the labour market. In these fields decisions can

even be taken by a qualified majority. However, in areas such as social security and the social protection of workers, and with respect to financial contributions for the promotion of employment and job creation, the Council would only be able to act unanimously (Article 3 of the Agreement).

Overall, one could say that the Maastricht Treaty, and its Protocol and Agreement on Social Policy, demonstrate a greater awareness of the social dimension of the EU than was previously the case. However, with some exceptions (for example, the ESF), full competencies remain restricted. Yet, at least for the 11 member states that signed the Agreement on Social Policy, the fight against exclusion is somewhat easier to embark on than other policy areas. To some extent, however, this is quite astonishing, as this approach is not in line with what would be a logical policy approach – a logical approach would be one that takes account of the basic logical chain underpinning social policy. This logical chain holds that we educate and train people to ensure that they can be adequately inserted into the labour force. Such an insertion should give these people the opportunity to gain a primary income. This income in turn enables people to have command over resources to guarantee their social participation. Yet, when this logical chain is interrupted because of unemployment or incapacity to work, social protection systems operate to provide replacement income in order not to endanger social participation. Meanwhile, restorative actions, such as work mediation, retraining and even partial reemployment schemes, are activated with the aim of securing rapid reinsertion into the labour market, thereby restoring the logical chain. When both the reinsertion devices and the income protection schemes are inadequate, however, the risk of exclusion materialises. So what is astonishing with the European approach is that exclusion, the last step in the logical chain, can more easily be addressed at the European level than the phases that precede it.

On closer consideration, however, it is far from clear how this European social policy approach should be judged. A first interpretation could be that this approach is quite in line with the subsidiarity principle as laid down in Article 3b of the Maastricht Treaty. This article says that

> ... in areas which do not fall within its exclusive
> competence, the Community shall take action,

in accordance with the principle of subsidiarity, only if and in so far as the objectives of the proposed action cannot be sufficiently achieved by the Member States and can therefore, by reason of the scale or effects of the proposed action, be better achieved by the Community.

One could interpret this to mean that the EU is not entitled to interfere in social policy matters until situations of exclusion show that the member states are unable to confront the situation adequately. A second interpretation, however, would be that even the Maastricht Treaty has defined EU competencies in the social field in a highly inadequate way. In fact, if the preservation of our logical chain is the ultimate objective for social policy then preventive employment policies and restorative reintegration policies should get priority over curative benefit schemes and over actions to curb exclusion. We see that the EU gradually grows into an economic, monetary and even fiscal community. At the same time the core policy level, not only in economic affairs but also with respect to employment opportunities, gradually shifts to the European level. This being the case, the basic choices with respect to social protection should, to a growing extent, be taken at the European level. The existence of situations of exclusion should then be considered as proof that the competencies given to the EU level are far from adequate. The European Commission White Paper on 'Growth, competitiveness and employment' could be considered as a first indicator for this line of thought (European Commission, 1993b).

An important development manifests itself also at the national level. The post-war welfare state was elaborated under the condition of full employment. Recent decades, however, have shown, first a steady increase of the unemployment rate and afterwards, high unemployment figures and high numbers of long-term unemployed (Room et al, 1990; European Commission, 1994a). Doubts are growing as to the possibilities of curbing this trend significantly and of reinserting the unemployed. Even if successful macroeconomic policies and intensive employment policies should succeed, the odds are that in the short and medium term a significant proportion of the active population cannot be reinserted into the labour market (European Commission, 1993a). This category will remain under attack. Our logical chain suggests that, even if they could not be reinserted into the labour market, they would at least get adequate income support to secure their social insertion in society. However, in spite of deficient labour demand, the work ethic and attempts to preserve a high incentive to work produce pressures to limit their benefit levels (Jehoel-Gijsbers and Vissers, 1995). The effect will be double-sided – not only will their income position and hence their material basis for social participation be undermined, but in addition, processes of mental retreat will be further intensified (Jehoel-Gijsbers and Heinen, 1991). Hence, social policy authorities at the local level are confronted with the double challenge of ensuring adequate income support and of replacing availability for work with availability for social integration as the ultimate entitlement condition. What is at stake is a renewed operationalisation of the last link of the logical chain, in order to safeguard social participation. Here again (the prevention of) exclusion is at the centre of attention.

Finally, the spatial dimension is receiving growing attention. At the EU level the Regional, Social and Cohesion Funds are being reassessed as instruments for curbing regional disparities. Also, at the lower levels of urban and rural policies, processes of multidimensional decline, of social demoralisation and even social unrest call for attention. Hence the notion of spatial exclusion has been launched, referring not so much to spaces where there are poor persons but to 'poor spaces' themselves. As the Poverty 3 programme has shown, such a space may be a poor region, a poor 'island' surrounded by a developed region, an urban ghetto or a shanty town. In such cases, the approach cannot be focused only on persons and groups, but has also to take account of the whole community. The notion of target groups, although not necessarily inappropriate, becomes incomplete, since ultimately the target group is the community of the space as a whole. For similar reasons, in such contexts the current notion of a programme to combat poverty shifts closer to that of a local development programme (Bruto da Costa et al, 1994, pp 8-9). Yet, both at the macro level of the European regions (NUTS 1 level) and at the meso level of urban and rural areas (NUTS 2 and 3 levels) there is a growing need for adequate indicators on which to base preferential policy treatment and its monitoring.[1]

So, the European as well as the local level are confronted with the issue of social exclusion. Both levels have to tackle important challenges for which major policy options present themselves. The measurement and analysis of social exclusion are no longer an interesting analytical and research topic but an issue that is full of policy relevance. In addition to this, there is a growing awareness of the spatial dimension of social exclusion. Also, with respect to this aspect, a growing need for adequate information presents itself as a prerequisite for valid policy making.

A conceptual matrix

In the realm of analysis and research, 'social exclusion' is a rather new concept. At first sight it was launched at the European level as a practical alternative to the old poverty concept. The latter, in fact, still lingered on in the abbreviated 'Poverty 3' notion of the European Community Programme to Foster Economic and Social Integration .... Yet, from soon after the social exclusion concept was first used, the European Commission stuck systematically to it. The original reason for this shift seems to have been political, as the member states (who have a guaranteed minimum income deemed sufficient to cover basic needs) expressed reservations about the word poverty when applied to their respective countries. 'Social exclusion' would then be a more adequate and less accusing expression to designate to the existing problems and definitions (Bruto da Costa et al, 1994, p 3). However, as the new concept seemed to refer more to the dynamic aspect of process that is at the basis of poverty and as it bore a less unidimensional connotation with the income dimension of poverty, the concept of social exclusion was soon accepted in action research and policy statements. For researchers, the question remains whether it is a useful concept and how it can be distinguished from older core concepts, such as poverty and deprivation. I suggest that the concept of social exclusion, as it has been documented so far, has two distinct connotations: its comprehensiveness and its dynamic character. Together these connotations make it a difficult, but at the same time, a very useful concept.

Comprehensiveness

According to Ringen, poverty can be defined and measured in two ways: directly (in terms of living conditions and consumption) and indirectly (in terms of income) (Ringen, 1988). A direct definition of poverty is one in terms of deprivation: "... a standard of consumption which is below what is generally considered to be a decent minimum." (Ringen, 1988, p 354). (In addition, Ringen argues that adding the adjective 'relative' to deprivation is redundant as poverty – be it defined in subsistence [income] terms or in deprivation terms – is always 'relative' [p 353].) Such a definition is called direct because it focuses on the actual living conditions of persons and households. Measuring poverty using an income poverty line, on the other hand, is an indirect method: poverty is assessed on the basis of the disposable income of the household. Such an approach is called indirect because it is not the actual living conditions that are being measured but only one of the determinants of these conditions. Based on this distinction, Ringen made a harsh criticism of the prevalent research on poverty as it often combines a direct definition (in terms of consumption) with an indirect measurement instrument (income poverty line). Even Peter Townsend, who pioneered the relative deprivation approach, makes this mistake. He has defined it as follows:

> People are relatively deprived if they cannot obtain, at all or sufficiently, the conditions of life – that is, the diets, amenities, standards and services – which allow them to play the roles, participate in the relationships and follow the customary behaviour which is expected of them by virtue of their membership of society. (Townsend, 1993)

Yet his reasoning continues: "If they lack or are denied resources to obtain access to these conditions of life and so fulfil membership of society they may be said to be in poverty ...". Under the 'relative deprivation' approach, a threshold of income is conceived, according to size and type of family, below which withdrawal or exclusion from an active membership of society becomes disproportionately accentuated

(Townsend, 1993, p 36). So Townsend, although defining poverty directly in deprivation terms, soon switches to an indirect approach by looking for an income threshold. Veit Wilson comments that

> ... exclusion is meant here in the weak sense, that lack of income excludes people from social activities which cost money. That income threshold would be a poverty line. In practice, this is sometimes found to be a band of income rather than any hard line. (Veit Wilson, 1994)

One could add that in market economies, such as the EU member states, access to a certain standard of living depends upon the resources available to buy them in the market. In this sense, the monetary indicator, in fact, reflects a diversified set of items and should not be considered as a unidimensional indicator. In this sense also, the tendency of Townsend to translate a relative deprivation concept into disposable income terms should not be criticised too sharply.

Veit Wilson's comment is in line with the notions of poverty and social exclusion that emerged from the Poverty 3 programme. The action researchers of that programme pointed to a major difference between poverty and social exclusion in the sense that the former concept has to do with a lack of resources, whereas the latter is more comprehensive, and is about "much more than money" (Bruto da Costa et al, 1994, p 6). By making this distinction between poverty and social exclusion, these action researchers could point to the real meaning that implicitly had been given to poverty at the European level for almost two decades. Already in 1974 the European Council had defined poverty as referring to "individuals or families whose resources are so small as to exclude them from the minimum acceptable way of life of the Member State in which they live." (Bruto da Costa et al, 1994, p 2). This broader, deprivation meaning of poverty now came to be seen by the action researchers as 'social exclusion'.

Even if there is agreement that the concept of social exclusion encompasses a broader range than just income or financial resources, the dimensions that it embraces have still to be indicated. The Poverty 3 researchers, and especially the Irish researchers, suggest that social exclusion should be defined in terms of the failure of one or more of the following four systems:

- the democratic and legal system, which promotes civic integration

- the labour market, which promotes economic integration

- the welfare state system, promoting what may be called social integration

- the family and community system, which promotes interpersonal integration.

According to Commins:

> One's sense of belonging in society depends on all four systems. Civic integration means being an equal citizen in a democratic system. Economic integration means having a job, having a valued economic function, being able to pay your way. Social integration means being able to avail oneself of the social services provided by the state. Interpersonal integration means having family and friends, neighbours and social networks to provide care and companionship and moral support when these are needed. All four systems are therefore, important. In a way the four systems are complementary: when one or two are weak the others need to be strong. And the worst off are those for whom all systems have failed ....
> (Commins, 1993, p 4)

In the way they refer to major social institutions, these researchers show some affinity with Marshall's analysis of citizenship (Marshall, 1950). In the latter's view, citizenship includes civil, political and social rights. Social exclusion could then be conceived in terms of the denial – or non-realisation – of citizenship rights, as the European Observatory on Policies to Combat Social Exclusion tried to do (Room et al, 1991, pp 5-7; 1992, pp 14-18). The action researchers, however, do not explicitly refer to the citizenship rights that may be put at risk, but to the major social institutions through which these rights should be materialised.

So, the conceptual differences become somewhat clearer: there is the traditional concept of poverty, which by now is restricted to denote a lack of disposable income, and there is the comprehensive concept of social exclusion, that refers to a breakdown or malfunctioning of the major societal systems that should guarantee full citizenship. Poverty, then, is part of – a specific form of – social exclusion. The latter is broader and should not necessarily always encompass an element of poverty. In between poverty and social exclusion there is the concept of relative deprivation. In theory, relative deprivation is in line with the social exclusion concept; in practice, however, its operationalisation has generally rendered it a broader version of the poverty concept. This double face of relative deprivation raises the question as to whether we will succeed in operationalising social exclusion in a more unambiguous way.

Process

The rapporteurs of the third European poverty programme point out that the projects that address the distinction between poverty and social exclusion understand the latter as a process and poverty as an outcome (Bruto da Costa et al, 1994, p 5). On closer scrutiny it becomes clear, however, that both poverty and social exclusion can have a double connotation. On the one hand, there is a static connotation, referring to the situation that has emerged, the outcome, whether this is a lack of disposable income (poverty) or a multifaceted failure (social exclusion). On the other hand, both concepts refer to a situation that has resulted from a process. Multidimensional social exclusion may be the outcome of a more complex process than is the case in situations of pure income poverty; nevertheless, poverty is also typically the result of a process of impoverishment. Corresponding to the analytical distinction between the process and its outcome, there is a need for two concepts, in the case of poverty as well as in the case of social exclusion. The author suggests using poverty and deprivation to denote the outcome, the situation, and to use impoverishment and social exclusion to refer to the process.

Table 2.1: Concepts

	Static outcome	Dynamic process
Income	Poverty	Impoverishment
Multidimensional	Deprivation	Social exclusion

As for the difference between poverty and social exclusion in their static meanings (ie, between poverty and deprivation as we are here using the terms) there is already some empirical evidence that the realities to which they refer, differ and hence that it is worthwhile to make a distinction between them. To give one example: in an analysis that was done on Dutch data for 1988, the overlap between deprivation and poverty seemed to be far from perfect (Muffels et al, 1992). As Table 2.2 shows, only 30% of the income poor are also deprived; on the other hand, 7.6% of the non-poor are deprived in other than income terms.

Table 2.2: Population by deprivation* and poverty†
(The Netherlands, 1988)

	Deprived (%)	Not deprived (%)	Total
Poor	29.9	70.1	100
Not poor	7.6	92.4	100

(N = 13,771)

* According to Subjective Deprivation Line 5.5.
† According to European Statistical Minimum Standard.

Source: Central Bureau of Statistics (CBS), Dutch Socio-Economic Panel, as reported in Muffels et al (1992) p 202

Further analysis even showed that the relationship between different kinds of poverty lines is much stronger than between poverty and deprivation lines, indicating that although poverty and deprivation are related, they are far from identical and can be considered as being complements instead of substitutes (Muffels, 1993b).

As far as the processes of impoverishment and social exclusion are concerned, so far we have a lot of casuistic, in-depth information but are still lacking coherent empirical evidence. Yet, as far as impoverishment is concerned, panel analyses already give us some idea of the very complex mechanisms that are at work (a good recent overview and discussion of the issues involved is provided by Walker, 1994; see also Walker's contribution to this book). To take an example from the same data-set: for The Netherlands it appears that the very stable number of the poor we find in each year conceals remarkable processes of mobility in and out of poverty. In each of the years 1985-88 some 10% of the population was in poverty. Yet taking the four years under consideration, as much as 20% of the population was hit by poverty in at least one of these years. On the other hand, only 0.5% was in poverty during the whole period. So, important mobility mechanisms are at work that act as trampolines to get people out of poverty. There are, in fact, two major trampolines that generate new income sources: finding employment, and changes in household composition. To these two trampolines that help people to jump out of poverty, a third device should be mentioned that prevents people from falling into poverty. In fact, the major brake that prevents households from sliding down into poverty is the availability of earnings-related, above-minimum social security protection. This prevents the majority of elderly, disabled and short-term unemployed people from sliding down to the minimum protection level, to poverty and further down to a situation of multidimensional deprivation (Dirven and Berghman, 1991). All this confirms the basic logical chain that was referred to earlier. Meanwhile, and with a view to monitoring, it pleads for having poverty or deprivation incidence indicators replaced by some sort of mobility indicators. The analysis of odds-ratios over time are a first step in that direction. (Odds-ratios indicate the relative probability of the poor getting out of poverty. See Dirven and Berghman, 1991, p 61ff.)

The operationalisation

It may be clear that in its static-outcome meaning, social exclusion, (ie, deprivation) is characterised by its comprehensiveness, embracing the multidimensional aspects of living conditions, and that in its process meaning its dynamic character is emphasised. Yet when focusing on the measurement and analysis of the social exclusion concept, its operationalisation should be scrutinised. Later chapters in this volume will deal with aspects of this in more detail. Here, however, we can consider the ways in which this problem has been – and has not been – tackled so far by the European networks, and for that purpose in a comparative perspective.

One preliminary observation should be made: what we want to deal with is the measurement and analysis of social exclusion, or to be more precise, of deprivation (static) and social exclusion (dynamic). So, this is not the place to deal with income poverty and impoverishment as such, although they may be part of the broader discussion on deprivation/social exclusion. However, it may be appropriate to recall that the measurement and analysis of income poverty are also of relatively recent date, certainly in a European, comparative context. The Europass Project (European Research on Poverty and Social Security), which was launched in the framework of the second poverty programme in the mid-1980s, was the first to embark on this line systematically. (Its main results were published in Deleeck et al, 1992.) In this project different poverty standards were used according to a common framework in five member states and two regions (Belgium, The Netherlands, Luxembourg, Ireland, Greece, Lorraine [France] and Catalonia [Spain]). In addition, a simple version of a relative deprivation indicator was applied, and a modest panel approach (two waves in some of the member states/regions) was tested. The analysis focused on poverty line methodologies, on the incidence of poverty and deprivation and on the adequacy of social security transfers for reducing poverty. In a cross-sectional approach, part of this analysis was later repeated and extended to other countries in the framework of the preparation of the European Commission's first report on the Council Recommendation on the convergence of social protection objectives and policies (Council of the European Communities,

1992a; European Commission, 1994b). Moreover, the experience gained in these analyses was instrumental in the feasibility and pilot studies for the European Community Household Panel Survey, which has been launched by Eurostat, the statistical office of the European Commission (Von Rosenbladt, 1990). This office also coordinated some secondary comparative analyses of income surveys, enabling some rough estimates of the poverty incidence in the member states (Eurostat, 1990), and made some progress in elaborating ESSPROS (the European System of Integrated Social Protection Statistics) (Eurostat, 1992). The latter, however, concentrates on expenditure figures and is unable to provide evidence on poverty, let alone on deprivation.

So far the social exclusion concept has been explicitly dealt with in two European initiatives: in the Poverty 3 (action research) programme and in the monitoring activities of the Observatory on social exclusion. On top of that, however, one could argue that the Poverty 2/Europass Project and the current European Community Household Panel constitute a third kind of initiative, insofar as they explicitly try to address the issue of multidimensional deprivation. However, it is striking that these three lines of action operate on quite distinct levels. Whereas Europass and the European Community Household Panel focus on empirical research, the third poverty programme dealt with innovative and model action projects and the Observatory has been assessing national policies. It is of primary importance to be aware of these differences in approach and objectives. The question here is the extent to which these different approaches can together contribute to a discussion on the measurement and analysis of social exclusion; not least, to what extent the experience of Poverty 3 and of the Observatory can provide guidelines and suggest priorities for researchers.

In dealing with the static element of deprivation, some considerable progress has been made by researchers in devising a workable methodology. Starting from Townsend, and capitalising on Runciman's relative deprivation theory and Kapteyn's preference formation theory, Muffels has made substantial advances (Muffels, 1993b; see also Whelan, 1993; Muffels, 1993a). The question remains, however, whether he and his colleagues will be able to encompass the valid dimensions. On the dynamic element, on the other hand, almost everything has still to be done. As mentioned already, in the European context the first dynamic analyses on impoverishment are becoming available in the framework of panel analyses and it is to be hoped that the many possible practical obstacles (especially access to data) will not discourage researchers in their efforts with the European Community Household Panel. However, we remain far removed from comprehensive empirical analyses of the process of social exclusion.

The European Observatory was confronted with quite a challenge – to study policies to combat social exclusion. It agreed on a sensible definition by taking "social exclusion to refer, first, to multidimensional disadvantage, which is of substantial duration and which involves dissociation from the major social and occupational milieux of society" (Room et al, 1992). This is in line with the comprehensive character of what we defined as deprivation. The elements of 'substantial duration' and 'dissociation from the major milieux' are useful additions that are worth empirical verification. Moreover, 'dissociation from the major milieux' reminds us of the four societal systems the Poverty 3 researchers suggested. Yet, when trying to find data to document this definition for each of the member states, the Observatory soon had to discover – or rather to confirm – that the available data sources are highly inadequate in relation to cumulative and enduring disadvantage. A systematic comparative analysis was entirely beyond the scope of the Observatory, which had to confine itself to using available information by way of illustration.

However, the Observatory was not concerned with social exclusion as such, but with policies to combat it. This raised the question of which policies had to be taken into account. The Observatory was wise enough not to restrict itself to those policies that are explicitly targeted on those who are already excluded. In line with the logical chain described earlier in this chapter, it examined a wider range of policies. In the absence of firm empirical or theoretical evidence, and in order to have some point of reference that was not entirely alien to social policy making, it took the 'social rights of citizens' as a kind of yardstick (most explicitly in the third annual report: Robbins, 1994, ch 3, p 25ff). To the extent that social rights (and civil and political rights that paved the way) are a (quasi) legal confirmation of both the basic rights of the citizens and the basic obligations of society, they are a good source of inspiration and are worth further systematic scrutiny, to inspire the list of dimensions that should be taken into account when deprivation and social exclusion are operationalised. The focus on policies meant that the Observatory was also involved in monitoring their effectiveness and performance. Such activities may shed light on poverty and deprivation, both before and after the effects of policy are taken into account. This information is of the utmost importance for the analysis of the dynamics of impoverishment and social exclusion and for the spatial dimension of deprivation.

The Poverty 3 programme was more removed from measurement and analysis than the Observatory. However, its action projects became familiar with the social exclusion concept and were an important vehicle for applying and popularising the concept. The Irish Poverty 3 participants reported:

> Already the term social exclusion is beginning to be used in Irish policy discussion. If we use it deliberately rather than casually, conscious of the special connotations attached to it and not to other terms, it could give us new insights on social problems and incentives to do something different about them. (Commins, 1993, p 6)

In a similar way, in countries such as Belgium, France and Portugal, Poverty 3 was instrumental for making social exclusion and its multidimensional and dynamic connotations part of the social policy discourse.[2] In a similar way of mobilising consciousness the concept figured in the third poverty programme itself. From the moment the programme was launched three leading principles were put forward against which the activities and progress of the projects were to be assessed: multidimensionality, partnership and participation (Poverty 3, 1992). For the action projects, partnership and participation figured as the key objectives, although multidimensionality (which referred to the comprehensive character of deprivation/social exclusion) represented a source of inspiration for action. As for analysis, any systematic empirical evidence was hardly available, as could be expected from an action research programme (although this observation does not relate to the limited number of explicit research projects that were launched in the framework of Poverty 3). Nevertheless, the many descriptive and evaluative reports that were written on the social context of the projects, on their activities and performance, are a gold mine for hypotheses on deprivation and social exclusion. These reports deserve attentive scrutiny by researchers before embarking on the next wave of qualitative exploratory studies.

Conclusion

The European level has been decisive for the introduction and spreading of the concept of social exclusion. To some extent this is astonishing. According to a logical social policy chain, one might expect that the European level would get competence for overall guidance of general societal institutions, such as the labour market and income protection, rather than focusing on complex situations and processes of social marginalisation. The launching of the concept of social exclusion at the European level may have been triggered by political reasons. This, however, does not preclude the concept yielding a real improvement of the conceptual framework that was previously used in poverty and relative deprivation studies. The multidimensional and dynamic connotations that it carried pointed to the necessity of enlarging the research field in two directions. Instead of focusing poverty research on a static description of income shortages, it showed the need, on the one hand to encompass a multidimensional set of living conditions, on the other hand, the process that leads to poverty or deprivation. In the case of (income) poverty the process of impoverishment then becomes an explicit focus of research; in the case of (multidimensional) deprivation it is the process of social exclusion that is at stake. In these terms the study of social exclusion becomes the ultimate aim for researchers in this field.

The initiatives that were taken by the then European Community in the late 1980s and early 1990s have supported this enlarged focus. Given their scale and duration, the results of these initiatives were bound to remain limited. Nevertheless, the research activities that have been (co)financed by the

European Commission, the Observatory, as well as the European Community Programme to Foster Economic and Social Integration ... have been instrumental in promoting the concept of social exclusion in social policy discourse and in making some progress in analysis. The latter is worth continuing effort, not least because the analysis of social exclusion may assist analysis of many basic dimensions of European social life in its complex, dynamic and comparative aspects.

Notes

1. According to NUTS (Nomenclature des unités territoriales statistiques) the EU consists of member states (NUTS level 0), which are divided into regions (NUTS level 1). Each region is divided into subregions (NUTS level 2), which are further subdivided (NUTS level 3). See Eurostat (1991).

2. An example for Belgium is provided in Vranken et al (1994). For more country-specific evidence see the national reports of the European Observatory on Policies to Combat Social Exclusion and the reports of the Poverty 3 programme that are issued by Animation and Research EEIG in Lille, France.

three

IN WHAT SENSE IS POVERTY MULTIDIMENSIONAL?

Brendan J. Whelan and Christopher T. Whelan

Introduction

Much recent research has focused on the 'multidimensional' nature of poverty. For many, as Berghman in his contribution to this volume notes, the concept of 'social exclusion' is preferable to that of poverty, because it carries less unidimensional connotations and because it directs attention to the more dynamic processes that are involved in producing situations of disadvantage. We will argue that clear conceptual distinctions must be made in using the term 'multidimensionality' since it may relate to the causes, descriptions or consequences of poverty. Clearly no one would wish to deny that poverty arises from a variety of processes or that it is experienced as involving a great deal more than an income defect. Paradoxically, however, an insistence on multidimensionality at the level of measurement of poverty could have the effect of obscuring the dynamics processes involved, leaving us incapable of distinguishing between the consequences of poverty, social class and a variety of specific forms of discrimination and social exclusion. In this paper we will argue that in embarking on a new phase of research guided by the concept of 'social exclusion' we should make sure that we incorporate the insights that 'conventional' poverty research affords us into the relationship between resources and deprivation and the dynamics underlying accumulated disadvantage.

Our paper begins with a review of the common definitions of poverty and methods of measuring it. It goes on to argue that simply combining the dimensions of poverty into an overall measure is not fruitful in improving our understanding of the processes underlying social exclusion. The second part of the paper presents an analysis of Irish poverty data. First, we consider the effect of marginalisation from the labour market (which is sometimes construed as a 'dimension' of poverty) as a causative or predisposing factor. Secondly, we present an analysis of the effects of poverty on psychological and physical health. These examples illustrate the importance of clearly specifying the nature of the variables and relationships used in studying poverty and social exclusion.

The measurement of poverty

Basic definition

Poverty is a complex and multifaceted phenomenon and its measurement has given rise to much controversy. A wide variety of conceptual and empirical approaches have been suggested but none has found universal acceptance (for a detailed review of approaches, see Callan and Nolan, 1991). Probably the most commonly applied technique is that of the income-based poverty line. This may embody either a relative concept (eg, O'Higgins and Jenkins, 1989) or an absolute concept (eg, the 'official' poverty line as used in the United States). There are, however, a number of major difficulties with the use of current income in this context.

Some researchers have tried to overcome these problems by using total expenditure as a proxy for income (Teekens and Zaidi, 1989). Others have developed techniques for incorporating 'subjective' or 'consensual' elements in the derivation of the poverty line. These include the Leyden Poverty Line, the Subjective Poverty Line (Goedhart et al, 1977) and the Centre for Social Policy Poverty Line (Deleeck et al, 1989). Ringen (1988) criticised poverty research for defining poverty 'directly' (ie, by reference to deprivation or inadequate consumption levels) and measuring it 'indirectly' (ie, by reference to income levels).

The use of 'deprivation indicators' offers the possibility of measuring poverty directly. This approach attempts to assess poverty by collecting data on the extent to which households possess certain commodities, can engage in certain activities or are subjected to financial pressures of different kinds. The set of items used is often thought of as a set of 'necessities', that is, a set of goods and services access thought to be customary for all in the society concerned.

The deprivation indicators' approach derives from the classic definition of poverty given by Townsend (1979).

> Individuals, families and groups in the population can be said to be in poverty when they lack the resources to obtain the type of diet, participate in the activities and have the living conditions and amenities which are customary, or at least widely encouraged, or approved, in the societies to which they belong. They are, in effect, excluded from ordinary living patterns, customs and activities. (Townsend, 1979, p 31)

Within the overall concept of poverty he distinguished 12 major subcategories or dimensions:

- dietary

- clothing

- fuel and light

- household facilities

- housing conditions

- work conditions

- health

- education

- environment

- family activities

- recreation

- social relations.

Several features of this definition should be noted. First, poverty is seen as being *attributable to lack of material resources*. People who are unable to participate in various customary activities, due to factors such as ill-health, poor education or isolation, may well be described by some other term such as 'deprived', 'marginalised' or 'socially excluded', but can only be categorised as 'poor' if their difficulties are due to lack of material resources. Indeed, even when social scientists use one of these other terms, their main focus is still, in most cases, on those who are materially disadvantaged. The problems of persons or groups who are relatively well off from a material point of view but who suffer exclusion for other reasons (for instance, because of their colour, age or health status) need to be analysed using different techniques and focusing on different social processes. Secondly, the definition emphasises the multidimensionality of poverty in that deprivation, due to lack of material resources, may arise from a variety of causes, and may have consequences for all aspects of a person's life – material, social and cultural.

The dimensions of poverty

Townsend's study has generated an enormous volume of comment, criticism and further work. Whelan (1993) reviews over 40 surveys that utilised various types of non-monetary indicators of poverty. It was found that two of Townsend's dimensions (viz. fuel and light and work conditions) were not included in any of the final sets of items used in any of these studies. Furthermore, it was found necessary to add two further dimensions (financial stress and miscellaneous) to the list. Thus, the deprivation items used in the studies may be classified under the following 12 headings.

- dietary

- clothing

- household facilities and consumer durables

- housing conditions

- health

- education

- family activities

- recreation

- social relations

- location and environment

- financial stress

- miscellaneous other items.

Creating an index of poverty

A variety of methods have been used to analyse and combine the deprivation items into overall measures of poverty or social exclusion.

Unweighted summation

Townsend derives his 12-item deprivation index as follows:

- he selected the most appropriate items from the original set of 60 by examining the correlation of each item with income;

- the deprivation score was derived by simply summing the number of items that the respondent lacked.

The score so derived was not used directly but was mapped into the income variable to define a poverty line.

Mack and Lansley (1985) also used an unweighted summation of items to derive their scale. However, they impose a number of additional conditions:

- that the items included be 'necessities', that is, considered to be necessities by a majority of the sample interviewed and possessed by a majority of the sample;

- that possession of the item be negatively correlated with income;

- that allowance was made for 'tastes' by asking each respondent who lacked a particular item if they 'would like but could not afford it'.

Weighting and reference groups

Desai and Shah (1988) took the original Townsend data and subjected it to econometric analysis. Instead of thinking of 'goods' they propose the notion of consumption events, emphasising the time-specific nature of the poverty concept. The measure that they derive is compensatory. It also explicitly incorporates the notion of reference groups in assessing poverty levels.

Factor analytic and psychometric approaches

Gailly and Hausman (1984) present a method for deriving a deprivation scale by the use of a model originated by Rasch (1960). By analysing responses to 82 items (each thought to reflect deprivation across a number of aspects or domains of people's lives), this technique allows them to define a unidimensional scale for the measurement of poverty based on 32 of these items. Thus, an essential element in their concept of poverty is the cumulation of disadvantage over a number of domains. The items used comprise both 'hard' variables (eg, objective data on employment, income, housing, etc) and 'soft' variables (eg, respondents' reported difficulty in making ends meet; worries about future health).

The Social Deprivation Scale

Muffels (1993b) extends the Desai and Shah model in a number of ways. The Social Deprivation Scale (SDS) that he derives incorporates the ideas of preference interdependence and reference groups. Thus, the lack of a given consumption item is more serious (weighted more heavily) the more common the consumption of that item is in one's reference group. The reference group is defined empirically as households similar to the respondent's, in terms of overall deprivation score and age and education of the head of the household. This model is also compensatory in nature since possession of one item can, to some extent, counteract the lack of another one. To validate their scale, the author carries out a principal components analysis. This attempts to examine the structure of their 42 original deprivation items and Muffels finds that 15 dimensions can be distinguished:

- income/money resources

- facilities in the home

- mental and physical health status

- fixed housing costs

- durables

- quality of the dwelling

- hot meals

- employment

- facilities in the neighbourhood

- quality of the neighbourhood

- food and clothes

- education

- social contacts

- social participation

- luxuries.

It is concluded that taste and reference group influences are very important and cannot be neglected in explaining deprivation or hardship.

'Fundamental' versus 'middle class' deprivation

The approach to the measurement of poverty developed at the Economic and Social Research Institute (ESRI) takes as a starting point the definition of poverty as *exclusion* arising from *lack of resources* and proceeds to investigate how information on deprivation indicators *and* income can be used to incorporate both exclusion and lack of resources into the poverty measure (Callan et al, 1993; Nolan and Whelan, forthcoming). This approach takes into account Ringen's (1988) critique of reliance on income in measuring poverty, since the poor are identified using both a deprivation and an income criterion. Exclusion is measured directly together with an income criterion to exclude those who have a low standard of living for reasons other than a low income. Thus, while adhering consistently to a relative conception of poverty, these authors are in agreement with those such as Sen (1992), who argue that poverty is a very specific form of deprivation that must be distinguished from a range of life-style inequalities or differences.

In pursuing this approach Whelan et al (1991) examined 24 deprivation items comprising 20 of the original Mack and Lansley variables and four indicators of financial stress. By the use of factor analysis, they confirmed the existence of three basic factors that they termed

- 'fundamental' or basic life-style deprivation

- 'middle class' or secondary life-style deprivation

- housing deprivation.

They consider the effect of these factors on a variety of measures of economic and psychological distress and show that primary deprivation bears "a particularly striking relationship to feelings of economic strain". Recent work by Callan et al (1993) extends this analysis. They show that both income and deprivation must be studied in order to fully understand the nature of poverty. The approach starts with a clear notion of resources as the causally prior variable and then seeks to establish the extent of deprivation of socially defined necessities arising from a lack of resources.

Households are defined as in poverty where they fall below a specified income line (for example, 60% of average disposable household) *and* experience an enforced absence of basic life-style items relating to food, clothing and heat. Subsequent work based on this approach has sought to develop an understanding of the determinants of different dimensions of life-style deprivation. More generally, it has sought to elucidate the processes of accumulation and erosion of resources that underlie these relationships, including the strategies open to households to deal with periods of material hardship, such as running down savings or other assets, or availing themselves of help from family or friends.

The need for conceptual clarity

We now go on to illustrate some insights into the nature of poverty and social exclusion that can be obtained by using this approach. We will argue that simply identifying several dimensions (through factor analysis or other techniques) does not per se enable us to decide the importance that should be attributed to particular dimensions. Indeed, the inclusion of determinants and outcomes in the same analytic schema may well hinder our capacity to understand the dynamics of social change and the processes by which certain social groups are excluded. If the identification of distinct dimensions of exclusion is to be fruitful we must direct our attention to the somewhat different factors that are involved in producing the different types of deprivation and consider the variable consequences of specific types of exclusion.

We present two illustrations of the value of this approach: one focusing on a causal or predisposing factor (labour market marginality), and a second addressing the issue of the effects of poverty on physical and mental health. We are, of course, conscious that these are only illustrations; a comprehensive treatment of the main causes and consequences would run to several volumes and would cover such additional factors as housing, education, ethnic origin, location and social participation, etc.

Labour market marginalisation, erosion or resources and life-style deprivation

In our work on poverty in Ireland, drawing on the ESRI 1987 national survey of 3,000 households, we examine the relationship of labour market marginality to a range of outcomes, which include income, other resources and life-style deprivation (Whelan et al, 1992; Whelan, forthcoming). Our work draws on the recent literature dealing with the possible emergence of an underclass. We start from Smith's (1992, p 5) definition of an underclass as "those family units having no stable relationship with legitimate gainful employment". In the interests of conceptual clarity, we chose in our analysis to reserve the term 'underclass' for situations involving socio-cultural effects contributing to vicious cycle processes (Whelan, 1996). Instead, we concentrate on a group termed the 'marginalised working class', defined as follows:

- The head of household is in the working class (ie, in CASMIN classes IIIb, VI and VIIa+b, which contain lower grades: see Erikson and Goldthorpe, 1993, pp 35-47).

- (a) The head of household has been unemployed for two years or more or (b) has spent 20% or more of their potential labour market time since leaving full-time education unemployed and has been in the labour market for at least five years.

- In the case of married respondents, the spouse of the head of household is not in employment.

- In addition, where the head of household is currently employed and has not experienced a spell of unemployment in the previous 12 months the household is excluded.

Such households constitute 11% of non-farm households where the head of household is less than 65 (Whelan, forthcoming).

Our focus on working class marginalisation involves a choice between the differing responses to the challenge raised for class analysis by large-scale and long-term unemployment. Thus, for Runciman (1990, p 88) the long-term unemployed are among those "whose roles place them more or less permanently at the economic level where benefits are paid by the state to those unable to participate in the labour market" and are placed in a residual category and fall *outside* the class schema. This definition, as Morris and Irwin (1992, p 402) note, fails to engage with conventional class analysis and with the fact that vulnerability to unemployment is a feature of location in the working class. Approaches that obscure this connection undermine our ability to understand the dynamics of labour market experience (Morris, 1993, p 408; 1995, pp 107-10). Thus, as Marshall et al (forthcoming) argue, critiques of the treatment of the unemployed in class analysis frequently involve the tendency to think of class in static rather than dynamic terms or as structure rather than as a process. The fact that people are not in employment at a particular point in time does not imply that they have dropped out of the class structure or that their previous class experience has become irrelevant.

In our subsequent analysis we distinguish between the middle class, the non-marginalised working class and the marginalised working class and employ the term 'class situation' to refer to this distinction. Our findings confirm that, in assessing the impact of labour market marginalisation, it is necessary to distinguish between different types of life-style deprivation and to identify a range of resources. The measures of resources available to us include:

- equivalent disposable household income

- deposits

- net house value.

We also distinguish between the following dimensions of deprivation:

- Basic deprivation, consisting of the *enforced* absence of items such as food, clothes and heat, which the majority of our respondents considered to be necessities.

- Secondary deprivation, which involves the *enforced* absence of items such as a car, telephone or participation in leisure activities.

- Housing and household durables, consisting of the *enforced* absence of items relating to housing quality and facilities (Callan et al, 1993).

Poverty is then defined as involving scoring above zero on the basic deprivation scale *and* falling below the 60% relative income line.

From Table 3.1 we can see that household income varies systematically across the categories of our classification ranging, in decile terms, from 7.53 for the middle class to 2.54 for the marginalised working class. A similar pattern is observed in relation to net housing values and an even more extreme degree of differentiation is found in relation to savings. The marginalised working class constitute a group that is characterised not only by a shortfall in current income but also by the erosion of, or failure to accumulate, long-term resources. The consequences of this depletion is captured best in the basic deprivation measure. For those households exposed to labour market marginalisation the primary deprivations score reaches 2.71, a level that is almost four times that of the non-marginalised working class and over eight times that of the middle class. Marginalisation is also associated with the highest observed levels of secondary and housing deprivation. However, in both cases, the type of marginalisation has a more modest impact. As the final column makes clear, what is most distinctive about the marginalised working class is the extent to which they experience poverty. Less than 4% of middle class households fall below the poverty line; the figure then jumps dramatically to two out of three for the marginalised working class.

Table 3.1: Resources, life-style and poverty by class situation

	Income decile (%)	Savings (£)	Net house value (£)	Basic deprivation (%)	Secondary deprivation (%)	Housing deprivation (%)	% poor
Middle class	7.53	2,925	26,215	0.33	1.36	0.13	3.7
Non-marginalised working class	5.41	1,491	17,249	0.79	2.91	0.38	17.5
Marginalised working class	2.54	292	7,800	2.71	4.83	0.77	66.7

Source: Whelan (forthcoming)

Consequences of labour marginality and basic deprivation

In this section, the relationship between labour market, marginalisation, life-style deprivation and certain aspects of physical and mental health will be examined. The objective is not to provide a detailed explanation of health inequalities, since an adequate discussion of issues relating to roles of selection and structural and cultural differences would take us well beyond the scope of this paper (Blane et al, 1993; Blaxter, 1990; Davey-Smith et al, 1990; Wilkinson, 1986). For the purposes of this paper, it is sufficient to show that specific indicators of physical and mental health (of a kind likely to be included in multidimensional measures of poverty) are associated with labour market marginality and basic deprivation in a manner that suggests that somewhat different underlying processes are involved.

Our measure of physical health status was derived from responses to the following question: 'Do you have any major illness, physical disability of infirmity that has troubled you for at least the past year or that is likely to go on troubling you in the future?'

This type of question on chronic illness has been widely used in surveys elsewhere (eg, in the UK General Household Survey and in regular health surveys carried out in France and the Scandinavian countries). Blaxter (1989) categorises this type of question as fitting into what she terms the 'medical model', since, although self-reported rather than clinically assessed, ill-health is being defined in terms of deviation from physiological norms rather than limitations to functioning or subjectively in terms of the individual's perceptions and experiences. While self-reporting might be thought likely to be problematic, where comparisons have been made the agreement with doctors' assessment or medical records has been high (Blaxter, 1989, pp 209-10). Substantially higher rates of self-reported chronic illness in the lower rather than in the higher social classes have been found in various countries, the gap generally being particularly pronounced in the middle age ranges.

To provide information about psychological health, the personal questionnaire also included a version of the widely used General Health Questionnaire (GHQ). This comprised a 12-item set of questions, which are designed to give information about the respondent's current mental state. These are six positive and six negative items, and each consists of a question asking whether the respondent has experienced a partial symptom or behaviour pattern. The GHQ was designed by Goldberg (1972) as a screening test for detecting minor psychiatric disorders in the community. For ease of presentation the results of analysis are reported in terms of a distinction between those scoring three or above and all others. This provides the most appropriate threshold score for distinguishing between those who are likely to be classified as non-psychotic psychiatric cases and all others.

In looking at health relationships we recognise that there is a possibility that the direction of causality may run from ill-health to marginality and exclusion. The evidence suggests that this is more likely to be the case in relation to physical health than to psychological ill-health. We are interested in comparing differences in the causal processes underlying the different types of health and the nature of the findings was such that the conclusions were, if anything, strengthened by the possibility of reverse causality. Furthermore, while for ease of presentation we may refer to the effects on physical and mental health, we are, of course, conscious that neither of these is a unitary phenomenon.

The analysis includes all adults in non-agricultural occupations where the head of household is aged less than 65. In Table 3.2 the percentage of cases reporting psychological distress distributed across class situation is shown, along with a basic deprivation score. The figure climbs gradually from a minimum of 11% among the middle class to an intermediate level of 18% among the non-marginalised working class and finally reaches a maximum of 30% among the marginalised working class. Similarly, the level of psychological distress rises steadily as the degree of primary deprivation experienced by the household increases; only 9% of individuals in households suffering an enforced lack of none of these items are found above the GHQ threshold, compared to 43% of those who are members of households with a score of two or more.

Table 3.2: Psychological distress and physical illness by basic life-style deprivation and class situation of household

	Basic deprivation scale				Class situation		
	0	1	2	3+	Middle class	Non-marginalised working class	Marginalised working class
% above GHQ threshold	9	20	30	43	11	18	30
% reporting major illness	11	17	20	21	9	16	18

Source: Whelan (forthcoming)

Elsewhere it is shown that if one assigns causal priority to primary life-style deprivation over both other dimensions, and to secondary deprivation over housing deprivation, then primary deprivation accounts for the vast bulk of the influence of life-style deprivation on psychological distress; although secondary deprivation appears to have a modest independent influence. Psychological distress is particularly responsive to extremes of life-style or labour market situation. Further analysis shows that among those in households experiencing primary deprivation the influence of class situation is modest. However, for all others it continues to play a crucial role (Whelan, 1992; 1994).

The situation in relation to physical health is rather different. Our indicator of physical ill-health relates to self-reported long-standing illness, physical disability or infirmity. Table 3.2 shows that the major contrast is between those in middle class and working class households and between those in households experiencing enforced deprivation of some of the primary items and all others. The finding suggests that in relation to this indicator, shared aspects of the experience and culture of the working class are more important than the extent of current differentiation, in terms of extreme labour market deprivation or labour market marginality.

Before concluding that working class marginalisation sheds little light on variations in physical illness, it should, however, be taken into account that the influences on physical health may develop over a much longer time period than is the case in relation to psychological distress. In particular, it is necessary to consider that childhood economic circumstances may be a relevant influence (Lundberg, 1991; 1993). The available evidence allows us to distinguish between those individuals who grew up in households experiencing great difficulty in making ends meet and all others. In Table 3.3 the impact of this factor on physical health status while controlling for class situation is shown. Within each class category those reared in situations of extreme financial strain were significantly more likely to report ill-health. This relationship cannot be explained away by the fact that older groups are more likely to have experienced such circumstances. The influence of economic hardship in childhood is thus not simply a consequence of its relationship to current class situation nor, as further analysis shows, its association with class origins. Lundberg (1991, p 160) suggests that

> ... economic hardship during childhood may be a factor which affects life chances throughout the various stages of the life-cycle. Hardship, may for instance, influence the time spent in school, the nature of the first job, and the later opportunities on the labour market etc. If this is the case, poor living conditions early in life will increase the risk of starting out on the wrong path in life in terms of both health risks and other living conditions.

The results suggest that our measure of childhood economic circumstances is tapping processes of accumulatory disadvantage over and above those captured by our measures of class situation and class origin. The significance of this finding is enhanced by the fact that, as is clear from Table 3.4, marginalised working class households containing children aged under 15 suffer extreme rates of poverty, with almost four out of five falling below our poverty line. Thus while labour market marginality is not a decisive factor in relation to our current measure of physical status, it seems highly probable that it is making a substantial contribution to class inequalities in health among the future generations of adults.

Conclusion

This paper has argued that better conceptual clarity is required when one speaks of the 'multidimensional' nature of poverty and social exclusion. We have suggested that the causes, nature and consequences of these social processes each include many aspects or dimensions. It is therefore crucial to develop a more differentiated understanding of where poverty arises, how it can be described and what are its consequences. Of course, within any such schema there may exist 'feed-back loops' operating in such a way that certain factors, originally conceived of as consequences of poverty, tend to exacerbate a poor person's situation. For instance, in the analysis presented above, ill-health was conceptualised as a consequence of deprivation. It could well be that prolonged illness may also lead to lower resources and hence to even greater levels of poverty.

Table 3.3: Physical illness by family's economic circumstances when person was growing up and class situation*

| Family's economic circumstances | Middle class | Class situation | |
		Non-marginalised working class	Marginalised working class
Great difficulty in making ends meet	14	23	23
Other	8	14	16

*   These figures represent the percentage of people reporting major physical illness.

Source: Whelan (1992; 1994)

Table 3.4   Poverty by class situation for households with children under 15

	% poor
Middle class	2.9
Non-marginalised working class	20.0
Marginalised working class	78.7

How can this improved understanding be developed in future research? We have argued that such research should include both good measures of income and of the level of deprivation. A good deal of work has been done in different countries in developing sets of indices of deprivation. Empirical cross-national research, such as the European Community Household

Panel, which is currently under way, offer the opportunity to harmonise and refine this set of indicators. The combination of the income and deprivation indicator approach offer the opportunity both to measure poverty more accurately and to provide a more complete picture of the life-styles of the poor.

In adopting this approach one is led naturally to emphasise the importance of a dynamic approach, that is, towards understanding how social exclusion occurs within a time perspective. This has also been underlined by other contributors to this volume, such as Paugam. From the point of view of future research, there is more at stake here than just an argument for improving the availability of panel data, important though this is. Given the long gestation period of the panel surveys now being set up, it will be a decade before we can use them to study even the medium-term dynamics of poverty. In the meantime, we can examine short-term fluctuations. However, we can also use retrospective questions to gain some insights into the longer term processes. The analysis presented above of labour market marginalisation is a simple example of how retrospective data can be used in this way. The crucial thing is the emphasis on understanding how exclusion functions in an intertemporal context.

four

THE SPIRAL OF PRECARIOUSNESS: A MULTIDIMENSIONAL APPROACH TO THE PROCESS OF SOCIAL DISQUALIFICATION IN FRANCE

Serge Paugam

Introduction

When consciousness of the phenomenon of 'new poverty' dawned during the 1980s, researchers and experts were led to analyse the income and living conditions of 'poor' or 'excluded' people. The object was usually to home in on this social group quantitatively – generally on the basis of an income threshold – and to distinguish it from other sections of the population.

Besides the inevitably arbitrary character of accepted statistical definitions for measuring poverty in this way, the scope of these studies was relatively limited for at least two reasons. The first is related to the sociological evidence that the 'poor' do not form a very homogenous social entity; that is to say, there are several strata within this population. In France, the results of studies of the beneficiaries of the minimum income (Revenue Minimum d'Insertion [RMI]) have confirmed this social heterogeneity. The second reason lies in the fact that poverty is a multidimensional phenomenon, which today corresponds less to a state, than to a process (Paugam, 1991; 1993). Consequently any static definition of poverty tends to lump together, within the same overall category, sections of the population whose situation is heterogeneous, and to obscure the basic question as to the process by which the problems of individuals or of households progressively accumulate, from its origins to its effects in the medium to long term. In order to analyse the inequalities presented by the risk of social exclusion among the working population (18 to 64 years of age)[1] we propose first to study the correlations among several indicators of economic and social precariousness (precarious employment, marital instability, economic poverty, inadequate social and family life, inadequate support networks and low levels of participation in social activities) and, secondly, to identify those population groups where there is the highest cumulation of handicaps. This research (based on the results of an enquiry by the Institut National de la Statistique et des Etudes Economiques (INSEE) into the living conditions of households in 1986/87, commonly known as the study 'Situations of disadvantage'[2]) is a contribution to the analysis of poverty as social disqualification, defined as a process which, step by step, can force various sections of the population into the sphere of occupational inactivity and assistance, by increasing their risk of a progressive accumulation of problems or handicaps.

The correlations observed[3]

Different situations in relation to employment are today organised in a hierarchy, not just according to levels of responsibility and power in the place of work, but also increasingly according to the degree of stability of the job, and the extent of social and economic advantage acquired through the occupation.

Five situations relating to employment

At least five situations can be distinguished:

- holders of a job, who consider that they do not risk losing it within the next two years (stable job not under threat);

- holders of a job who have been in work for more than a year, but who think they risk losing it within the next two years (stable job under threat);

- people who have changed job or who have had a period of unemployment in the year preceding the study, who have a precarious or intermittent job, who think that they are at risk of losing it within the next two years (unstable job);

- people who have been unemployed for less than two years;

- those unemployed for more than two years.

This presentation, which differs noticeably from the accepted traditional administrative criteria for characterising the differing status of employment and unemployment, allows one to go beyond the classic contrast between employment and unemployment, and to take better account of the realities of the employment market.[4]

Stable jobs not under threat represent 51.6% of employees in the sample; stable jobs under threat, 28.5%; unstable jobs, 7.8%; unemployment for less than two years, 6.8%; and unemployment for more than two years, 5.3%. The analysis of the demographic and social characteristics of the corresponding populations has underlined the very marked differences between them. People with jobs that are not under threat are generally in good health, live in comfortable housing and have many professional advantages (higher education qualifications). People who say their job is under threat are all, by their age, occupation, and status, in the less dynamic and protected sectors of the labour market, which makes them more vulnerable to economic fluctuations. People with jobs that are unstable do not all have difficulty in getting another job – this is only a case with a fraction of them. On the other hand, the others can be regarded overall as employed but working in sectors of the labour market, which rely on considerable mobility between firms, in the building industry or public works, for example. Among the unemployed, those whose unemployment is of more than two year's duration are clearly more disadvantaged than the others. This occurs more frequently among women and older people. The proportion of foreigners without educational qualifications and people living in poor housing is also higher.

These five situations (from stable jobs not under threat to unemployment for more than two years), relate, to a certain extent, back to the social divisions that are appearing in contemporary French society. What is striking is that they are very closely correlated with the outward appearance of the home. The lower the status in relation to employment, the higher the probability of living in a dwelling of poor appearance. If these different situations are not static – an individual can move successively from one to the other – they reflect the heterogeneity of social conditions.

Instability of the conjugal relationship

Occupational status thus defined is correlated with the conjugal trajectory built up from individual biographies in the studies (Martin, 1994). Instability of employment or unemployment is a factor that holds back the formation of a partnership as well as fertility, but there are differences according to sex; the likelihood of men living without a spouse if their employment situation is precarious, is noticeably stronger than for women in the same situation. Despite the development of sexual equality, not having a job remains less degrading for a woman, especially if she is living with a partner and has children. A strong correlation can also be observed between precariousness of employment and the instability of partnerships. Conjugal breakdown increases in a regular way according to the degree of precariousness of the job, but it is clearly more frequent in couples where it is the man who is confronted by employment problems. These results serve to underline that the instability of the family is today reinforced by the difficulties of being absorbed back into employment, experienced by a growing number of sectors of the population (de Singly, 1993; Kaufman, 1993).

Decline in income

If disturbances in conjugal life are linked, at least in part, to the precariousness of the occupational situation, it is, among other things, because the instability of the job and unemployment are manifest by a noticeable decline in income. People in difficulty in the employment market are, in fact, seeing their occupational income decline markedly. The share of social benefits in the disposable income of the household increases according to the degree of occupational precariousness. The proportion of households whose share of transfers is greater than half of the disposable income varies between about 4% for heads of the household in stable jobs not under threat to 75% for heads of household who have been unemployed for more than two years. The per capita disposable income is also, as one might expect, correlated to a high degree with the situation in relation to the job (see Table 4.1). These are the people unemployed for more than two years who are experiencing the most unfavourable situation: 40% of them are living in a household whose income, at the time of the survey, was less than 2,100FF per month.[5]

Furthermore, the risk of economic poverty is greater when the head of the household has experienced conjugal breakdown, including when he is living in a reconstituted partnership. Finally, it should be remembered that the proportion of low income households increases with the number of children, and most of all when there are three children or more. In fact, for large families the stability of the employment situation of the head of household is not always a sufficient condition for escaping from economic poverty (despite the social benefits that they receive).

The steep decline in income associated with occupational instability or unemployment results, for many households, in enormous financial problems, either for the purchase of goods essential to survival (food, health), or for housing (rent and charges) (Herpin, 1992). These problems become worse with conjugal breakdown. Large families are also particularly affected by this. Precariousness of employment also increases the likelihood of living in uncomfortable housing, and of being deprived of certain basic amenities.

Table 4.1: Economic poverty according to the employment situation (%)

	Not poor	Poor*	Very poor†	All poor/very poor	Total
Stable job not under threat	94.4	4	1.6	5.6	100
Stable job under threat	87.6	8.9	3.5	12.4	100
Unstable job	80.6	12.9	6.5	19.4	100
Unemployed less than 2 years	73.4	15.7	10.9	26.6	100
Unemployed more than 2 years	59.8	24.8	15.4	40.2	100
Overall	88.2	7.9	3.9	11.8	100

* Proportion of people living in a household where the per capita disposable income at the survey date was between 1,400FF and 2,100FF per month.

† Proportion of people living in a household where the per capita disposable income at the survey date was less than 1,400FF per month.

Source: INSEE study: 'Situations of disadvantage' (1986-87)

Coverage: All workers from 18-64 years of age

Decline in social life

Finally, precariousness in employment can be accompanied by a noticeable reduction in the intensity of social life.[6] It can cause relationships with other family members living outside the household to become more distant. The proportion of people having no relationship with their family increases sharply according to the precariousness of their job. Men are more affected than women by this process, which can lead to isolation, and withdrawal into oneself. This process also disproportionately affects people aged between 35 and 50 years (see Table 4.2). The hardship of precariousness of employment is, in fact, more grievous when it strikes people at the heart of their active life. It is experienced as an expression of a fundamental social disqualification. The possibility of being supported by family and friends and participation in social life also diminish according to the degree of occupational precariousness.

It can be concluded from Table 4.2 that the risk of breakdown in social relations is proportional to difficulties in the employment market. To a large extent, this phenomenon explains the current malaise and disintegration of social cohesion in disadvantaged neighbourhoods in which there is unemployment on a very large scale.

It should not, of course, be concluded too quickly that the 'social vacuum' has overtaken every suburb, and that there is no longer any sign of organised social life in working class areas. However, if reference is made to accounts by sociologists and ethnologists in the 1950s and 1960s (see, for example, Hoggart, 1957), it seems clear that the intensity of social relationships in these neighbourhoods has decreased sharply. Community life has been transformed by the effects of social differentiation in the working class world: certain upwardly mobile groups have moved out of the neighbourhood. In contrast, others have experienced a drop in status and become impoverished (Schwartz, 1990). More and more households have no other opportunity but to live in run-down estates. Often they internalise a negative identity and withdraw into themselves by seeking to distinguish themselves from their neighbours. When people know how family reputations are formed, they have every reason to remain silent and disguise as far as possible the worries of daily life. For many, the hope is that they will find a job and move out of the area (Paugam, 1995).

Evaluation of the risk of exclusion

Taking several dimensions into consideration, precariousness appears to be a diverse phenomenon that affects many sectors of the population. The strength of the links between the employment situation and other dimensions of economic and social life (family, income, living conditions and social contacts) could suggest that those people in situations of occupational precariousness – whether they are in an insecure job or are unemployed – have a good chance of becoming excluded from society. It is true that the analysis carried out has led to the drawing up of a hierarchy of situations from the most advantageous to the most precarious in each of the areas studied, and since the results converge, it is tempting to conclude that, for example, all long-term unemployed are experiencing a situation on the borderline of social exclusion. In reality it is not this simple, and if the observed statistical correlation is a sign of some form of social determinism, it cannot be interpreted as strictly affecting every individual. Nor does it mean that, even among this group who have, collectively, many problems and handicaps, there are no forms of compensation for the lack of participation in the labour market: family solidarity, for example, or a support network within the community or among friends, which offers to a greater or lesser degree a sort of protection from the process of social exclusion. It is therefore important to study the inequalities in the risk of social exclusion, distinguishing different population groups according to the cumulative strength of their problems, and examining, on the basis of the indicators used in the correlation analysis, those sectors most threatened with the passage from one stage to the next of social exclusion. This approach is, in fact, complementary to the qualitative studies that have been carried out on this topic.

Table 4.2: Absence of family social links* by sex and age, and according to employment situation

	Stable job not under threat[1]	Stable job under threat[2]	Unstable job[3]	Unemployed less than 2 years[4]	Unemployed more than 2 years[5]	All figures[6]	RMI[7]
Men							
-25 years	9.8	9.1	11.3	13.7	ns	11.7	–
25-34 years	5.7	7.1	7.9	14.5	21.9	7.1	19.0
35-49 years	7.7	12.0	24.1	11.6	32.6	10.7	32.9
50 + years	6.6	9.4	ns	9.8	19.6	9.1	23.3
Overall	7.0	9.9	13.8	12.8	25.2	9.4	25.4

	Stable job not under threat[1]	Stable job under threat[2]	Unstable Job[3]	Unemployed less than 2 years[4]	Unemployed more than 2 years[5]	All figures[6]	RMI[7]
Women							
-25 years	9.1	8.0	14.2	9.7	13.7	10.8	–
25-34 years	6.3	5.6	6.0	11.0	12.9	6.8	15.2
35-49 years	7.4	5.7	11.4	11.3	11.1	7.6	21.5
50 + years	6.5	8.2	ns	ns	16.1	8.3	19.2
Overall	7.1	6.6	11.2	10.4	13.3	8.0	18.1

	Stable job not under threat[1]	Stable job under threat[2]	Unstable Job[3]	Unemployed less than 2 years[4]	Unemployed more than 2 years[5]	All figures[6]	RMI[7]
Both sexes							
-25 years	9.4	8.7	12.7	11.7	17.9	11.2	–
25-34 years	6.0	6.5	7.0	12.6	15.4	7.0	17.1
35-49 years	7.6	9.7	17.2	11.5	20.2	9.3	27.9
50 + years	6.6	8.9	18.4	9.7	17.6	8.8	21.6
Overall	7.0	8.6	12.5	11.6	17.7	8.8	22.1
Sample	3,977	2,192	600	524	406	7,699	1,990

* Proportion of people with no contact with their family outside their own household.

ns = figures not significant.

1-6 Source: INSEE study 'Situations of disadvantage' (1986-87).

7 Source: Centre d'Etude des Revenus et des Couts (CERC) study on recipients of minimum guaranteed income (RMI) 1990-91.

Coverage: Working population from 18-64 years of age.

Three types of population

The results of a factorial analysis of the correlations can be studied using Figure 4.1 (p 64) as a starting point. The positions of the different variables selected have been plotted along the two axes. The first axis contrasts people, on the right hand side, who have a stable job, strong family links, a high level of income and a comfortable home, and those people, on the left hand side of the diagram, who are unemployed for over two years, with a very low income, poor support networks, and a poor standard of housing. Those people who are part of a couple but who have not experienced conjugal breakdown, and also those who participate in community life and those who have had a happy childhood are to be found, as one might expect, on the right hand side, while those living alone following the breakdown of a relationship and those with no social life are found on the left hand side. These results confirm the analysis of correlations carried out in previous sections. It means that one can speak of a cumulation of disadvantageous situations. This axis is best defined as the axis of participation in social and economic life, since it places individuals on an economic scale (income, occupation, consumption) and on a scale of social participation (family and conjugal life, support networks, community life).

The second axis shows those persons in good health, situated in the lower half of the diagram, as against those in poor health in the upper half. Note also that those people living with family and friends, who have never lived in a conjugal relationship, are in the lower half of the diagram. The variables that have most influence on the definition of this second axis are linked to age and health. These variables are, of course, not independent of each other. Young people, who are found in the lower half of the diagram, are more likely than their elders to be in good health. On the other hand, their involvement in the labour market is less certain. It is for this reason that those within an unstable job and who have been unemployed for less than two years are to be found in the lower left hand side of the diagram.

The complementary (non-contributory) variables indicated in italics confirm the trends that have already been revealed by the analysis of the correlations. Difficulties in paying for food as well as paying for housing charges are indicated on the upper left hand side of the diagram. Those persons whose occupational inactivity has been most prolonged (more than five years) are also in this sector, while those who have been unemployed for the shortest period of time are in the lower half, although still to the left hand side. The hierarchy of educational qualifications is also positioned according to the horizontal axis. Those with the most educational qualifications are positioned to the extreme right of the diagram and those with no qualifications to the left. Still following the same logic, it can be seen that civil servants and intermediary professions are towards the more favourable end of the axis of economic and social participation, and unqualified workers are the furthest from this point. Finally, it should be noted that immigrants (reference to the nationality of the father) are also to be found in the left hand side of the diagram, in particular those who have as their country of origin a non-European Union (EU) state.

It is possible, as a result of this analysis, to define three main types of situation. The first corresponds to the ideal-typical situation of an individual who has a stable job and has, at the same time, numerous advantages that enable him to maintain and forge social links (in particular, a regular income, but also solid social and cultural assets). These elements reinforce each other and their conjunction may be termed 'social and economic integration'. The right hand side of the diagram corresponds most closely to this ideal type. It comprises the most advantaged sections of society, but also the middle classes who have increased in importance in French society in the last 30 years. Those people with stable but insecure jobs are on the borderline of this ideal.

The other two types of situation may be defined by reference to the first. The second type is characterised by *fragility*. It may be defined as the situation where there is a fairly high degree of precariousness in relation to employment and weak social contacts, as a direct result of the instability of relations with the world of work. The lower left hand section of the diagram is the segment where those who have insecure social and economic links will be found. This will include many young people, and especially very young people still living at the parental home and waiting for entry into the social and economic world. The obstacles that they meet when trying to attain a secure occupational position forces them to delay conjugal relations and renders their social and family relationships more fragile. Their insecurity is, in fact, proportional to the risk, of which they are well aware, that with the passing years, they will not be able to attain the ideal of the first situation, and the fear that their experience may, in fact, be one of long periods of unemployment.

The third type of situation has two main characteristics: first, a retreat from the labour market, and second, poverty in economic and social terms. Those persons who fall within this category are most often older people who have had a career. They rely on social benefits and support from social workers to cope with their difficulties, and their social life can, in some cases, be reduced to contacts with their children and their immediate neighbours. The upper left hand portion of the diagram represents this type of poverty, which is at the edges of social exclusion. However, it must be remembered that those persons who are most excluded (those who no longer have any involvement with the employment market, or with their family, and who are weighed down at the same time by an accumulation of handicaps – lack of housing, health problems, no social services support, etc) are not represented in the 'Situations of disadvantage' survey. The people included in this study do, for example, still have a home, even if it is in a very poor state. However, for these people there is always the risk of experiencing the most extreme form of poverty.

The sections of the population most exposed to social exclusion

In order to identify those sections of society that are most threatened by the process of social exclusion (among these three types of situation), the indicator of economic poverty used earlier will be taken up again and completed by the addition of a global indicator of poverty of relationships. This latter is a synthesis of the three indicators explored above: family relations, social support networks, and life in the community. Three levels have been defined according to the degree of poverty of relationships: (1) not poor; (2) poor; (3) very poor (see Table 4.3). The proportions across the whole of the scale are as follows: 68% for the first, 25% for the second and 7% for the third.

Of course, this poverty of relationships, or relational poverty, has a different effect according to whether an individual has a stable job or not, since occupational activity is in itself a form of social interaction. However, it is interesting to note that 26% of people with a stable job not under threat have, outside of their work, very poor social relations, be they of family, friends, or in the community. If these persons were to lose their jobs, it is easy to imagine that they would soon become isolated and worn down by unemployment. It is true that poverty of relationships is proportional to the degree of occupational precariousness. This form of poverty affects one person in four with a stable job, but one in every two unemployed persons. It is clear that the ability to socialise and maintain social links is gradually worn away as the employment situation deteriorates. However, it should be observed at this point that there is a similarity between the position of those with an unstable job and those who have been unemployed for less than two years. These two situations are also, it will be recalled, to be found in the same section of Figure 4.1. They are characteristic of what we have termed 'fragility'.

In basing our analysis on economic poverty and poverty of relationships, we can try to measure the risk of social exclusion for each of the three main types of situation drawn from the factorial analysis of correlations, starting from the indicator that best combines the two – namely, the employment situation. Tables 4.1 and 4.2 allow us to identify individuals in a state of economic and relational poverty among:

- the population in stable employment (who most resemble the first type);

- the population in unstable employment or who have been unemployed for a period of less than two years (which is nearest to the second type of situation);

- the population who have been unemployed for more than two years (which is closest to the third type of situation).

Figure 4.1: Factorial analysis of correlations for the active population aged 18-64

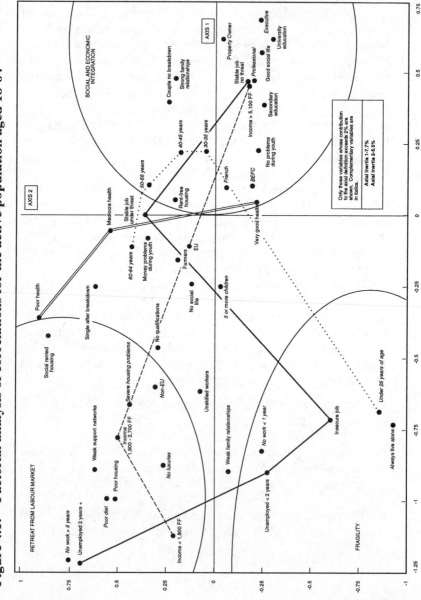

Table 4.3: Relational poverty* according to the employment situation (%)

	Non-poor (a)	Poor (b)	Very poor (c)	All poor/very poor	Total
Stable job not under threat	74.2	21.6	4.2	25.8	100
Stable job under threat	63.6	28.6	7.8	36.4	100
Unstable job	61.5	27.5	11.0	38.5	100
Unemployed less than 2 years	61.5	27.1	11.4	38.5	100
Unemployed more than 2 years	50.7	31.8	17.5	49.3	100
Overall	68.0	25.0	7.0	32.0	100

Source: INSEE study: 'Situations of disadvantage' (1986-87).

Coverage: All workers from 18-64 years of age

* The non-poor population (a) corresponds to people whose family life and supportive relationships are strong whatever the intensity of their participation in community life. The poor population (b) corresponds to people whose family social life and supportive relationships are average, whatever the intensity of their participation in community life; or weak, on condition that in this case they have a link with community life. The very poor population (c) corresponds to people whose family life and supportive relationships are weak and who are not members of any community.

To measure the risk of social exclusion of the whole section of the population with a stable job may seem at first a rather curious thing to do. Certain authors state that the fact of stable employment is sufficient to protect people from the risk of social exclusion. We work on the hypothesis that it is possible that vulnerable people exist within the section of the population with secure employment, even though, for these people, the risk of social exclusion is less than for those people who are furthest removed from the employment market.

Among those sectors of the population with a stable job, there is only a small minority in a situation of economic and relational poverty (3.3%). Men form the majority in this group (62% approximately, as against 56% for the whole of the section of the population in stable employment). Also over-represented are people over 50 years of age (35% against 21% for the entire group). The group is composed mainly of couples with children (58%) who have not experienced a breakdown in their relationship (61.6%). Almost one individual in four within this small segment has a father of non-EU nationality, as against a mere 5.8% for the whole group of the population with stable employment. Agricultural and manual workers are also over-represented. More than 55% of this small segment do not have any educational qualifications and 40% live in poor housing conditions. A high number have also had problems with money during their youth. These characteristics permit the identi-fication of a population group that has often been defined by the concept of 'working class poverty' (Barthe, 1987), in the sense that it is the cumulative difficulties of the world of work, but also outside of it, principally as a result of the inadequate economic, social and cultural capital available to this group, which creates the problems. This form of poverty is also traditional. Sociologists specialising in research into the working class and the shrinking peasantry have bestowed particular attention on this form of poverty. It is notable that it is this type of population group that has been most affected by industrial restructuring and developments within the agricultural world.

People who are in a situation of economic and relational poverty among the population group who are in insecure employment or who have been unemployed for less than two years are proportionately more numerous (10%). Their sociodemographic characteristics are also different. The proportion of men within this group is still high, but those under 25 are markedly in evidence (45.1% as compared with 40.6% for this population group as a whole). Economic and relational poverty also affects a high proportion of unmarried persons who live with their family or friends, There are some characteristics similar to those of 'working class poverty': a high proportion of people with a father who is a national of a non-EU state, over-representation of unskilled workers, of those with no educational qualifications, of those who are poorly housed (in the sense of the external poverty of the housing). There are also many people within this group who have had a childhood marked by poverty. The main difference between this second group by comparison with the first is one of age. It could almost be said that this group is composed of the adult children of the traditionally poor households. The latter knew a time when integration into the world of work was a step taken with ease. Their children, on the other hand, experience real difficulties in obtaining stable employment and no longer identify with the declining working class world. The uncertainty of their occupational future constitutes a real obstacle to the economic autonomy of these young people, and one response is to delay leaving the family home, or to abandon the idea altogether. Job security is, particularly for men of a working class background, the precondition of independence and the gateway to the social world (Galland, 1984).

Among the population group of people unemployed for more than two years, there is another increase in the number of people in a situation of economic and relational precariousness – a level of 22.4%. The proportion of men is higher than the proportion of men overall in this generally feminine population group, yet even here the proportion of women is higher (almost 54%). Most of these women are between 35 and 49 years of age (38.4%). The proportion of couples with children who have not experienced conjugal breakdown is very low. Single parent families are numerous, as are single people living with family and friends. Immigrants whose father is of a non-EU state are also over-represented. The proportion of manual and unskilled workers is 46.1% and for 15.4% there has been no means of identifying a trade due to lack of any clearly identifiable occupational experience. Those with no educational qualifications, in poor housing, and those who experienced problems during their youth are also high in number, even exceeding the high levels of the previous group. Here is the section of the population that is closest to extreme poverty. Their only possibility seems to be to live a life of reliance on social assistance, with the ever-present risk of watching their situation deteriorate ever further.

These three sections of the population all have two handicaps – economic and relational poverty – but, as we have seen, they do not constitute, in spite of certain shared objective similarities, one homogenous social stratum. There are differences between them: a generation gap and a difference linked to the different stage of social exclusion in which they find themselves. The concept of 'working class poverty' cannot usefully be used to describe the first type, as it has as one of its defining characteristics a stable job, which guarantees some level of integration. This first population group would be least capable of coping with the loss of employment. Potential fragility could easily become real. The absence of a job, especially for this generation who have developed a social life through work, would represent a deep humiliation and would lead, in the short term, to a high level of dependence on social assistance.

The people in the second type of population group run the risk of being pulled away from the labour market before they have experienced any stability. The majority of people in an insecure job or at the start of a period of unemployment experience a sort of fragility that results from the uncertainty of the future. For many people this is the first stage of the process of social exclusion. For some it is only a temporary step backwards, since it may correspond to the first stage of their work career, from which a better step is taken. For others, it is quite the opposite: lasting longer and accompanied by numerous failures in the search for secure employment. This is often the case for those people who already have serious difficulties. This phase of fragility can become a progressive accumulation of problems which may, in the long term, lead to discouragement and to a retreat from the employment market.

Finally, the third population group that has been identified among those people who have been unemployed for at least two years is a situation of fundamental social exclusion. Not all people on the outside of the employment market lack their own private support network. Certain people may not fall into economic poverty. There are various strategies to compensate for the lack of involvement in the employment market, especially for women, such as family relationships and help from social workers. Some of this group find a form of stability in this dependence on social services. On the other hand, there are others who, in this situation outside of the employment market, with the cumulative handicaps of economic and relational poverty, are already very close to the ultimate stage of the process of social exclusion, which is characterised by the breaking of elementary ties with society. It is difficult to evaluate the quantitative importance of this last stage, since those people who are socially excluded to the highest degree, such as homeless people, are not represented in statistical surveys taken of the whole population. It can, however, be estimated that 1% of those in the survey will have experience of this level of social exclusion.[7]

The results of this study confirm the risk of the accumulation of handicaps for the ever-increasing number of people in a situation of precariousness, and permit analysis of the factors in this process of social exclusion. They also give an opportunity to question the popular idea that everyone can be affected by social exclusion. The expression 'it will never happen to me' is the result of an optical illusion. Although very widespread at present, it is more the product of a collective anxiety in the face of unemployment, than a rigorous analysis of statistical surveys. It is certain that the case of the civil servant who is made redundant, and at the same time suffers a marital breakdown, loses his home, breaks contact with his family and goes down the rungs of the social ladder one by one until he finds himself on the street, is no longer exceptional. Charitable organisations are dealing more and more with people who have suffered a serious social displacement. It must not be deduced from this that the risk of exclusion strikes all individuals in an identical fashion independent of their social situation. There are various forms of precariousness spread across French society, and it is not true that in all cases they are the result of accumulated problems. It would be false to say that no one is protected from the risk of social exclusion. The thesis of the complete disappearance of traditional inequalities does not stand up to rigorous examination. It could even be said to hide from view the emergence of new phenomena of segregation in the areas of schooling, employment and housing.

The limitations of public action

In the course of this analysis, questions may be asked about the effectiveness of social benefits and preventive policies. The number of people in France (including partners and children supported by the household) who escape financial precariousness due to different mechanisms of social protection can be estimated as approximately 12 to 13 million. For about 7.6 million of these, the per capita disposable income lies between the level of the sum of the minimum income (2,250FF) and that of the minimum state retirement pension (3,130FF). For 5 million of the rest, this income lies between 1 and 1.3 times the minimum state retirement pension. These figures reflect the importance of social benefits in France and the effectiveness of the system of social protection in limiting poverty, in the economic sense of the term. In terms of the battle against exclusion, however, this system still has gaps.

The first gap results from the considerable rigidity of the social protection system, whose main structures had been worked out in earlier decades, not to confront evolving processes triggered off by the breakdown of employment and family, but to compensate for long-standing problems, risks or handicaps. This system turns out to be ineffective as a whole in preventing the risk of fragility or withdrawal from the employment market, which, as we have seen, is currently affecting large sections of the population.

This is the reason why the authorities are trying increasingly to introduce social protection measures into a general policy for the prevention of exclusion. In particular, it is a matter of searching for solutions that promote a link between a guarantee of resources and action for integration. The law on the minimum income, passed on 1st December 1988, falls within this logic. Its double object is to secure appropriate means of existence for the most disadvantaged people, and to encourage them to undertake for themselves the necessary steps to cease needing assistance. Numerous opportunities for integration have been tried out at a local level sufficient to allow the widespread application of such arrangements. After five years of experience however, it must be emphasised that, in spite of all the efforts, few benefit claimants have found a job, at least in the competitive sector of the economy. An accelerated increase in the number of people receiving this benefit has been evident – a fact which is causing concern for the authorities (Paugam, 1993)

It is clear that, to a large extent, the success of these experiments results from the ability to define a recognisable policy in consultation with business, the social partners and the actors who are now involved within the framework of training and integration into employment. Without a profound transformation of the operating conditions of the employment market, it is probable that in the present economic situation, solutions for integration will become increasingly uncertain.

The prevention of exclusion depends also on other public policies that it would be appropriate to conduct simultaneously, especially the battle against educational failure, the construction of social housing adapted to the special needs of households, and the setting up of a development programme for disadvantaged neighbourhoods. More generally, the battle against social exclusion requires a rethinking of the coordination between the different political authorities. Any appraisal of the situation that portrays the 'excluded' as being apart from and against the rest of the population is in itself an obstacle to the fight against social exclusion. It leads to a compartmentalised approach, always after the event and characterised by the search for emergency solutions for a social group that is elusive, because it is unstable and heterogeneous. The fight against social exclusion (if it is defined as a general policy of prevention of a process that begins with fragility and can lead to the breaking of all social ties), requires rather, a simultaneous and dynamic attack on the weaknesses of the education system, on the failings of professional training, on the voids in employment and housing policies and on the excessive spatial disparities. In this sense, the fight against social exclusion involves a battle against those social inequalities that are contrary to notions of citizenship, both the more traditional inequalities and those that are more recent and more complex and that affect new sectors of the population. Without a policy of prevention, the latter are likely to experience a progressive cumulation of difficulties and handicaps comparable to those that we have analysed in this paper. There is, in fact, a considerable risk that, if these initiatives fail at national and local levels, the number of people disqualified socially will rise again, and the present system will establish a trend towards an institutionalised social dualism whose initial symptoms are already easily recognised.

However, since this process of social exclusion can be seen in very similar forms in the main countries of Western Europe (see Appendix 4.1), it is equally important that there be cross-national cooperation in order to assess the effectiveness of the different policies that are in place, with a view to anticipating and thereby better managing their effects.

APPENDIX 4.1: PRECARIOUSNESS AND THE RISK OF SOCIAL EXCLUSION IN EUROPE

Preliminary results of a comparative study

Although the structural causes of the process of social exclusion are very similar in the countries of western Europe, there can be clear differences in the forms of social exclusion that develop, depending on the specific pattern of economic development and the labour market, the strength of social ties, and the level of public intervention on behalf of disadvantaged groups. Recent exploratory research on the cumulation of handicaps associated with the precariousness of employment has been carried out for the European Commission by the Centre d'Etude des Revenus et des Couts (CERC).[8]

After critical analysis of the statistical data available for the study of poverty in the sense of social exclusion, the study turns to the construction of roughly similar indicators for seven countries (Germany, Denmark, Spain, France, United Kingdom, Italy, The Netherlands).[9] It was, of course, impossible, as a result of the diversity of data analysed, to identify identical indicators for the seven countries. It is clear that in the multidimensional surveys used as a basis for the data, the questions were rarely put in the same form from one country to another. In addition, each data source had a few inaccuracies and the precise definition of the indicators could not always be the same. In certain cases it was necessary to approximate. Nevertheless, in spite of this sort of problem, the collaboration elaborated 12 indicators.

The indicators cover the greater part of the fields in the multidimensional surveys: employment, income, housing conditions, health, conjugal and family life, social life, and finally the problems encountered in youth.[10] Working from these indicators, the first statistical analysis was carried out. In each country, the indicators were cross-tabulated and a correlation test was run on each table. The survey sample was limited to the working population, defined as those in employment and those seeking work and claiming benefits.

The results of this research have shown convergence, but also quite wide divergence between the countries. Among the areas of convergence, there are some that are not surprising. Precariousness of employment is positively linked to paucity of income and poor living conditions. The likelihood of living singly or going through marital breakdown is increased in all countries for those people in a precarious situation in the employment market. Employment instability and unemployment increases the likelihood of breaking social ties, becoming dependant on state benefit and experiencing health problems.

The clearest areas of divergence are in the social networks. Precariousness of employment does not necessarily lead to a weakening of family ties or of the individual's support network in all countries. In Spain and The Netherlands, those who are unemployed have the same level of relationship with their families as those who are working. This is also the case in Italy. In these countries, and also in Denmark, the networks of family and friends appear to be strong, even when individuals are faced by numerous problems. On the other hand, for France and the UK, instability of employment and unemployment are likely to lead to a weakening of family and social relations. In these countries, the process of social exclusion is more radical. Finally, one other area of divergence merits special attention. There is no correlation in Denmark between the employment situation and problems experienced in youth; however, in France and the UK this correlation is very strong. This result could lead to the hypothesis that poverty is not inherited in the Scandinavian countries as in the other European countries. These results should, however, be analysed with care, as not all statistical analysis has yet been completed.

Table 4.4: Sociodemographic characteristics of the population in situation of economic and relational poverty according to position in the employment market

Sociodemographic characteristics	Employment situation					
	Stable job		Unstable job and unemployed < 2 years		Unemployed > 2 years	
	Population in situation of economic and relational poverty (a)	Total population in stable job	Population in situation of economic and relational poverty (a)	Total population in unstable job unemployed > 2 years	Population in situation of economic and relational poverty (a)	Total population unemployed > 2 years
Profession/trade						
Agricultural	28.6	5.1	–	0.6	1.1	4.9
Businessmen	8.7	7.3	1.8	3.7	–	6.6
Executives	0.5	13.4	1.8	5.3	1.1	11.4
Professionals	4.4	20.6	7.9	13.0	–	18.5
Salaried	19.4	27.5	22.1	33.1	23.1	28.5
Skilled workers	16.5	17.0	19.5	19.9	13.2	17.3
Unskilled workers	21.9	9.1	39.8	20.8	46.1	11.9
Undeclared	–	–	7.1	3.6	15.4	0.9

Sociodemographic characteristics	Employment situation					
	Stable job		Unstable job and unemployed < 2 years		Unemployed > 2 years	
	Population in situation of economic and relational poverty (a)	Total population in stable job	Population in situation of economic and relational poverty (a)	Total population in unstable job unemployed > 2 years	Population in situation of economic and relational poverty (a)	Total population unemployed > 2 years
Qualifications						
None	54.4	20.1	48.7	28.8	56.0	41.6
CEP	20.4	16.1	11.5	12.0	15.4	20.5
BEPC	5.3	14.2	12.4	18.1	5.5	11.6
CAP/BEP	14.6	20.0	19.4	20.7	22.0	21.9
BAC	2.9	11.9	7.1	11.0	–	2.7
University	2.4	17.7	0.9	9.4	1.1	1.7
Housing						
Rich	11.5	31.9	11.5	31.9	12.1	23.2
Average	48.7	50.1	48.7	50.1	35.2	46.3
Poor	39.8	18.0	39.8	18.0	52.7	30.5

Life in youth						
No problems	46.1	56.8	39.8	50.7	36.2	43.6
Family problems	5.4	8.6	12.4	12.7	17.6	14.3
Money problems	39.3	25.3	22.8	22.8	30.8	27.6
Money and family	9.2	9.3	19.5	13.8	15.4	14.5
Sample	206	6,169	113	1,124	91	406

CEP: Certificate for Primary Schools; BEPC: Certificate for Lower Secondary School Studies; CAP/BEP: Certificate for Professional Aptitude/Professional Studies Certificate; BAC: Final Secondary School Diploma.

Source: INSEE study: 'Situations of disadvantage' (1986-87)
Coverage: All workers from 18-64 years of age

Notes

1. Those people who have a job or who are seeking work and claiming benefits. The decision not to take into account those who are not actively seeking work, including older people in particular, is a result of the difficulty in using the same indicators for population groups whose life-style is different.

2. This study is currently the best available source in France for the study of precariousness and the risk of exclusion on a national scale because of its multidimensional character. The questionnaire was composed of more than 2,000 questions that were put either to the head of the household, or to a person over 18 years of age drawn at random from the household. Carried out over a sample of more than 13,000 households, this enquiry brings together themes that are generally tackled in separate, specialised studies: employment, income, housing, family life, health, social life, etc. This source, however, does have one limitation. If the snapshot of French society that it gives is of high quality (97% of the population resident in metropolitan France are covered), it does not touch the most desocialised people (for example, those with no fixed abode). The main part of the survey covers only 'ordinary households'. It may be that this limitation is no obstacle when studying the factors and processes behind social and economic precariousness, as distinct from outright exclusion, but it must be borne in mind when the results are being interpreted.

3. These correlations have been tested by means of various regression analyses. For details see Paugam et al (1993) pp 62-63, 161-63.

4. Note that this approach, which distinguishes several individual situations by employment status, makes it more difficult to then take account of differences arising from the composition of the household and in particular the occupational status of the partner of the head of household. In addition, the survey upon which this is based does not

give as much information on the partner and other members of the household as on the person surveyed.

5. This corresponds, after updating in line with the evolution of monthly salaries net of social contributions, to approximately 2,700FF in 1994.

6. This finding is not new. See Lazarfeld et al (1970); Schnapper (1981). For a general analysis of social life in France, reference can be made to much more recent studies, such as Héran (1988) and Forsé (1993).

7. It can be estimated that 15-20% of the recipients of the minimum guaranteed income experience this situation of exclusion.

8. See Paugam et al (1994).

9. The sources used come from the following studies: Germany (German Socio-Economic Panel); Denmark (Danish Welfare Survey); Spain (Estiles de Vida); France (Conditions de vie des menages/Situations défavorisées); UK (Social Change and Economic Life Initiative); Italy (Social Networks and Support Systems); The Netherlands (Life Situation Surveys).

10. The information relating to these different fields does not always exist within the sources for each individual questioned, in particular, for the Italian and Spanish studies. In order to carry out the maximum of cross-checking on the same individuals, the researchers have had to choose the most complete source, that is, the source that covered the most domains.

five

BETWEEN SURVEY AND SOCIAL SERVICES ANALYSIS: AN INQUIRY 'ON TWO LINES AND THREE LEVELS'

Francesca Zajczyk

Introduction

Towards the end of the 1980s there was renewed interest in the study of poverty, requiring researchers to confront various conceptual and definition problems. During the period since then efforts have been made in Italy and elsewhere to deepen theoretical reflection on the subject, but it is impossible to ignore the fact that the boundaries of the notion of poverty are so hazy and variegated that determining who is poor and who is not is still a very complex operation, from a theoretical as well as from an empirical point of view.

In everyday speech, 'poverty' means 'a condition of extreme economic difficulty', a condition in which the resources available are so scarce that they do not allow satisfaction of the primary needs for survival. The problem is that this concept, so clear to lay opinion and in popular literature, becomes much more complicated when transformed into an instrument for researchers and policy makers. On the one hand, there is the idea of poverty as a condition of material deprivation. On the other hand, poverty can be taken as involving a plurality of elements, each in itself plausible, but difficult to bring together into the unitary picture necessary for practical policy. When talking about poverty, we speak more and more of paths, sequences, longer or shorter time-spans of transition, the results of which differ greatly according to the sequence of events that form more or less vicious circles, and in which there is a gradual accumulation of exclusion from the resources that people need, of social and institutional isolation. These ambiguities at the definition level have not yet been resolved (Negri, 1993) and, consequently, neither have the problems connected with the measurement of the phenomenon.

From a practical point of view, it is possible to classify the principal methods of research employed until now into three main types. The most common, at least up to the mid-1980s, involved secondary analysis of an ecological type, of existing data, collected in larger or smaller territorial units. More widespread now, especially in studies at national and regional levels, is the sample survey; and we shall, in due course, see how many variations there may be when using the questionnaire. Finally – and this is the method most frequently used in local surveys or in a limited territory – there are the analyses of beneficiaries or users of services.

Ecological research using secondary analysis

The ecological approach can be very useful in providing a context that integrates information on quality and quantity gathered with other survey instruments.[1] However, ecological research, by itself, does not allow us to answer such questions as:

- who are the poor?

- which are the pathways leading to deprivation?

- how can we deal with or prevent them?

Ecological research may, at the most, be useful when comparing territories in relation to their general level of well-being or 'quality of life'. Furthermore, when looking at least at the specific situation in Italy, we must acknowledge the grave lack of sources of statistics when reconstructing the quantity of poverty. This deficit is very obvious when studying urban poverty within individual municipalities.

Sample surveys

There are many ways of carrying out this type of survey, but all involve the presentation of a questionnaire to a sample of the population.

First of all, there are surveys on household consumption and expenditure, widespread in all industrialised countries. These surveys commonly form the basis for elaboration of poverty estimates: for example, in Italy, they are the only kind of research directed towards the measurement of poverty (Commissione d'indagine sulla povertà e l'emarginazione, 1985; 1992). The problem with this kind of research is that income level is not necessarily a good indicator of poverty. Income implies measurement of status, which is not poverty, need, exclusion or social marginalisation: it is a description of the income spent by different family types compared to the mean or median living standard in the country concerned. On the one hand, not all those who find themselves below the poverty level are, in reality, poor; on the other hand, there are others who are poor but who are not counted among the poor because statistics are calculated on a basis that is not really reliable – that is, on a level of income that is arbitrarily defined as a threshold to divide the poor from the non-poor (equal for all, independent of the context). Thus, for example, many elderly people have a low level of consumption, but their manner of life may vary according to age, the type of access they have to services, their state of health, and the extent to which they can count on their family, etc.

Two further observations are appropriate here. The first concerns the specification of the threshold; the second concerns the type of monetary indicator used. Generally, there is no doubt that the choice of a conventional indicator has the advantage of making data comparable. However, it is still necessary to consider whether we can really affirm that those who dispose of an income or consumption level less than or equal to 50% of the national average, are poor. For example, the level of 655,000 lire monthly per capita for Italian families may be a little or a lot. Quite apart from the arbitrariness involved in establishing the threshold, a second problem (which is connected with the researcher's freedom of choice) derives from the use of income rather than expenditure data. For example, in Italy the percentage of poor calculated on the basis of income data (6% of Italian families – ISTAT, 1993) is roughly half of that calculated on the basis of expenditure (15% of Italian families – Sarpellon, 1992).

For the moment I am not interested in whether one indicator is better than another – what I wish to underline is that 'poverty', including even economic poverty, which is the most easily and clearly definable, is not clearly definable at all in reality. In fact, "a measure cannot easily be more precise than the concept it represents" (Carbonaro, 1993, quoting Sen).[2] For example, it is self-evident that the evaluation of a threshold cannot be absolute. This, in fact, depends on a number of factors (demographic aspects, the presence of solidarity networks, specific characteristics of the nuclear family, etc), which inevitably result in differentiated consumption requirements. It also depends on the context. "The same level of income gives rise to considerably different conditions of life, depending on whether the families concerned live in a large city in the North or a rural area of the South" (Sgritta and Innocenzi, 1993).

> The incapacity of the threshold method to take account of territorial differences is very evident, especially in strongly dualistic contexts such as Italy, characterised by different levels of access to the informal economy and to the resources distributed by the State. (Morlicchio and Spano', 1992)

Among sample surveys which are concerned with social exclusion and aspects of poverty, a growing emphasis is being given to indicators of deprivation, both of a material and social nature. This line of research attempts to distinguish the poor from the non-poor, by means of joint analysis of three sorts of data, relating to:

- the quantity of goods, services and resources owned

- access to certain activities

- conditions of stress due to various economic reasons.

The items utilised are generally thought of as being 'primary goods and services', which are therefore 'necessary', their availability considered normal in the context concerned. So, although the conceptual knots are far from being untied, elsewhere in Europe we find something that does not exist in Italy – widespread attempts to measure and analyse poverty that go beyond the simple use of monetary resources. Even if, on the whole, the European scene appears to be rather confused and is not homogeneous in the quality of the work being done, we should recognise that the last 10 years have undoubtedly been fertile. Among other things, we should not overlook the research into conditions of life or well-being, connected to debates on economic growth, development of welfare and its effects on the living standards of individuals and the community (Nussbaum and Sen, 1993).

As the research literature on poverty reveals, the measurement of well-being and lines of deprivation can be placed either in an objective or subjective context. The former supposes the existence of an external agent (the politician, the researcher) who identifies a representative function of social welfare and makes an evaluation on the basis of statistical or econometric analyses. This kind of approach, which according to Sen's definition could be called 'standard evaluation', is opposed by the subjective approach or 'self-evaluation', which concerns the judgement of the single person on his own standard of living relative to that of others (Sen, 1993). Here, the analysis of poverty does not consist so much in the determination of needs and of the resources necessary to satisfy them, but rather in the recognition of grades of satisfaction obtained by a certain level of income, which can vary from one individual to another.

We will consider briefly the conceptual and empirical problems faced by the first, objective, type of survey (we are well aware that it is the approach that has been most commonly adopted up until now). At a general level, some scholars observe – and this is one of the major criticisms directed against Townsend – that

> ... objective methods are based on a concept of
> the function of well-being decided by some Big
> Brother. If such a function of well-being does
> not coincide with the individual's perception of
> well-being, there is the risk that individuals be
> defined poor even when they do not feel so and
> vice versa. (Van Praag, 1984)

There are, then, two more specific criticisms of these so-called 'objective' surveys.[3] The first criticism is concerned with the question as to the criteria for choosing the items on which to base the scale of deprivation and, in particular, whether the necessity of an article should be judged on the basis of an objective social criterion rather than the subjective judgement of the researcher. In other words, criticism is directed at the arbitrariness of the method of selecting indicators when constructing the index of deprivation. The second, and perhaps more important point, relates to the non-availability of certain goods because of the free choice of the person concerned, rather than a scarcity of resources. Various pieces of research have shown that many non-poor heads of families lack a considerable number of commodities previously judged to be necessities, putting in question whether they were indeed essential. Townsend (the question could be extended to others using the same approach) is accused of having completely overlooked the role of free choice, and, therefore, of the subjective scale of values to which every individual refers when making decisions, giving importance only to the objective scarcity of resources.

At this point Sen's reflections on the real possibility of obtaining objective information are relevant (Sen, 1993).[4] He argues that the self-evaluation approach involves each person judging his own standard of living relative to that of others. A person may consider it to be higher than that of his neighbour, even if in terms of general contemporary standards his standard of living could be considered inferior. There is clearly no paradox in this case, as two different questions may normally receive two different answers. If contemporary standards are amply shared, then the two sets of replies may in most cases not diverge and the approach of self-evaluation would then tend to produce the same results obtained when applying standard evaluation.

In reality, when undertaking research, this dilemma remains open, just as when Townsend posed himself the problem of which criterion to adopt when defining a set of deprivation indicators that could represent necessary goods or resources. As we know, Townsend opted for an abstract, theoretical, apparently neutral approach and defined his set as "necessary goods and services" on the basis of his own judgement. He defended his position, arguing that some people do not control their sentiments, the variables on which judgement is based and that an aspect of 'false consciousness' may play a role in defining what is considered necessary. A related line of debate among researchers is whether a subjective feeling of deprivation should be considered a necessary condition for saying that someone is poor, bearing in mind that subjective feelings may be influenced by the general level of satisfaction in the population at that moment.

There are also problematic aspects with the work of those who apply the subjective method, in line with the model of Van Praag. The first concerns the assumption that to the different verbal qualifications used in defining income (insufficient, sufficient, etc) there correspond "the same answers, that is that every verbal definition has the same emotional significance for all individuals, in such a way that an interpersonal comparison can be made between levels of well-being" (Cosimo, 1991). This assumption of homogeneity is indispensable to the theoretical framework adopted in this approach. The second problem is that the questions asked refer to *family* income, while the answers are given by a sole member of the family. It is assumed that the interviewed person automatically has the same perception as his family.

In the types of survey described so far, poverty is generally assumed to be a static condition, belonging to a specific moment in time and not the result of a process, which may involve not only phases of entry to and exit from poverty, but also periods of chronic poverty. Most research tends, therefore, to present the condition of poverty at the time of the survey, and there are few examples of studies which, at a cross-national level, aim to monitor the process of impoverishment and, perhaps, the eventual return to normality. This objective is, however, followed by the longitudinal panels. Among such studies are the Socio-Economic Panel (SEP) of the University of

Wisconsin, the British Household Panel Study from 1991 and the study *Living standards during unemployment* (Heady and Smyth, 1989), well known to scholars in this field. Undoubtedly, this approach is methodologically important for its attention to the processes by which people enter and leave conditions of poverty; furthermore, these surveys are widely used by researchers to test the validity of the various methods of compiling deprivation indexes. Apart from this, however, this type of research remains of limited use when it comes to analysing the social structure of poverty, and the results have not contributed greatly to a more general comprehension of the phenomenon. It is also particularly expensive.

We thus find ourselves before a major contradiction that expresses the relationship between theoretical elaboration and empirical application. On the one hand (that of theoretical reflection), there is a growing consciousness of the importance of the dynamic dimension,

> ... both for the comprehension of the phenomenon in future development, and for its prevention. The so-called stressful events, and above all their concatenation constitute the dimension which should be understood, at least in order to intervene adequately in terms of repair if not to be able to prevent the process of social abandonment in itself. (Kazepov, 1994)

On the other hand (the empirical application), there is a proliferation of surveys, mostly on samples, which continue to consider poverty as a status. At the most, there is an attempt to improve the capacity for measuring poverty by enlarging the range of problem areas that are surveyed and, therefore, of the indicators to be employed, and during the phase of analysis, to improve the reading and interpretation by applying more sophisticated techniques. The result, however, is that there are no great differences in the results as far as general evidence is concerned; there is more probability of defining as poor those groups that are at a disadvantage, in particular, in terms of economic indicators. Furthermore, perhaps because the samples are too small to allow study of small groups, there is no particular effort to develop typologies other than in terms of groups that are easily characterised (eg, the elderly, single people, women with children, etc).

Analyses of service users and beneficiaries

Finally, we come to the last method identified at the beginning of this chapter – the analysis of poverty through study of the users and beneficiaries of social assistance or benefits distributed to individuals who are considered to be in economic need.

Firstly, it should be said that such data about users generally represents an important instrument for studies at the local, provincial and municipal levels, which have not been reached – at least in Italy, nor, often, in other countries – by national surveys. Therefore, data on public services and voluntary structures, especially Catholic ones (fundamental in Italy in the field of assistance) fill an important gap in the official system of investigation and allow a more detailed knowledge of different local situations. However, this information is not just important at a static and descriptive level, even if this is the most obvious and frequent. Rather, it may be used in a dynamic way, in order to reconstruct the process of impoverishment (an undertaking which is, for example, being carried out in Bremen, Germany – see the chapter by Buhr and Leibfried).

However, this source of information involves more than one peril, when it is used for making statistical estimates of poverty. The first question is essentially of a conceptual nature and refers to the relation between the state of poverty and the condition of being assisted. We find ourselves, in fact, before a paradox. On the one hand, it is not necessarily true that users of specific services are poor. In fact, not all the elderly who receive means-tested benefits are poor, nor are the drug addicts or handicapped, etc. Certainly, the marginalisation and social exclusion common to some conditions may be the ante-chamber to poverty, but it is also true that recourse to certain services, while being a sure sign of social disadvantage, does not necessarily signify a condition of absolute poverty. On the other hand, however, we also know that, at least for some kinds of service, the users who turn to them are only the tip of the iceberg, which has a hidden side not easily definable and therefore measurable.

The second question concerns the effect that a particular welfare system has on the institutional fabric of assistance services. For example, as is well known, welfare in Italy, as well as being based on a conservative system that highlights the relation between the state and the family, is particularly weak (it is characterised by an extremely fragmented system of assistance, not only between public and private, but also within the public sector itself). It is evident that the image of poverty that is derived from this situation risks being partial and distorted; and that with a system fragmented in this way, and defining a priori the categories of service, we end up prejudging the type of persons to be assisted (minors, drug addicts, handicapped, elderly infirm, etc), independent of the path that led them to their state of need.

The third question, finally, concerns the difficulty of bringing together the results of surveys based on data obtained from these services. In fact, at least as far as Italy is concerned, these data are not at all homogeneous – there is no coordination in the way they are obtained from the various services and, even more grave and important, there is no national framework of laws on social assistance. This absence "has left a high level of liberty to local authorities, giving rise to different institutional regulations on social assistance, heterogeneous among themselves, so that any comparability is quite problematic" (Kazepov, 1994). With the data categories thus depending so heavily on the choices made by social practitioners, it becomes difficult to analyse developments over time or to compare different local realities.

Methodological innovations in the Italian situation

From the examination carried out so far of the principal methods of studying social exclusion, the picture that emerges of the types of research is a rather varied one. At the same time, this research is strictly limited as far as the effective measurement of poverty is concerned. It is not so much a matter of the quality of one survey as opposed to another: each may in fact, bring interesting insights. Rather, the fact is that, aside from the specific context, the empirical studies in Europe do not substantially differ from the search for a 'poverty line'. They are an attempt to identify, albeit with a variety of different indicators and analytical techniques, a condition of poverty seen as something more than just a deficit of material resources. Nevertheless, social fragmentation and differentiation on the one hand, and on the other, the interpretation of poverty as the result of a complex process of cumulative deprivation, have since the beginning of the 1990s been leading towards new trajectories of analysis. The dynamic aspect of impoverishment, and of the entrance and exit from a situation of need, becomes more and more important both for understanding the phenomenon in its evolution, and for its prevention. In other words, the conditions of poverty are characterised by a process that has a static structure. In this process, to the initial conditions of deprivation (a death in the family, the addiction to drugs, the loss of a job, the impossibility of conceiving, the experience of abuse) follow responses that produce other conditions, in which the initial ones are reinforced and yet other factors of deprivation are involved. Poverty is not, therefore, a static condition but a degenerative syndrome, a process in which different crises come one after another.

The most effective instrument for detecting poverty not as a static condition belonging to a specific temporal span, but as the result of a process that can include phases of entrance and exit from poverty, is the longitudinal panel (ie, a survey that is capable of monitoring the same group of individuals or families, over a period of time). There are, however, few examples of studies that seek to follow the path of 'social drift' or the eventual return to normality. In the United States such studies have been in use for the longest period of time (in particular, the SEP, University of Wisconsin). In the European countries, where a dynamic research approach to the study of poverty is now being attempted on a larger scale, Germany leads the way. Apart from the classic longitudinal panel, the work at the University of Bremen (see Buhr and Leibfried's chapter) is particularly interesting. Between 1983 and 1989 the Bremen Group carried out a study on a sample of 10% of the users of urban welfare. This approach consists in processing information periodically gathered by the public administration, with the aim of defining the relationship between the main causes of the condition of need and the duration of the use of social services (Kazepov, 1994). This is, however, a very expensive approach, that in addition limits the consideration of information on the processes of impoverishment to the standard information recorded by the public administration (Kazepov et al, 1995).

In Italy, partly because of the organisational and institutional deficiencies of the social security system, the biographical study of crisis has been attempted through the reconstruction of events by means of retrospective interviews. The first and most significant of these studies, analysing the process by which social needs are created and met, is the one undertaken in the Veneto Region (Mauri et al, 1993). The innovative aspect of this study, as in the study of the Bremen Group, lies not so much in the quantitative description of the long-term and short-term poor (although this is usually the main goal of panel studies), as in the attention given to the temporal chains of events, conditions and sequences that mark the itinerary of the different phases of the life-cycle. It consists, in particular, of a survey in 'two lines and three levels', which integrates general quantitative research instruments with the qualitative analysis of biographies. This approach is inspired by an interpretation of poverty and social exclusion not only as a multidimensional and relative concept, but also and, above all, as a dynamic one. The first line consists in a classical general social survey, in which interviews using a structured questionnaire were conducted with a random two-stage sample of a population of (Venetian) families. These interviews were directed to the reconstruction of the strategies used for facing the difficult situations that may occur during the life-cycle of a so-called 'normal' family. The survey compared two segments of the population: the normal aproblematic families on the one hand (in other words, the majority of the families included in the stratified two-stage sample of the Venetian study, families that in the interviews did not reveal any particular problems), and the normal problematic families on the other (the minority of families included in the general sample, which in the interviews revealed the presence of major family problems).

This was the first line of investigation in the survey, examining the areas of health and well-being (normality) or at the most, of contingent areas of crisis and disadvantage (problematic normality). But it is well known that a study of poverty or disadvantage (or, equally, a study of well-being or quality of life) must not overlook the areas of declared pathology (that is, of the critical situations dealt with by the public welfare system), as well as the areas of chronic or irreversible conditions of suffering or discomfort. It is precisely to capture the 'state of being' of other populations in respect of these very themes, that a second line of investigation was adopted through the selection of a non-probabilistic sample of problematic and 'marked' families (ie, families already assigned to some agency of the welfare system). In particular, this sample involved:

- families with at least one person aged more than 75;

- families with at least three children aged less than 14 (selected, as in the general sample, through the same two-stage sample of the registry office);

- families with handicapped members (extracted from lists obtained from the local sociohealth units or from organisations operating in this sector);

- families in a state of financial hardship, supported economically by the local authorities in their own homes (extracted from the lists of the social assistance units of the local administration).

These four large groups were presented with a structured questionnaire, virtually identical to that of the random sample, within which, however, three narrative windows were opened (the interview continued in an unstructured form) relating to the following themes:

- first, the organisational problems that have arisen in the family and the events that the family has perceived as problems in recent years, along with the organisational changes they have adopted to confront these situations (in terms of jobs, study and work-projects);

- second, the family problems that may have contributed to the situation of crisis (the sequence and timing of their outbreak and the requests that the family has made for aid);

- third, the economic problems that have arisen in the family, their relevance and the ways of coping with them and their general expectations for the future.

These two lines of study aim, therefore, to reach multiple fragments of the population that experience their structural and existential tensions in very different ways. To allow the highest comparability among different segments, the study sequence of the second line consisted of two phases. The first (the narrative windows) aimed at supplying raw material for a more sensitive, detailed, qualitative interpretation of the survival processes at the 'border' of poverty. The other (structured phase), aimed at constructing a first, tentative bridge between segments of the normal population (unknown to the agencies monitoring and regulating welfare) and the population of 'service-users'.

The first advantage, or at least one of the innovative aspects of the two-line methodology described above, is the possibility of reaching, with the highest comparability possible, a multiplicity of populations. The second advantage is that this type of study focuses its attention on processes and dynamic elements. In particular, the use of a transverse view of the different population segments brings us back to the processes of impoverishment. The four problematic control groups illustrate factors that differ greatly in a hypothetical 'drift-process'. If the presence of non-self-sufficient or handicapped members of the family is a significant factor in the risk of marginalisation, and if the presence of severe economic problems is an indicator of the acceleration of this process, the presence of a large number of offspring is not by itself a decisive risk factor. But its combination with other events or conditions or behaviours can create combinations that are difficult to cope with. The temporal variable can be decisive in the movement from situations of so-called normality to situations of poverty, as the 'events' gradually reduce and finally extinguish available resources. The focus on poverty as a process, therefore, focuses attention on the temporal chains of events and conditions that push forward individuals who are at risk or that aggravate or render persistent their social marginalisation.

The third advantage is that this type of study is not limited to a descriptive analysis, but attempts a more interpretative reading. The term 'process' evokes the image of a chain of cause–effect relations. However, it is difficult to speak of an aetiology of poverty, because the arrival at a situation of poverty cannot be traced to a single chain of cause–effect relations for two sorts of interrelated reasons: first, because different forms of poverty may be the outcome of identical starting conditions (above all for border-line situations); and secondly, because an identical final state (extreme poverty) may be the point of arrival of different causal chains, each one sufficient, but none of which by itself is necessary (Micheli and Laffi, 1994).

Notwithstanding the complexity of the causes, in the Venetian survey an attempt has been made to reconstruct a set of indicators to recognise those critical events whose arrival most frequently causes a qualitative increase in an individual's vulnerability. First, from the comparison of the sample's normal aproblematic families with its problematic families, at least six elements can be identified which differentiate problematic families:

- greater housing mobility

- an over-average incidence of health emergencies and related need for social assistance

- a high level of requests for assistance and of perception of need

- much higher frequency in the use of day centres, retirement homes and basic social services

- higher levels of perception of status deterioration (especially economic)

- higher support for the privatisation of public services.

Secondly, for all the six family groups interviewed, 20 indicators predictive of 'risk-conditions' have been selected and translated into probabilistic terms.

Let us consider what these data reveal. It is clear that widowhood characterises families with an elderly member (four times the average) and that it is also very frequent in poor families. In these families the loss of the partner may have been the key event in the worsening of their conditions. Housing deficiencies also characterise poor families.

It is not surprising that among poor families there is a high probability (nine times higher than the average) of risk when a family member has a past history of drug abuse. Drug abuse, episodes of nervous breakdown and chronic deficit in the household budget at the end of the month are strong predictors of a risk situation (especially among families that do not have access to welfare services).

Reduced levels of communication in a household are also a strong signal of impending poverty (among poor families it occurs four times more often than in the average family). However, the presence in the family of an elderly or a handicapped person or of many young children seems to enhance the network of inter-family relationships. So, this is a case in which an important resource for the confrontation of crisis situations, communication and mutual relationships among family members, can become a bond.

This has implications for the interpretation that can be given to an aetiology of poverty. If poverty is explained as a cumulative process, then an unsatisfactory job, unemployment and a low pension are often necessary but insufficient conditions for a concatenation of events, resulting in conditions of multiple deprivation. Therefore, we should not look for 'the' causes of poverty, but rather for the 'inus-causes' (insufficient but necessary part of a condition that is itself unnecessary but sufficient) of particular drift processes. But if a single inus-cause then recurs in a larger number of 'sufficient minimal conditions', it will often occur together with crisis situations – it will be a reliable warning of the presence of a crisis situation. If, for phenomena as complex as poverty, a single unique cause cannot be determined, it is nonetheless possible to rank a group of inus-causes that are more probable than others, and therefore to draw a ranking list of predictive indicators that may be considered more reliable than others.

Table 5.1:   Twenty indicators predictive of specific crisis situations

	NA $P(e)^5$	NP $P(X)$ $= i.n$	ANZ 5.5 i.n	PRO 7.4 i.n	POV 2.2 i.n	HAN 1.7 i.n
Widowhood	4.8	1.06	4.01	0.73	2.68	0.33
Separation/divorce	1.2	1	0.67	0.42	7	0.67
No high school graduate adults	71.9	1.02	1.07	1.05	1.34	1.1
One/more unemployed adults	6.7	0.74	0.6	1.69	9.82	2.36
Partner with an unskilled job	36.7	0.91	1.57	1.01	2.11	0.61
Father with an unskilled job	45.6	1.03	1.36	0.86	1.84	1.07
Family with 7 children or more	15.5	1	1.56	1.4	1.44	1.14
First-born at < 20 years age	12.2	1.16	1	1.07	1.61	1.03
Home with 3 rooms at most	20.2	0.99	0.87	0.86	2.71	0.95
Home without privacy	9.9	1.01	0.95	3.52	3.09	2.48
Unemployment benefit in the last 5 years	19.5	0.83	0.81	1.41	2.48	1.71
Monthly budget in deficit	8.6	2.08	1.62	2.02	6.57	1.83
Incurable invalids at home	4.9	1.06	2.59	0.88	1.98	3.96
Toxicomaniacs at home	1.1	1.27	1.45	1.27	8.82	1.64
Nervous breakdowns at home	2.2	1.28	2.86	1.95	5.82	6.82
Children failing at school	21.4	1.02	1.44	0.37	1.87	1.55
Worsening status perception	11.4	1.07	1.54	1.14	2.59	1.38
2+ family members receiving social assistance	4.7	1.17	3.04	0.3	7.02	4.85
Low levels of communication at home	7	1.06	0.69	0.41	3.68	0.5
Low levels of communication outside	17.7	0.92	0.99	1.06	1.73	1.29

Note: Included in the random sample of the families of the Venetian region: NA = normal aproblematic families and NP = normal problematic families.

'Marked problematic families': ANZ = families with at least one elderly person; PRO = families with at least 3 children under 14; POV = families in a condition of financial hardship; HAN = families with a handicapped member.

Table 5.2 shows a range of the seven specific predictors[6] considered 'most reliable'; in other words, of the seven most frequent inus-causes.

The three situations at the 'border' of poverty – an elderly family member, families with many children, the presence of a handicapped person – seem to have three specific important predictive indicators: widowhood, the lack of adequate housing, and nervous breakdown. In a picture as intrinsically multifactorial as that of families in financial hardship, on the contrary, at least two events distinguish themselves as reliable predictors: episodes of unemployment and drug-addiction.

The multidimensionality of poverty makes creating a bridge between scenarios (quantitative, general) and biographies (qualitative, particular) necessary. To do this, it is, of course, also necessary to have an interpretative model that unifies processes of crisis and of marginalisation of the population. A necessary, if not in itself sufficient, condition for the achievement of effective results, lies in having a clear project regarding the organisation and coordination of survey instruments. It should be borne in mind that historically, the major surveys on poverty (from the Parliamentary surveys on the South of Italy to studies of poverty in London at the beginning of the century – Booth, 1903) have always put together documentary material and a variegated array of research methods (statistical, sociological, anthropological).

Conclusion

In order to understand poverty, we need to use any type of data that can contribute to the construction of the above mentioned structural and institutional context: data on the labour market, on health conditions, on the use of time. In other words, as pointed out by Micheli and Laffi (1994), it is necessary to "throw a bridge between (quantitative, general) scenarios and (qualitative, particular) biographies." It is only by considering both spheres, that we can hope to reconstruct theoretical– methodological itineraries that will allow us both to estimate – even if approximately – the number of poor, and to define and narrow down concepts that have some validity. This certainly is an operation that demands a great ability to synthesise, or a model that can unify crisis processes and population marginalisation. This requires an ambitious project for the organisation and coordination of survey instruments strongly oriented towards this goal. Ambitious but necessary, because this represents the only way to generalise the analysis of the processes of social exclusion, and to reduce the danger of gross misinterpretations, especially for the analysis of vulnerable groups.

Table 5.2: Seven specific predictors for each marked family

Fam. with aged P(X) = 5.5% (ANZ)	P(X|e)
Widowhood	22.05
2+ family members receiving social assistance	16.72
Nervous breakdowns at home	15.73
Incurable invalids at home	14.25
Monthly budget in deficit	8.91
Family with 7 children or more	8.58
Worsening status perception	8.47
Fam. in a state of financial hardship P(X) = 2.2% (POV)	
One/more unemployed adults	21.6
Toxicomaniacs at home	19.4
2+ family members receiving social assistance	15.44
Separation/divorce	15.4
Monthly budget in deficit	14.45
Nervous breakdowns at home	12.8
Low levels of communication at home	8.1
Fam. with children P(X) = 7.4% (PRO)	
Home without privacy	26.05
Monthly budget in deficit	14.95
Nervous breakdowns at home	14.43
One/more unemployed adults	12.51
Unemployment benefit in the last 5 years	10.43
Family with 7 children or more	10.36
First-born at < 20 years age	7.92
Fam. with handicap P(X) = 1.7% (HAN)	
Nervous breakdowns at home	11.59
2+ family members receiving social assistance	8.25
Incurable invalids at home	6.73
Home without privacy	4.22
One or more unemployed adults	4.01
Unemployment benefit in the last 5 years	2.91
Children failing at school	2.64

Notes

1. Actually, analyses of this type do not have poverty as their specific object, but, rather, the more general theme of 'inequality', analysed through sectoral data, for example, labour market, housing conditions.

2. Among other things, some of the quality controls carried out by ISTAT in the survey on consumption, upon which the poverty line is calculated, have brought about the lowering of this quota to 12%.

3. These questions are the same as those raised by several scholars regarding Townsend's original work (1979).

4. On the other hand, Carbonaro (1993) has also recently argued that the terms 'subjective' and 'objective', now commonly used to designate the two paths of research, are not lacking in ambiguity: "after all, it cannot be understood why a line of poverty determined on the basis of the opinions of a population sample should be less objective (or more subjective) than the one fixed by experts or organs of public administration".

5. P(e) indicates the probability of occurrence of a certain critical event/factor, estimated according to the frequency of this critical event/factor in the random sample of the families of the Venetian region. P(e|X), on the other hand, is the probability that the same critical event/factor can be found outside the considered sample, that is, in the segment of population X, which means related to one of the six specific groups of families. Therefore, index number (i.n) means the frequency of a critical event in the subpopulation X, compared to the frequency of the same event in the whole population: i.n = P(e|X)/P(e). For the definition of P(X) see note 6.

6. The list of predictive indicators has been made with the help of Bayes' postulate, which allows us to translate the prior probabilities of occurrence of a certain event into posterior

probabilities, strengthened or weakened on the basis of some auxiliary information. $P(X)$ is the probability of observing, among families of the Veneto region, a family belonging to the segment X (poor, with handicap or even only problematic): a probability that is estimated through the corresponding frequency in the general sample, or on the basis of external information. The aim is to know the probability of finding a family of the segment X when in this family a problematic event is observed: the higher $(P(X|e)$ compared to $P(X)$, the more the event is a good diagnostic aid to improve the understanding of the peculiar problematic situation of the segment X; that is to say it is a good predictive indicator of X. The Bayes' postulate says that: $P(X|e) = [P(e|X) \cdot P(X)]/P(e)$; the predictive capability of e, specifically for the X segment of crisis, can therefore be found on the basis of statistics already available.

six

THE DYNAMICS OF POVERTY AND SOCIAL EXCLUSION

Robert Walker

Introduction

Poverty and social exclusion mean different things to different people. This 'overidentification' of terms is both a strength and a weakness. One advantage is that variations in interpretation can be embraced and hidden within a single word, whereas, if they were to be made explicit, they might prevent agreement and inhibit policy advance. Unfortunately the differences in the meanings attached to the term 'poverty' have now become so extreme within the European policy arena, with some actors denying its existence, others bemoaning its rapid growth and most concerned by the financial and fiscal implications of any coherent policy response, that its use has been shelved. For the time being social exclusion survives as a sufficiently ambiguous term to facilitate a continuing dialogue about matters that some would equate with, or, at least, include within, the concept of, poverty. However, the overidentification of terms can also lead to a degree of confusion and intellectual anarchy that prevents the possibility of measurement and analysis and, as a consequence, precludes the development of appropriate policy responses.

In his introduction to this book, Room discusses the disparate origins of the terms poverty and social exclusion.

- The concept of 'poverty', as used in most policy discourse, has its origins in a liberal vision prevalent in Britain in the late nineteenth century. Within this paradigm, society was viewed as a set of individuals engaged in economic competition, which resulted in some having incomes large in relation to their needs while others risked destitution. Policy aimed to ensure that those in the latter category, occupying the lowest position in the distribution of income to needs ratios, had the minimum resources necessary for survival.

- The term 'social exclusion' has different, French, origins. It derives from the idea of society as a status hierarchy comprising people bound together by rights and obligations that reflect, and are defined with respect to, a shared moral order. Exclusion is the state of detachment from this moral order and can be brought about by many factors, including limited income.

Simple but important insights into the relationship between poverty and social exclusion result from making time explicit in the conceptualisation, definition and measurement of the two concepts. For example, the personal experience of poor people is largely determined by the structure of poverty, its distribution within society and over time. Short spells of poverty are not only inherently less destructive than long ones, but, if experienced by different people, they mean that the poor frequently change places with the non-poor and that comparatively large numbers of people experience poverty. From this shared experience may come a common understanding that can provide the political support for policies to address the problem. Alternatively, a shared fear of poverty might act to atomise society, as each looks after their own. Either way, the situation is very different when poverty predominantly occurs in long spells. In such circumstances, comparatively few people experience poverty and the remainder rightly believe that there is little risk of them becoming poor. The poor have virtually no chance of escaping from poverty and, therefore, little allegiance to the wider community with which they have little in common, and from which they are unlikely to receive much political support. In such a scenario the experience of poverty comes very close to that of social exclusion.

    The thesis developed in this chapter is that the failure to take adequate account of time causes us to understate the extent to which poverty touches the lives of people, to misunderstand the real nature of social exclusion and thereby to continue with polices that are at best ameliorative and, at worst, exacerbate the problem. By way of response we *begin* the process of making time explicit. From an initial focus on poverty, specifically its definition and measurement, the chapter progresses, via a consideration of the experience of poor people and causation, to explore certain of the relationships between poverty and social exclusion. Some policy implications of the analysis are discussed in the final section.

Definition and measurement

Breaking with convention, this section deals with issues of measurement ahead of discussion about meaning. The reason is that some of the problems encountered, taking explicit account of time in measurement, cause one to question prior assumptions about the nature of poverty and social exclusion.[1]

The accounting period

Let us initially couch the discussion in terms familiar to those of us brought up to think about poverty first and social exclusion second. Poverty is usually defined in terms of a shortfall in resources relative to a legitimate set of needs. Clearly much has been written about the appropriate definitions of resources and needs although the debate about the rights and wrongs remains vigorous (Citro and Michael, 1995; Poverty Summit, 1992; Bradshaw, 1993). Less has been said about the choice of the accounting period over which resources and needs are measured, although this can radically affect the recorded level of poverty.

Lengthening the accounting period has the effect of reducing the cross-sectional poverty rate. This happens because averaging over time evens out the temporary mismatches between income and needs, lessens the degree of dispersion in the population and hence reduces the proportion of individuals appearing in the tails of the income to needs distribution. Moreover, there is an in-built asymmetry in the averaging process, since windfall income will inflate the average resources a person with low income has, more than a temporary shortfall will deflate the average income of someone at the opposite end of the distribution (Walker, 1991).

The consequences of changing the accounting period, which can be considerable, depend on the stability of peoples' needs and the volatility of income flows. Measures of poverty will be more sensitive to the choice of accounting period in situations where circumstances are less stable. Given the recent development of a flexible labour market across Europe creating more precarious employment, one can presume that measures have become increasingly susceptible to the choice of accounting period.

As the accounting period is extended, so the resultant estimates of poverty asymptotically approach the level of permanent poverty. This is because the shortfalls in income received by people who experience the shortest spells of poverty are the first to be offset by the higher income received during more prosperous periods. It follows, also, that the longer the accounting period over which needs are matched against resources, the more the characteristics of people deemed to be poor reflect those of people who, if not permanently poor, are in the midst of a very long spell.

There is considerable evidence from the United States that decisions about the choice of accounting period have non-trivial consequences. Reducing the accounting period from one year to one month results in a 24% increase in the official US poverty rate, while expanding the period from one year to six years halves the number of Caucasian white women who are counted as poor (Walker, 1994). While the topic has received less attention in Europe, life-time incomes have been modelled on British data and compared with annual incomes (Falkingham and Hills, 1994). Consistent with theory, Figure 6.1 (p 106) reveals that income measured over the life-time is much more egalitarian than annual income; indeed, depending on the measure used, inequality is reduced by between a third and a half. Employing precisely the same data and fixing an individual poverty line at 50% of median income, the poverty rate is approximately halved.

Figure 6.1   Annual and life-time incomes in the United Kingdom

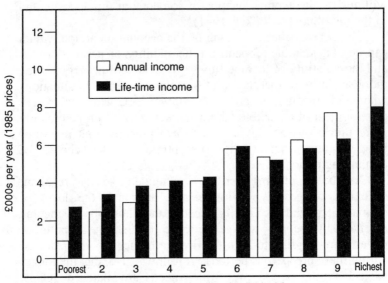

Source: Falkingham and Hills (1994)

There is probably no correct choice of accounting period. Different measures may need to be applied reflecting the purposes of the enquiry. Pragmatic considerations concerning the kind of information that is available will inevitably also apply. If the objective is to estimate the demand on a social assistance scheme aimed at the destitute and designed to obviate the need for them to depend on charity, then a short accounting period, probably no longer than a day, may be appropriate. However, if the concern is with the practicality of relying on private pension provision to eradicate poverty in old age, then the opposite is true.

Prevalence

Assumptions about time are typically implicit in cross-sectional measures, but need to be made explicit in a more dynamic view of poverty and social exclusion. In addition to decisions about the accounting period, which still have to be made, it is also necessary to choose the period over which poverty or exclusion is to be observed. Often the observation period is determined solely by the length of time for which longitudinal data is available, although this usually has inestimable consequences on the resultant analysis.

Prevalence, the proportion of a population that experiences a spell of poverty during a given period, is the longitudinal equivalent of the cross-sectional poverty rate and suffers similar limitations. Prevalence is very sensitive to the length of the observation period; recorded values increase as the observation period is extended because of the enhanced opportunity to observe a greater proportion of short-term poverty.

However, this sensitivity offers a powerful tool for further investigating the nature of poverty and for making comparisons between different areas or countries. If recorded prevalence rises linearly and rapidly as the observation period is increased, this indicates that poverty is principally experienced in short spells by different people. Figure 6.2, for example (p 108), arrays the numbers of people recorded as ever receiving social assistance in four Swedish municipalities when the observation period is expanded from one to nine years. It shows that, depending on the locality, between 4% and 10% of people of working age make a claim for social assistance in any particular year, which is consistent with the widely accepted view that poverty in Sweden is comparatively rare and that social assistance fulfils a largely residual function. However, the fact anywhere between 14% and 28% of the working age population will make a successful claim on social assistance in the longer term acts as an important corrective to the initial assumption. Moreover, it is evident that while the proportion claiming benefit is lower in Lund than in Malmo, people tend to receive benefit for longer (the slope of the curve is flatter). These differences might reflect variations in the underlying reasons for needing to claim social assistance or differences in the nature of the provision in the two municipalities.

Given a fixed observation period, prevalence is determined by the total volume of poverty, the length of spells and the degree to which they are recurrent. The lower bound is set by the situation where the same group of people is continuously in poverty. The upper bound describes the situation where poverty approaches a once in a life-time event and where spells of poverty are as short as the global sum of poverty allows. Values in between imply a variable proportion of the population is experiencing repeated spells of poverty of varying lengths.

Figure 6.2   Percentage of population receiving social assistance in four municipalities in Sweden*

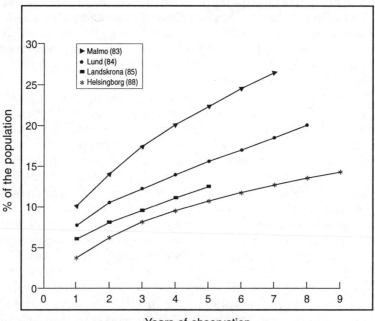

Years of observation

*   The observation period for Malmo is 1983-89, for Lund 1984-92, for Landskrona 1985-92, and for Helsingborg 1988-92.

Source: Salonen (1993)

Traditional discourse on poverty has implicitly assumed the kind of poverty associated with minimum, or at least minimal, prevalence. The poor have tended to be contrasted with the non-poor, as if the two groups never changed places, that is, as if the poor were permanently poor. Certainly, this concept underlies the rhetoric concerning the supposed growth in long-term dependency on benefits and is implicit in much of the discussion on social exclusion; to become detached from social structures is a fate not generally given to instant remedies. While prevalence measures for European countries are as yet rare, it is already clear that (thankfully) permanent poverty is likely to prove to be exceptional. For example, first results from the British Household Panel Study show that half of the individuals who appear in the bottom decile of the equivalised income distribution in one year have left by the second (Webb, 1995). Likewise, Dutch data relating to the mid-1980s, show half of all spells of poverty lasting for less than a year (Muffels et al, 1992).

Much more common (if the US experience is found to be repeated in European countries), is the reoccurrence of poverty. This phenomenon has already been documented with respect to social assistance receipt. Salonen (1993), working in Helsingborg in Sweden, recognised four different patterns of usage over a five-year period. Only 8% of recipients were permanent users, whereas 82% were variously categorised as occasional (42%), sporadic (19%) or recurrent (21%) users. Likewise, in Bremen, Germany, 40% of people claiming social assistance over a six-year period did so on at least two occasions (Brückner, 1995).

At least some of the people who experience repeated spells of poverty or periods on benefit are moving in and out of employment. They are trying, albeit with limited success, to cling on to at least one of the pivotal social structures that foster integration. It remains to be established what proportion of such people experience intermittent, or indeed permanent, exclusion from other aspects of social life on account of their repeated poverty.

What is already apparent is that in shifting attention from the cross-sectional poverty rate to a longitudinal measure of prevalence, one is forced to recognise the different patterning of poverty over time. This, in turn, raises the question of whether these different patterns, in fact, index different kinds of poverty or social exclusion. If so, then our traditional cross-sectional measures have led us to combine the sociological equivalents of cabbages and kings with potentially disastrous consequences for policy development.

Duration and severity

The arrival of panel data inevitably triggers an interest in the duration of poverty, even though other dimensions of temporal patterning may turn out to be more important. Moreover, duration cannot wisely be studied in isolation from severity, the extent to which income falls short of needs. Two measures of duration are commonly used, spell length and accumulated duration – the total duration of poverty experienced over a given period – and both, like prevalence, are highly sensitive to the length of the observation period.

Table 6.1 compares the distribution of children's poverty in Germany and the US, using an accounting period of one year and a six-year observation period (1984-89). What is immediately apparent is the contrast between a high and a low wage economy; not only is the prevalence of children's poverty much lower in Germany than in the US (20% compared with 32%), cumulative durations are significantly shorter with German children being 35 times less likely to be poor in all six years than their US counterparts.

Table 6.1:   Poverty among children in Germany and the USA, 1984-89 (%)

Duration of poverty*	Germany (%)	USA (%)
No poverty	76.7	80.1
One year	9.5	7.5
Two years	5.5	4.7
Three years	3.7	3.5
Four years	2.5	2.1
Five years	1.6	1.8
Six years	0.5	0.2

* 50% of median post transfer incomes.

Source: Daly (1994)

Initial impressions require some qualification. First, it would be wrong to underplay the importance of long-term poverty in Germany. After all, even on the figures presented, a fifth of the German children who experienced poverty were poor for a least half of the six-year period. Moreover, the figures presented understate true durations, because some of the spells will have begun before 1984 (left-hand censorship), while others will have continued after 1989. Another difficulty with cumulative duration is that it conflates different sequences of poverty. A single three-year spell is, for example, equated with six spells of six months spread over many years even though, as already noted, such different patterns may index entirely different social experiences. Spell censorship similarly affects attempts to establish the mean length of spells. Ignoring censorship results in an underestimate of the true length of spells. On the other hand, if the observation period is short, a bias in the opposite direction can be significant, as there is a higher probability of including long spells in the observation period than short ones.

When panel data first became available in the US these problems resulted in a frustrating political debate about the extent of long-term poverty. Fortunately simulation techniques have been developed that overcome some of the difficulties. Table 6.2 (p 112) illustrates the significance of some of the potential biases with reference to the time spent on Family Credit, a British means-tested benefit available only to families with children in which at least one person is in employment. The shortest period of observation is provided by a point in time measure, the current caseload. Ignoring censorship and counting only the time spent on benefit to date reveals that most people have been on benefit for less than six months and virtually none for more than four years. But adjusting for censorship and asking how long members of the current caseload will eventually remain on benefit provides a radically different picture, for it seems that as many as 30% will still be on benefit after six years.

However, the current caseload reflects the accumulation of long-term claimants and thereby does not adequately reflect the turnover of short-term cases. To take account of this, one needs to ask how long new claimants will have spent on benefit before they leave. The answer is that 47% of them will have left benefit after only six months, with just 8% remaining on benefit for six years or more (Table 6.2).

These different perspectives on duration, although adding complexity to the measurement problem, again help to clarify the social meaning of poverty. The Family Credit example reveals that although most spells of benefit receipt are short, covering transitory circumstances, a large part of the total benefit expenditure goes to the small number of people with wages that are continuously below the means-tested threshold. Longitudinal data for both The Netherlands and Germany reveal a similar pattern – although most spells of poverty are short, a large part of the total poverty gap is accounted for by the small number of people who are in the midst of very long spells of poverty.

Table 6.2:   Stock and flow estimates of duration: spells on Family Credit (UK) (%)

	Observed length for current stock (%)	Predicted length of completed spells for current stock (%)	Predicted length of completed spells for those starting a spell (%)
6	57	15	47
12	19	12	18
18	10	10	10
24	5	5	6
30	4	8	5
36	4	5	2
42	2	2	1
48	0	2	1
54	–	2	1
60	–	2	1
66	–	3	1
72	–	30	8

Note: do not sum due to rounding.
Source: adapted from Walker (1994)

A truly satisfactory measure of poverty would combine duration with severity, lack of resources in relation to need. There is, as Atkinson (1984, p 15) has argued, "some level of income deficiency which is serious enough even for short periods and a lesser extent of deprivation which becomes serious if it lasts long enough". However, income gap measures are rarely used even in cross-sectional studies (exceptions include Sen, 1982 and Muffels et al, 1992) and most combined measures that have been used follow the classic formulation:

$$P=YT$$

where Y is the income deficit and T is the length for which it lasts. This is essentially a static measure, for it fails to take account of changes in resources and needs over time.

However, devising a satisfactory alternative is by no means easy (Walker, 1994). Suffice to say that such a measure would need to take account of the depreciation in physical and social assets that may accompany an increasingly long spell of poverty. It would also reflect the sequencing of periods of poverty and relative prosperity and be able to distinguish whether a given shortfall in income is concentrated in a short spell or spread evenly across the observation period. Families may be most able to cope financially if poverty follows a prolonged period of affluence, although they may be less prepared psychologically, while the consequences of having no income at all during, for example, a three-month period, are likely to be very different from experiencing the same income deficit but spread over 12 months.

The fact that no comprehensive measure of this kind yet exists counsels against any belief that we understand what poverty is, let alone that we know the extent of poverty and its relationship to social exclusion.

The meanings of poverty

The attempt to find measures of poverty has highlighted the possibility that there may not be one form of poverty but many, each with different implications for social exclusion. Our growing understanding of these different kinds of experience comes mainly from qualitative research and the accounts of 'poor' people themselves. It emerges that, far from time simply being the medium in which poverty occurs, it helps to forge different experiences. Not only do people exchange places in the social order as spells of poverty start and finish, the fear of falling into poverty and the hope that it will one day end, a hope that sustains people but may fade over time, are all integral components of the experience of being poor.

The shared discipline

Although poverties may differ, they impose a common discipline. Merely to make ends meet on a low income requires effective money management. Moreover, this management also has a strong temporal component. Families facing an excess number of competing claims on limited resources typically respond by attempting to resequence the claims, deferring some until resources are available and holding on to a little cash in order to meet both known and unpredictable future expenses. Ironically, "when money is tight, managing the household spending [becomes] a full-time job" (Kempson et al, 1994).

In the UK it is typically the woman who carries the principal responsibility for budgeting, certainly when both partners are out of work. Management demands the setting of priorities with collective necessities (food, rent and fuel) typically being given higher priority than clothes, shoes or individual spending. However, while the woman almost invariably tries to 'ring fence' the money to be spent on food, this generally proves to be impractical since food is one of the few components of the budget that offers any degree of flexibility (Dobson et al, 1994; Walker et al, 1995).

Although welfare benefits are paid fortnightly, mothers typically shop for food weekly so that they can save money in case of unexpected demands and because food in the house is likely to be eaten. For the same reasons, women increase the frequency of their shopping when money is particularly short. Shopping is generally done alone in order to minimise expenditure. Searching for the cheapest items is time-consuming and difficult: when buying clothes, the choice is often between cost and quality, and hence durability, but typically there is no real alternative to cheapness (Middleton et al, 1994).

While families have no choice but to adapt their expenditures, preferences change much more slowly. As a consequence, for example, families struggle to continue to eat a mainstream diet by adopting cheaper imitations of conventional eating patterns. To radically rethink diet involves trial and error and there is no room for mistakes and waste on a low income. Moreover, change adds to the tensions and frustrations of poverty incomes that already deny people the sociability of eating out, the convenience of take-away foods and the satisfaction of entertaining (Dobson et al, 1994).

The process of becoming poor is deeply distressing, the memories of better times are vivid and the stigma, for example, felt in having to pass the supermarket by in favour of the discount store is painful to bear. Moreover, the process may not become any easier over time, not least because the financial cushioning carried over from more affluent days is rapidly exhausted (Morgan, 1994). Nevertheless, households do become more knowledgeable about how to manage on a low income and, in some cases, more practised at keeping within budget. Long-term recipients of benefits may become habituated to the constraints inherent in their predicament such that their frustrations become less explicit. For people who incessantly move on and off benefit the experience must be one of repeatedly dashed hopes and frustrated aspirations, when long-term planning is impossible or as likely as not to come to nothing.

Children's preferences and needs are almost invariably placed first by parents, both for altruistic and practical reasons (Middleton and Mitchell, 1994). They strongly believe that children should have access to a wide range of opportunities necessary for their social and intellectual development and, moreover, that they should not be singled out as a result of poverty. The latter concern raises in parents' minds the spectres of ostracism and bullying, while some parents additionally fear that, if they unable to meet the justifiable requests of their children, peer pressure may be such as to force their children to steal in order to be able to participate in the activities of childhood.

Certainly children appear to share a common culture of acquisition irrespective of parental incomes and, although children from low income homes may make less demands in deference to family circumstances, they may well be more likely to resort to tantrums and other forms of direct action when demanding things from parents. Low income parents feel themselves doubly disadvantaged in their financial dealings with children. They both have to say 'no' more often and to respond less consistently because of fluctuations in the family budget. In such cases, financial discipline over their children is exerted from necessity rather than from any decision about what is good or bad for their child to have or to do.

It is clear, therefore, that the seeds of social exclusion are inherent within the very experience of poverty: increased social isolation, reduced morale, deviant behaviours and even the experience of ostracism that are all linked more or less directly to the limited choice and restricted opportunities imposed by inadequate resources.

Patterns of experience

Given the social and personal consequences of living on a low income it is hardly surprising that, contrary to the concerns of some commentators, British evidence suggests that few people choose to remain poor or on benefit (Jordan et al, 1992). Instead, most poor people recognise that a full-time job or better paid work offers the best route out of poverty, although this mode of escape is denied to many on account of their age, lack of skills or childcare commitments (Dawes, 1993). While some people give up the search for work, and comparatively very few seek retraining, large numbers continue with the time-consuming, deeply alienating process of locating job vacancies, submitting applications and waiting to be judged acceptable or not for work.

With comparatively few well paid jobs available, people are forced to find alternative ways of maximising income. Based on the experiences of 74 low income families in three inner city areas in Britain, Kempson et al (1994, p 275) have identified a hierarchy of approaches, many offering only short-term solutions, ranging from the socially acceptable to the almost unacceptable (Figure 6.3). (Help from friends and relatives does not fit neatly into this hierarchy, since according to the nature of assistance, it spans the entire range.)

Figure 6.3: Hierarchy of options facing families with inadequate resources

Find better paid full-time work
Spend 'savings'
Claim benefit
Sell non-essential possessions
Find part-time work within earnings disregard
Use consumer credit for regular expenditure
Delay paying bills
Take casual work (often above the earnings disregard)
Cash insurance policies
Pawn valuables
Sell essential possessions
Charity
Petty crime
Begging (unacceptable)

In general, the options higher up the list are most subject to structural constraints. So, for example, respondents who have been in low paid work or have not worked for some time typically will not have savings to draw on. Families who adopt strategies further down the list, and engage in socially unacceptable behaviour as one clear manifestation of social exclusion, are more likely to have multiple debts and to be being actively pursued by creditors.

At any one time the 74 families were equally divided between those who were 'keeping their heads above water' and those who were 'drowning'; the latter were typically exposed to multiple debts with no prospect of things getting easier and confronted only by unacceptable options (Figure 6.4, p 118). Smaller numbers were clearly either 'sinking' or 'struggling to the surface'. Over time circumstances change, sometimes as the result of good luck or effective planning, more often because of events beyond the families' control. Families that had earlier been keeping their heads above water begin sinking, invariably as a result of a further drop in income. Likewise, some of those previously struggling to the surface manage to keep their head above water. The most common experience is that of financial instability and uncertainty while "the slide into difficulties [is] altogether quicker than struggling back to the surface" (Kempson et al, 1994, p 277).

Figure 6.4:   Trajectories of poor families

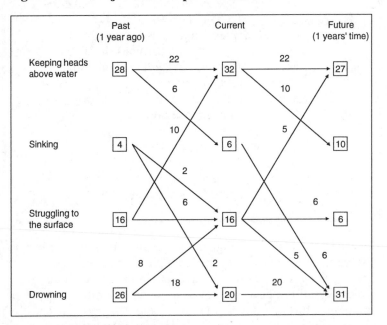

Source: Kempson et al (1994)

In Bremen, Germany, people who receive social assistance for a single short spell typically suffer only temporary loss of status and little reduction in individual autonomy. By contrast, those who move on and off benefit ('oscillators') face imminent loss of autonomy; they appear to inhabit the ever more precarious world of temporary employment and financial risk. Socially there is often little difference between the oscillators and those who have already lost status and become marginalised. One symbol of this marginalisation is evidenced by the gradual reduction in the notes added to their social assistance file.

When new to benefit, files are replete with details of support measures offered and implemented, but later the picture shifts to the routine handling of clients – almost a matter of shifting names on paper.

Some claimants in Bremen can receive assistance for long periods without loss of status or social exclusion. Primarily these people are pensioners who are not expected to move off benefit. Rather than suffer dependency as a result of claiming social assistance, benefit enhances autonomy by supplementing low pensions. This, however, is not the case for most long-term recipients, very few of whom manage to break free of the system through training or sheltered employment.

Evidence of this kind is beginning to suggest, therefore, that the different patterning of poverty over time, and the varying trajectories that people follow, imbue poverty with different social meanings and impart differential risks of social exclusion.

Causes of poverty and social exclusion

The major advances in our understanding of poverty and social exclusion that are likely to result from the arrival of better longitudinal data, and hence from being able to make temporal processes explicit, are in the area of causal theory. This is because panel data make it possible directly to observe cause and effect and to separate the sequences of events and behaviours involved. At the moment, however, we are still in a ground clearing phase. Although it is easy to show that earlier notions are overly simple and fail to take adequate account of the degree of change in society and in people's lives, coherent theoretical structures that take full account of studies of poverty dynamics have yet to emerge and, of course, data are often still unavailable.

Past debates about poverty have tended to reinforce a static view of poverty. At one end of the spectrum are those who view human frailty as the root cause of poverty. Individuals are believed to be poor as a consequence of their own capacities, attitudes and/or behaviour, which must change if poverty is to be reduced. Few proponents of this view see change occurring quickly, since it would entail developments such as the reconstitution of the nuclear family, the promotion of traditional family values, a fundamental restructuring and contraction of the welfare state and the coercive application of moral rectitude. In contrast, those who point to structural factors as the real cause of poverty offer a similarly pessimistic short-term scenario. Poverty reflects the prevalence of low paid jobs and processes in the labour market that push people into unemployment and economic inactivity. According to this view the incidence of poverty has much to do with the all embracing effects of class, mediated and largely compounded by gender and race, which exert their influence over income, wealth, education, career, family formation and inheritance. As a result, poverty is largely confined to the working class who "walk along economic paths that are familiar to their parents" (George and Howard, 1991, p 119).

Neither approach accords well with the enormous volatility in the financial and other circumstances of families in all sections of society that longitudinal research reveals. Substantial variations in income to needs ratios from one year to the next is almost common place. For example, individuals who entered the bottom decile of the UK equivalised income distribution between waves one and two of the British Household Panel Study averaged a 50% fall in income (Webb, 1995). Moreover, US context evidence suggests that there only a minority of the people who experience falls of this magnitude suffer poverty as a consequence (Burkhauser et al, 1989).

Also, as we have seen, longitudinal evidence suggests that the pattern and duration of poverty that people experience varies enormously. In studies to date it seems that the factors associated with an enhanced risk of ever becoming poor, or requiring to apply for social assistance, are also implicated in the incidence of poverty in its most severe and long-lasting forms (Walker, 1994). These include poor education, limited work experience, marital status, family size and race or ethnic origin. There is some evidence, too, that people who have suffered a spell of poverty, or have ever claimed social assistance, are more likely than others to experience additional spells. Whether this is because they are inherently more prone to poverty, for predominantly structural or attitudinal reasons, or whether the experience of poverty itself makes people more vulnerable, remains a moot point. So, too, does the issue of whether the simple fact of being on benefit, and/or poor, itself contributes to a person remaining poor. Research on this topic undertaken in different contexts suggests different answers which, again, may point to the differentiated experience of poverty.

The really important developments in understanding are likely to come from analyses of the triggers that precipitate poverty, the events associated with the end of spells and, in particular, the context in which they occur. There is growing evidence that the events that trigger poverty are widespread but that poverty is a comparatively rare outcome. This means that any comprehensive explanation of poverty has to take account not only of the probability that any particular event occurs but also of the probability that the event triggers a spell of poverty. Both probabilities are likely to vary dramatically between (groups of) individuals for reasons to do with personal characteristics and the plethora of structural factors associated with their prior social position and spatial location.

Table 6.3 (p 122) presents the results of an illustrative first step along this road to new explanations. Although the analysis that uses the Dutch Socio-Economic Panel is quite complex, and the data imperfect, it shows the importance of economic over demographic triggers. Becoming unemployed trebles the risk of poverty in The Netherlands, whereas people who have been widowed or become divorced are only twice as likely as other people to fall below the poverty line. However, these associations are not necessarily independent of structural characteristics, which are also shown to have an important influence on the risk of poverty. Being older, having better qualifications and higher socioeconomic status protect the Dutch against poverty, whereas being single or living alone increases the risk of becoming poor. Future analysis will need to investigate the interactions between the triggers and the structural circumstances in which people find themselves. Knowing the histories of the individuals, the sequence of events that have impacted on their lives and the changes that have affected others in the population should make it possible to disentangle the effects of personal and structural factors, and to construct theories that span micro and macro explanations.

Table 6.3: Routes in and out of poverty in The Netherlands (figures taken from the National Minimum Income Standard [NMSI])

Variables in the equation	Into poverty			Out of poverty		
	Pseudo ∝	Significance level	Exponent	Pseudo ∝	Significance level	Exponent
NMSI-ratio	0.1	4.5*	1.1	0.9	5.1*	2.5
Residual income	-0.1	-13.4	0.9	0.1	10.4*	1.1
Socioeconomic status						
employed	0	0	0	0	0	0
unemployed/disabled	0.8	8.6*	2.3	0.5	2.9*	1.6
retired	0.3	1.8	1.2	0.7	2.8*	2.0
social assistance	0.9	5.3*	2.6	-0.5	-1.9	0.6
no profession	1.4	11.9*	3.8	-0.8	-5.6*	0.5
Education level						
primary/sec. low educ.	0	0	0	0	0	0
secondary higher	-0.1	-2.3*	0.9	0.3	2.5*	1.3
tertiary	-0.5	-4.8	0.6	0.7	3.1*	2.0
university	-0.4	-2.7*	0.7	1.4	4.0*	3.9
Age class						
< 34 years	0	0	0	0	0	0
35-44	0.1	1.1	1.1	0.5	3.1*	1.6
45-54	0.4	4.4*	1.5	0.4	2.6*	1.5
55-64	-0.6	-5.5*	0.6	0.7	4.4*	2.1
65-74	-0.8	-6.2	0.5	0.9	3.4*	2.5
>= 75	-0.1	-5.2*	0.5	0.9	3.1*	2.5
Sex (dummy)	-0.1	-0.8	0.9	-0.4	-3.2*	0.6
Marital status						
married	0	0	0		ns	ns
divorced/widowed	0.2	1.4	1.2	ns	ns	ns
unmarried	0.4	3.5*	1.5	ns	ns	ns

Number of adults	0.3	2.3*	1.3	-0.2	-1.3	0.8
Number of children	0.4	5.0*	1.5	0.1	0.7	1.1
Dummy change n child	0.1	1.1	1.1	ns	ns	ns
Dummy change n adult	0.8	8.5*	2.2	ns	ns	ns
(Re)Marriage	ns	ns	ns	0.4	1.7	2.3
Separation/Divorce	0.4	2.2*	1.5	ns	ns	ns
Job gain	0.2	1.1	1.2	1.0	3.7*	2.6
Job loss	1.1	9.6*	2.9	-0.5	-1.3	0.6
No. of employed at t+1	-1.1	-24.6	0.3	0.7	11.8*	2.0
Change employed status						
no change	0	0	0	0	0	0
become employed	-0.7	-3.2*	0.5	1.6	6.0*	4.8
become unemployed	1.1	8.8*	3.0	-0.6	-2.1*	0.5
Time						
1985/86	ns	ns	ns	ns	ns	ns
1986/87	ns	ns	ns	ns	ns	ns
1987/88	0.0	-0.2	1.0	-0.6	-6.2*	0.5
Constant	-2.1	-11.5	0.1	-1.2	-4.6*	0.3

NMSI-ratio = the ratio of household income to the national minimum income standard (NMSI) at time t. NMSI is the threshold for social assistance payments.

Residual income = income other than labour or social security income at time t + 1.

Log-likelihood = 1,365 (out of poverty); - 5,290 (into poverty).

Pseudo R^2 = 0.21 (out of poverty); 0.16 (into poverty). N = 2,626 (out of poverty); 30,284 (into poverty).

* = significant if t-ratio > = 2.

Source: Muffels et al (1992)

However, the need to develop effective models of the processes that facilitate movements out of poverty is equally important if we are to better understand the nature of poverty and the attendant risks of social exclusion. We know, for example, that the prevailing level of unemployment is determined more by the speed at which people find jobs than by the rate of redundancies (Pissarides, 1986). Because the same may be true of the poverty rate, it is particularly important to investigate the barriers that prevent people escaping from poverty.

The Dutch evidence again points to the significance of employment as a route out of poverty: those who found a job were five times more likely to move out of poverty than those who did not, while education and prior economic status were also powerful predictors of the people most likely to escape poverty during the three-year period observed. In this Dutch case, however, the receipt of social assistance itself seems to be an important barrier, even when other socioeconomic, employment and demographic factors have been taken into account. Whether this reflects the loss of status and personal autonomy that may accompany receipt, the prior, unmeasured characteristics of those who claim benefit, or the attitudes of social and economic gate-keepers towards social assistance, recipients are among the next questions that need to be addressed. Assuming social exclusion (understood as detachment from mainstream social and moral structures) to be distinctly different from poverty, answers to questions of this kind hold out the possibility of determining whether poverty is either a necessary or sufficient precondition for social exclusion and, if not, what other considerations need to be taken into account.

To take a simple example, let us assume that one set of linkages between poverty and social exclusion can be conceptualised in terms of the trajectories that some people take between them. One such trajectory might take the form of slipping from poverty into social exclusion, a transition akin to moving from a state of 'keeping their heads above water' through 'sinking' to 'drowning'. This trajectory could be triggered by the loss of employment and compounded by structural factors. The objective chances of finding work and hence escaping poverty may be low. This fact may be understood by the family concerned and may serve to undermine the morale and hope that are essential if family members are to continue seeking work and trying to make ends meet. They may, as a consequence, have no choice but to employ strategies at the socially unacceptable end of the family's list of options and hence step outside society's norms.

Even before this point the family may have begun to become detached from social institutions and the multifaceted nature of social exclusion will have become evident. Preventative health care may have been neglected. The demands of mutual reciprocity may have limited visits to all but closest kin, while stress and depression may have added impetus to this social retreat. Lack of finance may have prevented children from engaging in the full range of intra- and extra-curriculum educational activities with significant implications for their educational and social development. They may even have reacted negatively to inconsistent economic socialisation that low income parents may necessarily provide. Confronted by the asocial behaviour to which the family has succumbed, the reaction of external organisations may confound attempts by the family to fight their social exclusion. Creditors may seek to repossess goods and landlords threaten eviction. Potential employers may be put off by inadequate personal references and social welfare agencies may move to more coercive policies. The process of social exclusion will have become vary hard to reverse.

It may be that trajectories such as these do not exist, but if they do, and their incidence and direction can be established, this will certainly illuminate our understanding of poverty, social exclusion and the relationship between them. However, this will also entail us learning more about the differentiation of poverty and about the incidence of its varying forms. First of all, we need to critically evaluate the emergent typologies, such as those discussed above, and to establish their validity as social concepts within the member states of Europe.[2] It is also important to ask whether the types of poverty are discrete, and perhaps associated with different aspects of social exclusion, or if one form is usually a precursor to another. We need further to investigate whether the sequencing of spells of poverty is important, if the severity and length of spells are dependant on the characteristics of earlier ones, and if the severity of poverty and the relationship with social exclusion varies systematically within spells. Only in this way will it be possible to devise and to target policy responses that are well attuned to the circumstances in which people find themselves.

Policy responses

We have already defined a long research agenda that follows from adopting an explicit focus on the dynamic nature of poverty and social exclusion. However, it is unnecessary to await answers to all those questions before considering what the impact of this new perspective might be on policy.

It is apparent that poverty is indeed dynamic: spells of poverty begin and end, most spells are mercifully short and the poor frequently do change places with the not so poor and even with the formerly prosperous. Recognition of these facts is an important antidote to the fatalism engendered by the view that 'the poor are always with us'. Instead of implementing ameliorative policies, which hark back to nineteenth-century ideals of relieving poverty, the imperative is for preventative action together with active intervention to bring spells of poverty to an early end.

The discovery that, although the prevalence of poverty-inducing events is high, poverty is rarely the result means that poverty must be understood in terms of the prior circumstances that allow the occurrence of an event to bring about a shortage of income in relation to need. As already noted, the prior circumstances are likely to reflect various combinations of structural and personal factors, which, when better understood, may well predicate a wide range of polices with short-term as well as strategic goals. In the interim, preventative policies, building on the experience of social and private insurance, have much to commend them (Walker et al, 1995).

Equally, if not more importantly, the fact that people are moving out of poverty all the time should enable us to draw policy lessons from contrasting the experiences of those who leave and those who remain behind. Already, studies of the dynamics of unemployment (Elias and Steiner, 1993; Gregg and Wadsworth, 1994) have pointed to certain key determinants of success, including aspects of job search behaviour, basic literacy and specific mixes of skills and experience that have begun to inform insertion policies. Other research has focused on the constellations of administrative, financial and other considerations that facilitate or inhibit movements off social assistance (Shaw et al, 1995). Indeed, the totally unexpected US finding that significant numbers of retirement pensioners move out of poverty has been replicated in the UK, pointing to potential solutions to even this most intractable form of poverty (Burkhauser et al, 1988; Ashworth et al, 1995).

More important still is the proposition that poverty differs not only in cause but in kind and that this may, in turn, predicate the introduction of differentiated policies. For example, if transient spells of poverty typically index a temporary departure from an otherwise prosperous life-time trajectory, they may be satisfactorily resolved by some form of bridging funding, perhaps linked to past or future income flows. Repeated spells of poverty in a life lived close to the margins of poverty, or recurrent spells of severe and long lasting hardship, clearly require a different policy response. Both may point to a tenuous relationship to the labour market and call for training or insertion policies that seek to break the sequence (Walker, 1994). The sudden fall in income coincident with some major life event may necessitate yet other approaches depending on the likely prognosis and whether or not the event constituted a potentially insurable risk.

A dynamic analysis also suggests that poverty and social exclusion are unlikely to be coterminous, either in time or prevalence. Poverty is probably neither a sufficient nor a necessary factor in social exclusion, although certain kinds of poverty may contribute to the risk of exclusion. Certainly the diagnostic features of poverty, shortage of money, limited choice and coping strategies that imply increasing isolation, portend the experience of social exclusion. However, the brevity of much poverty may mean that many people only suffer limited loss of status and autonomy. Lengthier and repeated spells of poverty present a greater risk of exclusion: families stand to lose the dignity that comes with self-determination as they find their best efforts are continually thwarted and their coping strategies are pushed beyond the acceptable, perhaps to such an extent that the locus of control shifts from the family to external social agencies. Social exclusion, in such cases, is a destination on a journey through poverty. Moreover, the risk of social exclusion may be heightened when poverty is highly concentrated and the gap between the social experiences of the poor and non-poor is most extreme. Tracing the trajectories from poverty into social exclusion, and determining the circumstances in which they are most likely to occur, offers the hope that one day it will be possible to identify quickly the people most at risk and to implement policies that stem their fall into the waiting abyss.

To conclude, time helps to mould the different experiences of poverty and social exclusion that will often be endured at different points in people's life-time trajectories. The trajectory followed in this chapter has been from poverty towards social exclusion. However, it should not be forgotten that unknown numbers of people move in the opposite direction from social exclusion into poverty – this is the theme of a chapter that has yet to be written.

Notes

1. This chapter draws on examples from a range of countries to illustrate *general* principles. However, it cannot be assumed that the precise circumstances that apply in one country will apply in another.

2. The new European Community Household Panel Survey (sponsored by Eurostat) means that this research agenda has now become a practical possibility.

seven

'WHAT A DIFFERENCE A DAY MAKES': THE SIGNIFICANCE FOR SOCIAL POLICY OF THE DURATION OF SOCIAL ASSISTANCE RECEIPT

Petra Buhr and Stephan Leibfried

Introduction

For a long time, 'duration' was neglected in research on poverty. Poverty research, commonly based on cross-sectional data, usually regarded poverty and social assistance payments as the unchangeable characteristics of people or groups of people. With the more recent dynamic research on poverty, a change of perspective has occurred. It is the analysis of the *courses* of poverty and social assistance, and therefore their source and development processes, that has become central, rather than their (static) circumstances at a point in time. It follows from this that poverty or social assistance payments are a changeable state, and in the course of the life of individuals several phases of social assistance and poverty can appear. This kind of dynamic approach is, for instance, evident in the research project 'Social assistance careers', which is being carried out at the University of Bremen.[1] The database is the Bremen 10% Longitudinal Survey of Social Assistance Files (LSA), which is being undertaken by the Senator for Health, Youth and Social Affairs in collaboration with the Centre for Social Policy and Special Research Unit 186. (With regard to the construction of the survey, see Buhr et al, 1990a; for the hypotheses and results of the project see Buhr et al, 1990b; Leisering and Zwick, 1990;

Buhr and Voges, 1991; Ludwig, 1992; Leisering and Voges, 1992).

With poverty research becoming more dynamic, the examination of the duration of social assistance payments has also become more prominent. It will now be shown that the question about the duration of social assistance is today being put in a way that is different to that used at the time when the Federal Social Assistance Law (BSHG)[2] first came into being; and that what at first glance appears to be the 'technical' problem of the measurement of duration, raises, in fact, a series of major social policy issues. In other words, the response to certain important, social and public policy-related questions (for instance, the definition of the scale of long-term poverty depends decisively on the concept of time that is used). In this paper we will not be going into the question of 'cross-sectional or longitudinal?', despite its importance. We are, however, starting from the view that the use of regularly established longitudinal data are appropriate in order to obtain reliable information about the duration of payments to the 'typical' recipient of social assistance, and the change in this 'typical person', as well as to determine thresholds for help in the run-up to long-term dependency. (On the controversy about the uses of dynamic poverty research and the differing meanings of cross-sectional and longitudinal data, see Busch-Geertsema and Ruhstrat, 1992, and Leisering, 1993. On the need for a dynamic estimate in poverty research and social reporting, see also Buhr and Ludwig 1991, and Leibfried and Voges, 1992.)

We will first describe the assumptions about duration that can be deduced from the BSHG, and how duration in public and social policy discussion is perceived. Hence, how long should social assistance continue and how long is it thought that payments of social assistance should last? We will then put forward the possibilities for measurement of duration, and examine these on the basis of their social policy significance. Five different functions of the measurement of duration will be distinguished. In this connection we will also pose the question as to how short-term and long-term payments can be distinguished. Finally, we will make clear the meaningfulness of differing concepts of duration, with results from our research project 'Social assistance careers'. In conclusion we will summarise the most important theses.

Assumptions about duration in the Federal Social Assistance Law: how long should social payments continue?

The BSHG, in contrast to the Promotion of Employment Law, or social assistance arrangements in many other countries, recognises no time limit on the duration of the payment of assistance, so that no general concept of duration and no designated scale is available with which the true situation can be measured. The 'spirit' of the law can be most easily gauged from the formula that social assistance shall be paid "for as short a time as possible and so long as necessary". Social assistance shall not be "equated with the payment of a retirement pension", and "people should not be allowed to carry on living on social assistance." The passing of the Law through the Federal Parliament stated as follows:

> Social assistance assumes that citizens wish to rely on themselves. It requires them to make genuine efforts to free themselves from public assistance. It would be doing them a disservice, if the extensive range of help led to the result, that financial considerations were such that it was better to become a long-term recipient than to remain in work. (Christian Democratic Union [CDU] MP Frau Niggermeyer at the first reading of BSHG on 4th May 1960, Federal German Parliament, 3rd period, Sitting 111, 6257)

The ideal case, which corresponds to this self-help assumption and to the origins of the BHSG, would be short term, but this self-help principle has itself already been broken by the BSHG. For several groups of recipients, the elderly, the unemployable, the disabled, and mothers with small children are accepted, so that social assistance must be paid for a longer time or even permanently, since it is not expected that they can earn their living by working. The Federal Parliament at that time stated:

> We are clear, that in spite of preventative help, a certain percentage of long-term recipients will be in need of help; I am thinking particularly of

certain groups of elderly people who cannot
become independent of social assistance
through insurance or their own provision.
(CDU MP Frau Niggermeyer at the first reading
of the BSHG on 4th May 1960, Federal
German Parliament, 3rd period, Sitting 111,
6257)

Therefore, no well-defined concept of duration can be deduced
from the BSHG. For various groups of recipients, different
assumptions about duration can, however, be indirectly inferred
(people without health limitations and family obligations, short
duration; women with small children, at least medium term until
the children are older; elderly and unemployable people with
any claim on other means of livelihood, permanent).

Time-related images of poverty in the public domain: the irrigidity and lack of empirical foundations

If today one questions the notion that social assistance in
practice fulfils its intended function, this also involves a
particular assumption about duration. It is accepted that social
assistance for many (especially old age pensioners, single
parents, and the long-term unemployed) has become a
permanent means of support. (On change in the functions of
social assistance, see Brueck, 1976; Wenzel and Leibfried,
1986.)

The design of social assistance as
individualised emergency help corresponds to
the provision of *only temporary support*. There
are therefore only coincidental needs, which
result from the adverse circumstances of fate.
This design, involving the hope that social
assistance as purely income assistance will
cease, because the prevailing social policy,
involving social insurance and welfare
provision, make long-term payments unnecessary, is, however, missing the target, as

has increasingly been shown, on account of the social structure. Single parents, the unemployed, and old age pensioners are often, for reasons which result on the one hand from the structure of their living circumstances, and on the other from their limited opportunities for change, dependent *permanently* or indeed for many years on social assistance as a *basic social support* (Wenzel and Leibfried, 1986, p 35 – emphasises in the original)

Furthermore, outside social policy 'discussion circles', the opinion predominated and continues to predominate that the payment of social assistance and poverty are essentially long-term phenomena and those affected are in every respect a permanently marginalised group. 'Once poor, always poor' – the message has been loud and clear from the end of the 1960s to the 1990s. "The vicious circle of poverty" was the headline in many periodicals at the beginning of 1993, when the Federation of German Trade Unions published figures on the new poor. The origin of such a perspective is connected with the fact that poverty in the 1960s and 1970s was perceived as, above all, a problem of fringe groups or the poverty of old age. (On the changing discourse and images of poverty, see Buhr et al, 1991.)

It will now be shown that this long-term perspective has remained unaltered, although the composition of social assistance claimants has changed considerably since the 1960s, and today there are more *potential short-term cases* than before. In 1963 more than 50% of the heads of household on social assistance (outside of institutions) were over 60 years old, while 87% were not employed. In 1988 the proportion of heads of households over 60 years old was only about 15%. Social assistance recipients are increasingly of a younger age group. Unemployment has long since overtaken inadequacy of old age pensions as a reason for social assistance. (On structural change in social assistance claimants, see Leisering and Zwick, 1990.) Thus, the thesis of social assistance as 'permanent basic support' has come into being at a point in time when the proportion of elderly and potential long-term dependants on social assistance has fallen, while the proportion of younger and middle age groups and the unemployed (a more capable short-term clientele, willing to help themselves) has increased.

It should be added that this assumption about duration stood for a long time on shaky empirical foundations, since no reliable data were available on the duration of social assistance. On the contrary, for a long time, duration was only examined in isolated studies and not as a subject in social policy practice. So the duration of social assistance, for example, was not identified in annual statistics on social assistance.   This will only change through a reform of social assistance statistics (see Buhr et al, 1992).   Only two special surveys from 1971 and 1982 give information about this.

The duration of social assistance can become a matter for debate only when variable periods of dependance on social assistance actually occur. If all or most of the recipients have no chance (because of old age or illness) to become independent once again, as was mostly the case at the time of the passing of the BSHG, then duration must not be, and was not then an issue. If, however, as today, the social assistance clientele is of a different composition, the concept of a differentiated duration, short term as well as long term, becomes more necessary and more meaningful.

Different concepts of the measurement of duration will now be considered.

Concepts of duration and their social policy significance

Presentation of different concepts of duration

Episodic concept (duration of the last linked payment): the Federal Statistical Office has, in special surveys, measured the duration of the last uninterrupted payment. This also appears in the reformed social assistance statistics – in other words, the duration of the last social assistance episode will be measured. A break of one day will be enough to create a new episode. It is the current problem, the immediate requirement for action, that stands in the foreground in this method of examination. Possible earlier periods of social assistance will not be taken into consideration.

Life-time related concepts: another possibility is to go over and to consider the whole length of time a person has previously been receiving social assistance, and whether the recipient has been able to stop receiving benefit more than once (discontinuity of social assistance payments). By this method, breaks in social assistance receipt also become evident. There are two possibilities:

- **The whole time period between the first and last payment (gross concept)**: here the time period over which the person has had contact with the social assistance office is measured, independent of whether or not there have been interruptions of payment. It can then be seen that, in spite of the periods of independence of social assistance, no long-term stability of income relationships can be achieved, and once again the path to the social assistance office must be taken.

- **The whole payment period (net concept)**: here the single time periods when payment has been made, which can be separated by times without social assistance, are added up over several years. In this way longer time periods than those of the episodic concept and shorter than the gross concept are revealed. Behind it lies the assumption, that, above all, the actual times of income poverty or direct contacts with the social assistance office are important.

As Table 7.1 shows, gross, net and episodic duration differ very sharply from one another.

Function of the measurement of duration

The duration of social assistance is, in practice, significant in a variety of respects. More especially we see five functions of the measurement of duration. In the first place, duration is an *indicator of problem situations* or *the need for help*, for behind particular types of duration or general time periods lie particular types of problem (and vice versa). With increasing time periods on social assistance particular problems can appear or deepen.

Secondly, duration can serve as an *intervention indicator*, and thus show where help is required.

This refers, on the one hand, to the kind of intervention. A simple example for time-related measures is the granting of social assistance as a loan, but other measures, such as paying out by computer or measures within the framework of help at work, can also be time-related. On the other hand, considerations of duration can determine the point in time for intervention and accordingly indicate an 'early warning system', the latest time when the situation must be dealt with, in order to avoid particular negative consequences of social assistance, or because it can be expected that the person concerned can no longer manage on his own resources. Thirdly, duration can also be used as an *indicator of burden*, both as to the financial costs for the administration and also the work efforts by the social worker. Fourthly, duration can be an *indicator of effectiveness* of the BSHG, for instance, retrospectively over the setting of the target that the recipient should become independent of social assistance as quickly as possible. Finally, duration also is significant for a *diagnosis of society*, because, for example, to describe the condition of the society as the 'two thirds/one third society' involves assumptions about duration (eg, permanent exclusion of a section of the population).

The individual concepts of duration distinguished earlier can now be evaluated in terms of these five functions. Where the predominantly episodic concept of the Federal Statistical Office is concerned, it is the immediate need for help and the current costs that are highlighted, in contrast to any life-time related concepts. Using this concept as an indicator of effectiveness, the type of problem and need for intervention is unproblematic, as long as gross, net and episodic duration approximate to each other (something that could be taken for granted in the 1960s more than it can today). However, as these three 'duration' concepts diverge, because of interruptions of payment (or to put it another way, unsuccessful 'escape' from social assistance), a purely episodic concept misses the problem cases. This is still more the case, if social assistance is not limited to cash payments but, as stipulated in the law, also includes personal and counselling help. Gross and net duration then become more appropriate indicators of the effectiveness of the BSHG, for types of need and forms of intervention.

Table 7.1: Schematic portrayal of the gross, net and episodic duration shown by an example of two cases in the Bremen 10% longitudinal survey of social assistance files

1/83	Observation period	4/89
	Number and duration of payment spells	

Case 1

| A | B | C | D | E | F |

Case 2

| G | H | I | J | K |

10/86

Explanation: Gross concept: time period between the first and last payments (1/83-4/89)

Net concept: sum of single payment time periods

Case 1: A + B + C + D + E + F; Case 2: G + H + I + J + K

Source: Senator for Health, Youth and Social Affairs; Centre for Social Policy and Special Research Unit 186 of the University of Bremen: Bremen LSA

Episodic concept: last connected payment (payment time period, ie, F and K). (Official concept of the Federal Statistical Office: a new payment time period is defined already after an interruption of one day.)

Longitudinal study: observation of the course of social assistance (whole case) of both cases from 1/83 until time point of enquiry 4/89.

Cross-section study: examination referring to time (vertical line); at one point 10/86, for example, case 2 is not in payment.

This is because the gross and net duration concepts take into account that in a person's life, multiple forms of social assistance may be required; these concepts therefore constitute stronger indicators for the likely course of problems than the episodic concept of the Federal Statistical Office. They refer to the causes of multiple social assistance payments, and hence why some people succeed better than others in becoming *permanently* independent of social assistance.

This becomes clear if one looks again at Table 7.1: if one were to depend only on the episodic concept, a 'distorted' picture would emerge. Both cases depicted here have had a number of social assistance payments. Altogether, the recipients of assistance have been in contact with the social security office for more than six years; however, the most recent payments last only two or nine months respectively. That is why the gross and net concepts are more appropriate than the episodic concept in portraying causes of social assistance, and in assessing the effectiveness of the BSHG with regard to the target of making people permanently independent of social assistance. On the other hand, one could argue that whoever repeatedly manages to leave social assistance will manage it once again.

Because the episodic duration is an indicator for the current financial cost of support, it can be used in conjunction with the net concept to estimate how much a recipient has cost overall in the course of his dealings with social assistance.

On the basis of our interviews with social assistance recipients we gained the impression that the people whose payments have been interrupted many times (so that the gross, net and episodic concepts diverge dramatically), are frequently the hard cases, 'multi-problem cases' (see Buhr, 1995; Ludwig, 1995), who have more than just financial problems. A 'continuous long-term case', someone who therefore receives social assistance uninterrupted over long time periods (no difference between gross and net duration), will presumably make less work, because it has become routine (eg, payment by computer) (see also Schwarz, 1995). In other words, behind different types of duration lie different problem situations for the social authorities – cases which are more or less difficult and cause more or less work. This result suggests that the duration of social assistance can also be an indicator of the workload on social assistance officials, thus yielding a method for revising these workloads on a differential basis.

The explosive force of measurement of duration for social policy is show particularly when duration is used as an indicator of effectiveness. As shown above, the individual concepts of duration deal quite differently with long-term use of social assistance. Correspondingly, differing 'portrayals of the effectiveness of policy' are possible: depending on one's political or ideological position, one will therefore either favour a concept which, like the episodic concept, concentrates on short durations, and thereby implies higher levels of effectiveness, successful policies or open social structures; alternatively, one favours a concept which, as in the case of the gross and net concepts, concentrates on longer duration and thereby reveals a lower degree of effectiveness of the policy.

Problems in drawing the boundary between short- and long-term payment

The question of when short-term payments cease and long-term payment begins is at first glance only of a more straightforward and technical nature. There are no unambiguous criteria for making this distinction. In different studies various boundaries are used, and these boundaries also change over time. Nevertheless, threshold values that define the transition to long-term payment (seen as problematic) are important (for instance, so as to be able to stipulate the point in time for intervention). Possible threshold values, which are listed in summary in Figure 7.1 (p 141), will now be considered.

The BSHG mentions the idea of 'short term' (para 15b), but without any further explanation. In the legal terminology this time period is understood, as a rule, to be up to six months. Unemployed people are deemed to be long-term unemployed after one year, a boundary which is also frequently regarded by practitioners in the social assistance field as the transition to long-term payment (Schwarz, 1995). Such or other *absolute boundaries* must, however, remain arbitrary, as long as they are not fleshed out with any particular content. In other words, it is necessary to take into account, after what time period of social assistance payment particular consequences follow for the person concerned (mental health, motivation, state of health, living conditions, etc) and for the authorities (costs, trouble), so that the critical boundaries or threshold values for intervention (eg, the introduction of measures to help find employment) can be determined. As far as we can see, precise thresholds were not, up until now, to be found in research either into unemployed people or into poverty.

In contrast to these absolute boundary values, *relative thresholds* set an individual time period on social assistance in relation to the individual's life-time or to the experience of other social assistance recipients. Related to the life-time, a time period from one to two years on social assistance has a relevance other than in relation to a short observation period. However, the problem of laying down particular boundaries also arises here. What amount of social assistance time is judged to be critical, as a proportion of life-time? Here too, the question should be asked as to whether the duration of social assistance should not be evaluated according to the stage of life of the person – is the duration of social assistance more fateful for younger people than for older people, and therefore should it be weighted correspondingly more strictly?

The individual duration of social assistance payments could also be related to the duration of payment of other social assistance recipients. It could, for instance, be laid down that those who remain longer than average in receipt of benefit should be regarded as a long-term case; or that the 10% or 20% of all recipients who remain longest in receipt of benefit need special help. It can also be laid down that long-term dependance begins where the probability of leaving assistance drops markedly. If, on the basis of empirical data about several cohorts, one established that the probability of leaving assistance after two years lay at only 10%, for example, this could be the critical boundary: that is, all those who after two years have still not escaped require help which is targeted on their needs, because there is now only a slight possibility that they can make the 'jump' on their own.

Figure 7.1: Possible boundaries between short- and long-term payment

---

1.   Objective boundaries.
1.1   Absolute boundaries.

Establishment of critical time points (1 year, 10 years) when short-term payment ceases and long-term payment begins.

1.2   Relative boundaries.
1.2.1   Boundaries with which individual social assistance and life-time are set in relationship.

Establishment of a critical proportion of the individual's life-time in receipt of social assistance: long-term payment begins, when on average a particular proportion of life (perhaps 50%) has been spent on social assistance.

1.2.2   Boundaries, which relate the individual period on social assistance to that of all other social assistance recipients.

Particular groups of social assistance recipients are ranked as short- or long-term claimants (perhaps the lower or upper quartile; or the upper or lower decile; or those above or below the average).

2.   Subjective boundaries.

Self-assessment by those concerned, on the basis of their estimate of the significance and consequences of social assistance payments.

These relative boundaries are dependant on the actual distribution of duration within a particular group of social assistance recipients and over a particular time period. At times when many recipients come off benefit relatively quickly, the intervention thresholds are correspondingly lower and more people receive the benefit of (targeted) help earlier; at times, when on average, longer periods are spent on social assistance, perhaps because of a poor economic situation, the thresholds are accordingly higher, and fewer people receive extra help (eg, training courses) at a later stage. The advantage of this kind of relative concept is that there is a good adaptation of assistance measures to existing means (it therefore works procyclically, rather than countercyclically). The disadvantage is that in individual cases the intervention threshold (precisely because of this procyclical process) may end up being significantly higher than would be demanded by observing the effectiveness of the social assistance that is being offered.

Finally, *subjective boundaries* could also be used, which are based on the self-assessment of the person concerned. The results of our interview indicate that subjective assumptions about time – dependant on the meaning that the individual attaches to social assistance, or else on the available resources that determine his perception of the likelihood of escaping – can differ from objective, absolute boundaries more or less strongly. So, a payment, which according to objective or relative criteria is seen as long term, could be assessed by the person concerned as 'temporary' or 'limited'. This is especially true for single parents, who define their receipt of social assistance as a transitory phase until their children reach school age (Buhr, 1995).

Alternative ways of measuring the duration of social assistance payments – an empirical example

Table 7.2 shows the varied distribution of long- and short-term payment, depending on which concept is used for measuring the duration of social assistance and for defining long- and short-term receipt. The data refer to 586 cases (administrative records) from a cohort of claimants (1983) in the LSA.

Table 7.2:   Long-term and short-term payments according to different concepts of duration

Threshold value	Duration concept		
	Gross	Net	Episodic
Short: up to 1 year	45%	55%	76%
Middle: 1-5 years	32%	34%	19%
Long: over 5 years	23%	11%	5%
Relative threshold of short-term payment ('lower 25%')	3 mths	2 mths	1 mth
Middle threshold ('50% median')	18 mths	9 mths	4 mths
Relative threshold of long-term payment ('upper 25%')	58 mths	30 mths	12 mths

Upper part of the table, gross concept column: up to one year 45%, over five years 23% of cases in the cohort of claimants in benefit in 1983.

Lower part of the table, column net concept: 25% of recipients removed after two months at the most. In comparison, 25% remain longer than 30 months in benefit.

Source: Senator for Health, Youth, and Social Affairs, Centre for Social Policy and Special Research Unit 186 of the University of Bremen: Bremen: LSA.

We distinguish between three concepts of duration (gross, net and episodic) and between two possibilities for distinguishing between long- and short-term receipt of social assistance: absolute boundaries (years) and relative boundaries (quartiles). The upper part of the table contains the percentage of cases having received social assistance for less than a year, one to five years and longer than five years. In the lower part of the table we show three relative thresholds, which show into which time period, a quarter, half and three quarters of all cases in payment fall. We have then defined the lower 25% as short-term claimants and the upper 25% as long-term claimants; that is, short-term payments cease where a quarter of the cases are taken out of benefit, and long-term payment begins where only a quarter are still in payment.

The highest proportion of short-term claimants (and the lowest relative threshold of the short-term payments) are show to be for the episodic concept; the lowest proportion of short-term claimants (but still nearly 50%) and the highest relative threshold of long-term payments appear under the gross concept 'what a difference a day makes'. These results again make clear that a purely episodic concept can bypass the problem cases; and they show the effect on social reporting that a break of one day in payment of social assistance can have. At the same time, however, it shows, independently of the duration concept used, that the short-term recipient is the predominant type of claimant. That also means that social assistance fulfils its aim of converting help to self-help for a large number of recipients, as these become independent of social assistance again after a relatively short time.

Conclusion

The new dynamic poverty research has directed attention more closely than before to the duration of social assistance. After closer analysis, 'time' turns out to be an important dimension that had previously been neglected, and had remained scientifically and politically unquestioned. Our concern was to show the problems of measurement and to analyse the social and social policy relevance of different concepts of duration.

As an indicator of effectiveness, types of need and intervention requirements, a concept of duration that measures the duration of social assistance throughout a life-time, and takes into account breaks and new payments, is preferable to a purely episodic concept. In order to indicate immediate needs for action and the current costs, however, an episodic concept can be meaningful.

A reform of official statistics should be concentrated on the *total duration* (gross and net concepts) as well as on the *episodic concepts*, thereby providing policy makers and administrators with better information. The introduction of data processing in the field of social assistance might also improve the quality of local social reporting.

Taking duration as an effectiveness indicator should not, however, obscure the fact that for particular groups (the elderly and disabled, for instance) the dictum 'the shorter the help, the more effective it is' does not and cannot apply. The results of our project also show that a prolonged duration of social assistance must not always inevitably go along with special problems, and thus, increased needs for intervention. This indicates the limits of duration of social assistance as an indicator of problems, interventions and effectiveness (Buhr and Leisering, 1995).

Notes

1. The project is being led by Stephan Leibfried and Wolfgang Voges. Petra Buhr, Lutz Leisering, Monika Ludwig and Michael Zwick are project collaborators.

2. The Federal Social Assistance Law (BSHG) is a means-tested programme for which everyone in need and who cannot help themselves is eligible. However, since 1993, people asking for asylum are treated in a special system. Social assistance consists of 'Hilfe zum Lebensunterhalt' (maintenance benefits) and 'Hilfe in besonderen Lebenslagen' (benefits for persons with special needs, eg, disabled persons). In our project, we concentrate on persons receiving maintenance benefits.

eight

SOCIAL EXCLUSION AND SPATIAL STRESS: THE CONNECTIONS

Hans Kristensen

Introduction

At a recent meeting in the Danish Ministry of Housing and Building, the development of spatial social indicators in connection with the surveillance of different housing estates and town sectors was discussed. After having debated different income groups, age profiles, business conditions, etc, one of the participants stated that in his opinion the best indicator was the make of cars in a parking lot on an ordinary evening. A housing area with a lot of old, rusty, worn-down Ladas and Skodas and a few (if any) BMWs was a sure sign of a problematic area. Although we, at the Danish Building Research Institute, have, for many years, researched into the development and solution of problems in housing areas we have, however, not applied this indicator. But I think that he is right – during our research work it has been easy to see whether one was in a well-functioning part of town or in an area with social problems. It is not only the parked cars that make an impression, but also the appearance of the houses, the degree of wear and tear, the conditions of the windows, the amount of garbage, the surface of the roads – all these physical features clearly indicate the socioeconomic conditions inside the houses as well as among the people moving about the neighbourhood.

The first realisation is that there *is* a connection between the social condition of a housing area and the physical appearance of a neighbourhood. In what follows I will summarise the connection between these social and physical aspects, based on research into social exclusion over the last decade and reconstruction attempts in different housing areas. Furthermore, I would like to discuss which indicators are capable of representing these processes and their results. In this connection I would specifically like to argue for indicators that can make the problems as well as their solution visible.

Development of problems

During the 1960s and 1970s the main problem of the Danish welfare society was not yet social exclusion, but rather the inequality reigning in the labour market as far as income was concerned. It was the working poor who became the centre of an extensive programme of research carried out by the Low Income Commission (LIC) (Lavindkomstkommissionen, 1982), which started its work in 1976. The small section of the population – yet on the increase – aged between 16 and 67, which was excluded from the labour market, was not considered a grave problem. The general attitude was that the welfare system ought to be able to take care of this group. But already during the five-year period of the LIC's work, ie, from 1976-81, a change took place. Unemployment was a reality and the exclusion from the labour market of more and more groups of society who were referred to different early retirement schemes or who became long-term unemployed was increasing. And now in the 1990s the fact that approximately one third of all persons aged between 16 and 67 are more or less permanently excluded from the labour market is without doubt the gravest social problem in Denmark (Kristensen, 1995).

The spatial distribution of social problems has also changed. Earlier, the mass of social problems was concentrated in specific neighbourhoods in and around the town centres, whereas the large, newly built social housing estates on the outskirts of cities were still populated by young families of workers and salaried employees. The new suburban housing areas had larger flats than previously, were better equipped and were surrounded by wide open green spaces. The flats of these housing estates are almost of a size (100-120 m²) corresponding to that of a Danish one-family house, so they were attractive in spite of the high rent. Since then, many of these housing estates in particular have had a hard time.   There has been an accelerating process whereby they have turned into slums and an accumulation of social and physical decay has taken place; in other words, a development of spatial stress has set in. During the same period, some of the older neighbourhoods were renovated, whereas others have undergone a gentrification process, so that some of the previous slum areas close to the town centres do not have as many social problems as the more recent suburban housing areas. Our studies of the slumming process are illustrated below, corresponding to the processes taking place in older neighbourhoods.

Figure 8.1:   Study of the slumming process

Resourceful families move out
Vacant flats – high percentage of moves
Problematic families move in
Few resources for the strengthening of the social life
Social decay, vandalism, crime
Branding, bad reputation
High rent
Fewer funds for maintenance
Physical decay
Building damages
Unemployment, more marginalised

The connection between social exclusion and spatial stress

From Figure 8.1 it is difficult to ascertain what started the processes in the large suburban social housing estates.   In Denmark it was, paradoxically, the growth of welfare provision and a very generous tax system during the 1960s and beginning of the 1970s that made the private one-family house attainable for almost everybody with a steady income, and more especially for two-income families. The consequence was that a large majority of Danish workers and salaried employees went from rented flats to owner-occupied homes. More than 55% of Danish householders live in owner-occupied homes, primarily one-family houses. Those who were left behind in rented flats were either financially badly off (for example, those who were already undergoing a process of exclusion), or those who already functioned less well, perhaps as they were already excluded. It was difficult for the housing corporations to rent out the vacant flats, and those who were looking for a flat or were helped by the municipality to obtain a flat, were often socially and financially weak persons or families. Gradually, this process of exchange made its mark on the estates: more vandalism, grafitti on the walls, broken windows in basements, filthiness on the stairways, and trees, bushes and flowers ruined. These events coincided with the building damage caused by the low quality, if novel, solutions adopted during the rapid industrialisation of the building process: leaking roofs, facade joints opening up, causing draught and moisture, windows beginning to rot, and the technical installations proving inadequate. There were no funds for necessary repairs and increased maintenance, as the economy of each estate is independent. Often maintenance was postponed or totally omitted. This made the poor appearance of the estates even more visible and was a signal to the tenants as well as to the outside world that here there was no future. This gradual branding and bad reputation led to more and more people and families, with a surplus of human as well as financial resources, choosing to move out. In this way the negative development process shown in Figure 8.1 perpetually reinforces itself. The physical, spatial and visible changes are closely connected to the destructive social processes taking place among the inhabitants, eventually leading to social exclusion. In Denmark, however, the process normally does not go as far as to make a person or a family destitute.

The importance of the dwelling

The main reason for the social exclusion process lies in the labour market. To combat this, exclusion has proved very difficult and the strategies followed often have more of the characteristics of general macroeconomic measures. On a more local level, and in more direct contact with the excluded or those in the process of becoming so, the dwelling becomes the fixed point in life that secures someone against a destructive social ejection. From being a place where one spends relatively few hours of leisure, the dwelling and the entire housing estate become to the excluded the place where one spends the entire day. Very few housing estates meet these requirements – here, the one-family house is much more adequate, although often economically unattainable for precisely those groups without work. The state of uneventfulness reigning on the large housing estates has become a grave problem. Most housing estates dating from the period 1960-75 got their inspiration from Le Corbusier's functionalist ideas: the dwelling as the framework for passive relaxation after a hard day's work, with large, light rooms from where one could contemplate quiet green lawns stretching up to the next 8-, 10- or 12-storey housing block several hundred metres away. On these well-planned housing estates there is no room for the small workshop, nor space for the little cafe, for the spontaneous, disordered life that people live when work no longer takes up the entire day. In addition, the housing estates dating from this period are often located far from neighbourhoods where less strict town planning has been carried out and where 50-100 years of minor and large modifications and additions to the original buildings have created a multiplicity of shops, workshops and cafes. The result is that many people on the new suburban housing estates do not only experience exclusion from the labour market, but also an isolation and paralysis in life within their dwelling.

An effort to improve the housing estates, to make them more attractive and more eventful, to create more activities, etc, is therefore a necessary effort to stop the destructive side of the social process of exclusion. This can be made independently of, but preferably parallel to, an effort to create jobs and reintegrate people into the labour market. These two forms of effort can strengthen each other and increase the chance of success. Since mid-1994 such efforts have been introduced on a relatively large scale in Denmark (Byudvalget, 1994). More than 200 housing estates will receive financial support to improve the physical appearance and to lower the rent (the latter in order to improve the competition from the one-family houses). At the same time a special social programme will be run on more than half of these estates.

Visibility

In the discussion about and the development of indicators of social exclusion, great weight is normally placed on various forms of statistics. These fit into the daily planning and administrative systems in charge of the areas and people with social problems. Both administrators, planners, and researchers are educated to 'see' the problems in a table or to 'read' them from an index. Not so for ordinary people and definitely not so for the typically excluded people. To these people figures and tables are part of the suppressive and alienating financial, administrative system that has played a role in the exclusion from which they are suffering. They read the decay and the exclusion process of the housing estates and the appearance of the neighbourhoods. They look at the decay of the houses, the state of trees and bushes, the filth in the streets and in the yards, the parked cars exposed to vandalism or about to rot. They also notice the drunkards and seedy types gathering in squares and other places and groups of noisy youngsters roaming the streets. These tangible, visible physical and social phenomena are the indicators that are decisive to ordinary people's judgement of the condition of an area and that, in reality, are also of great importance to the more professional forms of locally oriented efforts.

This means that an effort to prevent social exclusion in a specific area, an effort related to the spatial dimension, should consider to what extent and in which way this effort can be made visible. Just as the effects of registration of physical and social decay (dilapidated housing, filthy streets, groups of drunkards) indicates a downward movement in the problem spiral, a visible effort to improve an area can be of great value to the residents. Building renovation and reestablishment of the open spaces and roads, cleaning up, repairs, etc, can be seen as a sign that finally a change for the better is on the way. This optimism can support and strengthen more traditional socio-political and employment efforts.

In our investigations into more recent housing estates, where an extensive improvement of buildings as well as of open spaces has taken place, it appears that the inhabitants evaluate both improvements positively, with a tendency more often to comment upon the open spaces (these being more visible) than upon the improvements made to the buildings. In order to obtain an expression of satisfaction from more than 50% of the inhabitants, the buildings had to be changed considerably: new facades and new roofs triggered this degree of satisfaction. Maybe this is due to the fact that it is taken for granted that buildings are maintained, whereas the open spaces in this connection are looked upon as being more of a luxury. As it is less expensive to improve the open spaces than the buildings it is our conclusion that this effort ought to have a very high priority as an integrated part of a total physical and social re-establishment of a problematic area. Another positive fact was that it was possible to include the residents in the improvements of the open spaces, as many of the tasks did not require professional skills. For instance, the reshaping of the planted areas, the playgrounds, the paths, etc, could be carried out in cooperation with a few professionals and a number of amateurs (residents). When emphasis was put on the inclusion of unemployed youth in these projects, fewer cases of vandalism could be registered afterwards. Unfortunately, the long-term effect is more difficult to judge. But all in all, the conclusion is that a wider local commitment and an understanding of a development strategy in a socially burdened housing estate is secured by making part of the effort visible, ie, by integrating physical changes with the more sociopolitical strategy.

Indicators related to spatial and social dimensions

The development of indicators should partly consider the related spatial and social processes described by the problem spiral shown in Figure 8.1, and should partly include features of the physical environment, the economic conditions and the social structure of a given area. At the same time it should be possible for the parties who need them as a guiding tool to establish and to update the indicators. Consequently, it is of no use to suggest extensive (and costly) regular surveys as a main source of information for planning and guiding in economically-poor housing estates.

On the basis of an extensive research programme into problematic Danish housing estates, where both physical decay and social exclusion were visible prior to the start of the effort, we wish to point to the following types of indicators (Christiansen et al, 1993).

Local statistics

Danish housing corporations keep quite comprehensive accounts of what is going on in the field of subsidised housing. This accounting is local and is kept for each individual estate, from 20-30 dwellings up to about a 1,000 dwellings. With very few modifications in the existing accounting system information could be obtained regarding:

- breaking of the house-rules

- vandalism

- complaints from tenants

- 'moonlight' moves

- arrears of rent

- loss caused by vacant flats.

If the municipal social administration is included, it might be possible to get a registration of the extent of social cases on the estate. If the police are involved, the extent and type of reports on the estate in question can be recorded.

Only a few of these indicators are collected systematically at present, but during interviews with housing managers and social workers from the municipalities, references to increasing or declining 'tendencies' in these indicators were frequent. In spite of the very weak statistical base at present, the indicators were given high priority as direct measurements of the social situation on the estates. They are essential to the inhabitants' evaluation of the general social situation of the estate.

Central statistics

In Denmark an extensive central registration of personal data takes place, as all data concerning income, employment, etc, are collected and registered under a personal number in the Danish Central Bureau of Statistics. Furthermore, a central building register exists where extensive information about the size of the housing estate, the physical equipment and the size of the flats, renovations, etc, have been entered according to postal addresses. These various registers can be correlated, so that combined physical and social data pertaining to a given housing estate, a neighbourhood, an entire town, municipality or whatever geographical unit might be desired, can be obtained. From these sources we obtained data regarding:

- the age composition

- employment

- income

- nationality

- turnover of residents.

These indicators give more indirect information about the social situation, and in general their validity is dubious (while reliability is extremely high). The indicator that most strongly correlates with the perceived and expressed social problems concerns moves to and from the estates. When that figure exceeds 20-25% moves per year it is a sign of a rather poor social situation.

The easy access to these kind of statistics – although expenses in connection with data where several registers have to be combined can be prohibitive – has changed the discussion about indicators from a discussion about what can be obtained to a discussion of relevance.

Survey data

None of the previously mentioned data are a direct illustration of the attitudes, evaluations and preferences of the inhabitants. This kind of information, which might be of great importance to the restoration efforts, should be collected as survey data in the area in question. The extent of such a survey may vary, ranging from a questionnaire to actual interviews with one or all the inhabitants. In our work with problematic estates we interviewed a number of key people about their evaluation as to need and result. Simultaneously, we had asked the Institute of Social Research to carry out systematic and representative interviews with the inhabitants about the improvements carried out on the estates. In this way we obtained the following data:

- clublife and activities

- satisfaction/dissatisfaction with the estate

- noise and other nuisances on the estate

- evaluation of reputation

- wish to move (and if so, to where).

Out of these indicators the satisfaction/dissatisfaction expressed with the estate gives the best correlation with the other key-indicators and, especially, with the general impression obtained through the indicators, key-person interviews and our own observations. The satisfaction expressed has, however, to be on quite a high level, that is, above 90%. On some of the estates where problems prevailed after the improvement programmes were finished, 80-85% of the inhabitants expressed satisfaction. Our explanation for this relatively high figure is that you have to 'explain' to yourself, that you are relatively satisfied – whether in fact you are satisfied or not – as long as you have not moved out.

The final conclusion concerning these various types of data is that even relatively few and simple data collected over a number of years (for example, the frequency of moves on a certain estate), give a fairly good indication as to the general condition of an estate. It is also of vital importance to the sociopolitical efforts on an estate or a neighbourhood to know the age composition and the employment situation of residents.

However, one must keep in mind that it is also very important to work systematically with the physical characteristics, including the visible phenomena of an estate. In our work over the years, both in the old urban renewal areas and the more recent suburban estates, we have made a registration in figures and by taking photographs of the areas before and after renovation. As a supplement to the administrative staff or as a main indicator to the ordinary people a series of photographs illustrating buildings, streets and yards are more informative than the traditional statistical information. Furthermore, pictures are good at illustrating the efforts that have been made. If the photographic registration is to complete the total registration, it is important that this work is done by professionals who are trained at 'seeing'. In our research, this documentation was handled by an architect.

Conclusion

Within social sciences, and perhaps among those who work with social indicators, there is a tendency to refine the indicators and to build indexes where several factors are weighted together. This may be a useful development, but not necessarily so. When it is a question of the connection between physical, spatial phenomena, economic and social conditions, it is my experience that a series of relatively simple indicators, combined with in-depth interviews with key-persons from the estates in question or persons working with the estates and preferably also with a personal inspection of the area, give a fairly good indication of the degree of problems on the estate. It is also very useful to make a photographic registration of the estate in question in order to produce the optimal total picture of the condition in question. This complex data collection is thus a combination of rather traditional quantitative indications of the present total situation in the areas. It sometimes makes it difficult to say exactly what the key issue is that makes an estate problem-ridden – it also causes some problems regarding more traditional theory-building, as some of the qualitative data are of an impressionistic nature. But the same complexity does exist in the real life of the estates – and it is an attempt to catch this complexity that we have made.

If the indicators are to be utilised for the carrying through of an improvement depending on, for instance, the support from local politicians, it is of vital importance to use a combination of the various methods of documentation mentioned above (including photographic registration). When speaking about general sociopolitical efforts not entailing a spatial dimension (for instance, changes in social policies or in the labour market), this type of making things visible is not possible in the same way. But a pictorial coverage of this type of social problem has a very strong impact. Numerous television programmes covering social themes followed by political initiatives are proof that laws can be changed, in-depth investigations started, etc, when problems are shown with pictures. The risk attached to this type of documentation is that it only shows the visible. Therefore the traditional quantitative indicators should always be included in the planning and in the political decision making as the 'most heavy' documentation.

nine

MEASURING SOCIOECONOMIC DIFFERENCES WITHIN AREAS: A FRENCH ANALYSIS

Isa Aldeghi

Introduction

In order to address the problem of social exclusion within the European Union (EU), it is first necessary to identify the populations concerned and the areas that they occupy. The 'Poverty 3' programme aimed to develop specific actions to integrate these populations at the local level. It was a way of promoting actions in these areas and situating the problems in a local context. In the Poverty 3 programme the definition of poverty went beyond monetary considerations. The location of households was one of the factors to be considered in a multidimensional approach to exclusion (Tricart, 1994).

The phenomenon of pauperisation of certain areas of European territory can be interpreted as the geographical consequence of transformations in the labour market at an international level (Jordan, 1994). Within a conurbation and its surroundings, the different neighbourhoods do not resemble each other socially. Differences in the types of housing contribute to the social differentiation of neighbourhoods locally.

The analysis presented here of the social differentiation of villages and urban neighbourhoods was not initially designed to address the question of poverty or exclusion. The aim was to render visible the dividing lines at work in the social differentiation of a national territory. These tools will describe the whole of the French territory. Each area, rich or poor, urban or rural, Parisian or provincial, industrial or of the tertiary sector, can be located in an overall structure. This approach links national and local questions, considering each local situation as dependant on a broader system (Aldeghi and Tabard, 1988a). This approach therefore differs from that of Robson (see chapter 11), which aims to classify areas according to their level of disadvantage, using a methodology based on diverse indicators.

Explaining the location of social groups with regard to where businesses and administrations are situated

This paper focuses on an original approach to the projection on the ground of social inequalities in France. Since 1971, the research has been conducted under the direction of Nicole Tabard, research director in the Centre National de la Recherche Scientifique (CNRS). The work started at the Centre de Recherche pour l'Étude et l'Observation des Conditions de Vie (CREDOC) with the idea of optimising sampling and studying contextual influences on consumer behaviour. The Censuses analysed are from 1968, 1975, 1982 and 1990. I participated in this programme between 1985 and 1990, the date at which Nicole Tabard moved to the Institut National d'Études Statistiques et Économiques (INSEE), where the Census is produced and treated. She is now involved in the work of the social studies division ('Études sociales'). This programme has produced a way of describing France with reference to the differences of socioeconomic status of inhabitants in different areas.

The population that serves as a reference, the geographical units and the classification codes have evolved since the first applications. However, Tabard's work has remained based on the same approach to the problem. The analysis is centred on data concerning the distribution of inhabitants within the production system; and the location of firms and public establishments is considered as the generating principle of social differences between geographical units. This does not mean that other differences between areas are ignored (eg, types of families, age groups, housing characteristics, etc). However, this information is not used for developing the classification of areas. Each area is classified only with respect to the socioeconomic profile of its inhabitants through correspondence analysis followed by ascending clustering hierarchy. This aspect distinguishes the work from other research based on different criteria. To take recent examples in France, Mansuy and Marpsat (1991) based their spatial analysis on social position and types of families, while Catherine Rhein in the same year worked on types of housing (Rhein, 1991). In the United Kingdom, Robson uses various direct indicators of poverty while Green (1994) takes into consideration several indicators of poverty and wealth.

The approach followed by Tabard remains more multi-dimensional than hierarchical. In this perspective, it is not the concentration of a social category that best describes an area, but the associations between different social groups. For instance, working class areas will be considered differently according to whether workers are neighbours of supervisors, technicians or clerical staff. Furthermore, the classifications used to describe the socioeconomic position of inhabitants are based on the French standard classification of occupations ('Nomenclature des Professions-Catégories Sociales ou PCS'), which is a multi-dimensional tool. This classification combines several dimensions of social position, such as upper/lower class, paid employment/self-employed, skilled/non-skilled working class, craft work/industrial employment, agriculture/public/ sector/trade/education/health/transport, etc (see Desrosieres et al, 1983).

From the beginning, Tabard wished to describe social position as a combination of occupation and field of activity. This has only been undertaken since the 1982 Census, as it was necessary to analyse data on individuals and not just aggregate tables. It thus became possible to create an ad hoc classification. For instance, among the skilled craft workers, the construction workers are distinguished from bakers and butchers. Among the supervisory staff, metal workers are distinguished from those working in the construction, textile, chemical or electronics industries.

Studying the differences among neighbourhoods through the Census of Population

In France, there are relatively few data sources that allow the treatment of the status of areas. Traditionally, zones are contrasted according to their size, or their closeness to the centre (see Marpsat, 1986). National surveys using questionnaires are too small to be representative of a town, even less so of a neighbourhood, including times when the sample reaches several tens of thousands of people. Because of their exhaustiveness, censuses are precious sources of information. When towns are large enough, it is possible to perceive the differences from neighbourhood to neighbourhood. The work situation, the occupation and the field of activity is known for each inhabitant. However, no questions are asked about the level or regularity of income. Other administrative data are available concerning the groups of the population who are in difficulties: means-tested family allowance, job-seeker's allowance, minimum income (RMI), etc. These figures are available at the level of a town or village, but not for their subdivisions. In the near future, this will be possible, thanks to the Répertoire de Localisation Infra-Communale (REPLIC), a new INSEE system (see Marpsat, 1993). Unfortunately, the first experiments show that it is not yet possible to find the îlot (the smallest geographical area of the Census – see Vinot, 1993) for at least 20% of the addresses. The wish to make available data on neighbourhoods, especially for those experiencing difficulties, led to the creation of the Mission Villes in INSEE in 1991 (see Choffel, 1993).

Four poles

The most recently treated data are the 1990 Census of Population. France has been divided into 7,000 areas, each comprising between 3,000 and 12,000 inhabitants. Those areas can be neighbourhoods of big cities, whole towns if their size is between 5,000 and 10,000 inhabitants, or groups of small towns or villages of less than 5,000 inhabitants each, all in the same administrative district.

Each household is characterised socially by occupation and sector of activity into one of the 153 codes of the classification. The factor analyses and classifications are based on the socio-economic profile of the working and unemployed males considered as heads of household by the Census. The other households, those whose heads are retired, or female, etc, are included only at an illustrative level. The reasons for this choice will be developed after the presentation of the main results. Areas are classified into 33 types of neighbourhood, town or district. They will not all be described here, but they come together around four main poles: agricultural, working class, middle class and a 'high-level tertiary sector–advanced technology pole. (See Tabard, 1993a, and Appendix 9.1 for the list of these types.)

The agricultural and crafts pole (13% of French households)

Among the active male heads of households living in these areas, a quarter work in agriculture. Self-employed craftsmen are also numerous. There are a large number of manual workers, but not as many as in the working-class pole. One of the main results of the analyses of France appears here, that is to say, that manual workers often live in rural areas. Typical industries are those of timber, food-processing and the building trade. In these often rural districts, the largest proportion of old people are to be found. This pole may be divided into seven types.

The working-class pole (36% of French households)

Almost half of the working or unemployed male heads of households are manual workers. These workers are more often in branches of industry than the workers living in the agricultural and crafts pole, who more usually work in small production units. Not all the working-class areas are located in big cities – around one third of the inhabitants of this pole live in villages. Those who do not live in rural areas live in various sizes of towns, except for the Paris district. The north and north-east of France, with their old industries, are often in this pole. Except for rural areas, working-class pole areas are characterised by a decreasing population, in spite of the surplus of births over deaths. More people leave than come to the working-class areas.

This pole is divided into 12 types. In two of them, workers are neighbours with farmers and agricultural workers (but they are not as numerous as in the agricultural pole). The location is often rural and many householders own their houses. In the 10 other types of working-class area, the sectors of activity are often declining industries: mines, textile industry, steel works, etc. Large families and social housing are very common. The differences among these 10 types of areas result from the proportion of skilled people among workers, the balance between industrial and artisan workers, activity sectors and social categories other than working class. In some areas, workers live near retired workers, sometimes their neighbours are technicians or supervisors, sometimes they are clerical and service staff (especially civil servants).

The tertiary and technical middle-class pole (41% of French households)

Clerical and service staff, technicians and middle-level professionals in health, social welfare, administration and management are typical inhabitants of this pole. These areas are often neighbourhoods of large towns (except Paris). This pole is divided into nine types. Five of them contain many administrative middle-class people. These are urban districts, with many single-parent families. The four other types contain many middle-class production workers (especially technicians) and middle-class trades. These are outlying areas. The population has been growing rapidly in the last 20 years and there are substantial numbers of older people.

The 'high-level tertiary sector–advanced technology' pole (10% of French households)

In these areas, the owner-managers, professions and 'cadres' (management staff, engineers, senior civil servants, higher intellectual professions) form 44% of the working and unemployed male heads of households, as compared with 7% to 20% in the other poles. Companies providing services to other companies are over-represented. Those working in industry are in advanced technology firms. Most of the wealthy areas of France are in Paris or its better-off suburbs. In this area, however, there are also many foreign households, and single women living alone.

A visual representation of the social oppositions structuring the French territory

The principal oppositions at work in the analysis of geographical units may be represented in a two-dimensional diagram (Figure 9.1, p 174). The 7,000 units are still defined according to their socioeconomic profile. The classification of social positions remains the same, except that agriculture has been excluded. This enables one to go beyond the first opposition, that is, that of farming and non-farming areas. The diagram presents the first two elements of the factor analysis and illustrates the other social oppositions that characterise the differences between areas.

The main opposition, between the top and the base of the graphic, is hierarchical level. Owner-managers of large companies or companies providing services to other companies, non-medical professionals, and engineers in advanced technology firms are in very different areas than those containing industrial manual workers, especially unskilled ones. Craft manual workers are found in more areas than industrial manual workers; they live in less segregated areas and are not as far from middle-class and upper-class people as the industrial workers. However, craft manual workers live in areas having the highest level of working-class unemployment. Clerical, service staff and middle-level professionals live in socially intermediate areas between the wealthiest and the poorest areas.

The second opposition is illustrated from left to right, with trade and services to individuals on the left, and industry and technology on the right. The neighbourhoods where inhabitants work in the tertiary sector are on the left of the diagram. It may be administration, trade, services to inhabitants or crafts work, according to the hierarchical level. They are opposed to the areas where industrial workers live (bottom right) or to areas with engineers or technicians employed in advanced technology firms (top right). Services to companies may be projected on the left of the diagram.

The use of these typologies: the possibility of going beyond the socioeconomic dimension

As explained earlier, these typologies are based solely on the socioeconomic position of inhabitants. Their use, as has been shown in past works or in works to be published, goes well beyond these dimensions. Even though no information on the types of housing was included in the initial analysis, all the typologies show that the different kinds of neighbourhood (as defined by the social profile of their inhabitants) correspond to clearly different types of housing (age of buildings, opposition between towers and blocks and detached housing, the crowdedness of the housing, the opposition between owners, mortgage payers, council house tenants or private tenants). During the course of a study on the location of foreigners based on the Census data, the clustering of certain nationalities in specific types of neighbourhoods was observed, whereas other nationalities appeared to be more dispersed (Desplanques and Tabard, 1991). A survey of families associated with the 1992 Census showed differences of fertility in women belonging to comparable social milieu according to the social environments in which they live (Aldeghi and Tabard, 1988b).

These typologies could be suspected of having a tautological aspect. To simplify, the specificity of working-class areas might be simply attributed to the high proportion of working-class households in them. However, a 1987 study on the area of Essonne demonstrated that it was not tautological

(Aldeghi and Tabard, 1987). The sampling was based on the above mentioned typology of neighbourhoods. In each of five main types of neighbourhood, the same number of households belonging to three main social groups was interviewed. It was shown that differences exist among households of the same social categories that are related to their location as described by the typology. The differences found were those of geographical origin, social origin and level of salary (which is clearly higher for equivalent class when in a wealthy area). Purchasing behaviour, tendency to self-production, benefit from family networks or community help for improving housing or repairing cars, or alternatively dependance on a cash-based system, would vary strongly according to the social neighbourhood where given groups live.

'Priority districts' in the general framework of France

Thanks to the Mission Villes in INSEE, it is possible to produce statistics for the 500 urban districts in which, in 1993, priority programmes have been developed under agreements between local authorities and the representatives of central government. The priority district policy in France is not based on homogeneous criteria for the choice of neighbourhoods. Rather, it is the result of a political will at a local level to intervene in a part of the territory. However, local authorities do, of course, justify their request for state funding by reference to various objective indicators. Some of the common ones are the number of the unemployed, the state of housing, the proportion of young people without formal qualifications, etc.

Compared with the averages for France, or for the conurbation to which they belong, these priority districts are often close to the boundary of the urban unit. The inhabitants of these areas are often to be found in council flats in tower blocks built from 1949 to 1975. The population is young, with many large families and foreign households. The level of unemployment is high (see Castellan et al, 1992). Tabard situated these areas within the framework elaborated above (see Tabard, 1993b; 1993c). Two types of working-class areas contain a high proportion of their population in priority districts: type I12213, highly urban: "Very working class, craft manual workers but not self-employed, unemployment, priority district, emigration", and type I11: "Very working class, textile and clothing industries, unskilled workers, emigration". These two types are respectively in first and second place for the proportion of unemployed among male heads of households.

Comparing these priority areas with the rest of the town where they are to be found, Tabard reveals the specific characteristics associated with these neighbourhoods. Some of them have already been highlighted by Castellan et al (1992): the importance of high buildings, of council flats built from 1949 to 1974, the high proportion of households whose head is between 25 and 49 years of age, the importance of unemployment and the large proportion of foreign households. Other important characteristics are: the large proportion of skilled workers, and even more of unskilled workers; the preponderance of single-parent families or families with two parents and at least three children; and the high level of households without cars (which is striking, as most of these priority districts are far from town centres).

Similar results had been found for priority districts of the Île-de-France (this French region includes Paris), from the 1982 Census (see Aldeghi and Tabard, 1988a). From seven indicators, a score was attributed to each area, one mark being given each time an area reached the threshold observed for this criterion in the average of the priority districts. This method identified areas that were not classified as 'priority' by the local authority but had the same characteristics. Up until now, however, the same method has not been applied to 1990 Census data. Another way of selecting potential priority neigh-bourhoods is to start from the projection on the diagram (see Figure 9.1, p 174) of the priority districts. Most of them are situated in the bottom left area of the diagram, where inhabitants are often unskilled craft workers, and where unemployment figures are high. It is easy to list similar neighbourhoods that have not yet benefited from priority contracts.

For each town of at least 50,000 inhabitants, Tabard has projected the priority districts and the other districts onto this diagram, thereby providing an overview of the social position of French areas. Overall, the status of priority districts tends to be low when the other areas of the same town have a rather low status too.   Observed one by one, the situations are heterogeneous.   When the priority district is part of a rather poor town, it is either similar to the other neighbourhoods, or slightly poorer.   In this case, it is possible to speak of a continuity between areas of the town.   Sometimes, the social distance between the priority district and the other districts of the town is enormous.   Then it is possible to speak of rupture. In this case, a concentration of poor people in a few areas of rather wealthy cities may be observed.   In a few cases, the social status of priority districts does not seem especially low and it is possible to find much poorer neighbourhoods in the same towns that are not classified as priority districts.   It is not impossible that some of these ambiguous situations correspond to areas where pockets of poverty exist within the more varied framework of a large neighbourhood.

The reasons for selecting employed males as a basis for the analysis of the 1990 Census data

It is worth considering at this point the appropriateness of the choice of the reference population and, in particular, the exclusion of retired people and females (whether working, seeking work or homemakers).

In order to remain coherent with the general approach, which gives central importance to the location of employment, retired and other inactive groups (such as students) have not been retained in the active variables for the analysis.   Other phenomena affect the location of retired people.   First, companies where retired people formerly worked may have disappeared or moved.   Furthermore, the more comfortably-off are quite mobile on retirement; and the simultaneous presence of retired managers and middle-class people with shopkeepers and staff who provide services to them (especially catering staff) has created a specific type of area, well known for tourism and found by the sea or spas.   Retired farmers and former manual workers are less mobile, however – they often stay in the area where they worked, and are found close to non-retired farmers or workers, often in villages of declining population.

When considering the overall approach, it is harder to justify the absence of women in the population of reference, as in France 44% of the working population are women (according to the latest published figures from the French Employment Survey, *Enquête Emploi*, in March 1993). This absence was a choice in view of the limited means available for research. Earlier studies had shown that men are a better indicator of the social position of areas. First, the absence of some women from the labour market clouds an analysis of their social position. Second, women are concentrated in fewer social positions than men, who are more often managing directors of large companies, senior executives in the private sector or skilled and unskilled workers.

The question of the location of women was treated earlier, using 1982 Census data. Funding from the National Family Allowance Body ('Caisse Nationale d'Allocations Familiales') was used to conduct research on the relationship of women to work (Aldeghi and Tabard, 1988b). A simultaneous classification of men and women in couples proved to be unhelpful. Either a detailed classification contains too many items to be used at a local level, or a less detailed classification does not reveal accurate differences. The best methodology proved to be the creation of two separate tools of description of areas – one based on male employment, and the other on female employment. The subsequent crossing of the two typologies brings a more complete view of the oppositions between areas. The classification of areas differs slightly when the situations of men and women are examined separately. When only men are considered, the hierarchical dimension may be observed to be dominant. Among women, this dimension exists but is weaker than among men; the opposition between public and private sector is also important.

Among the interesting findings of this earlier research may be noted the systematic link between the level of female unemployment and the proportion of women at home not seeking work. In other words, the absence of some women from the labour market seems to be explained more by the lack of opportunities than by the desire to stay at home. Another correlation appears between the proportion of unqualified workers among women at work and the proportion of women at home or seeking jobs.

The falling differentiation between technological areas and tertiary areas in the 1980s

Seen from a static viewpoint, the social oppositions between zones are strong. What are the trends over time? Chenu and Tabard (1993) compared the results of towns and villages from the 1982 Census and from the 1990 Census. Four main trends were revealed that may be summarised as follows. The first is the reinforcement of social segregation in large urban centres already well-off in 1982. The proportion of managing directors and senior executives had the greatest increase in these towns between 1982 and 1990. The following two trends show the profile of two main types of middle-class towns or villages becoming more similar. The areas that are becoming more 'technological' (ie, in which can be observed a high rate of increase of technicians and supervisory staff) between 1982 and 1990 are areas that were mainly tertiary sector and trade in 1982. Conversely, the highest increase in craft workers, shopkeepers, services to individuals and civil servants may be found in areas that originally had a technological orientation. Finally, the fourth trend is the substitution of industrial workers by unskilled craft workers and employees. Those towns and villages had a strong industrial orientation in 1982 and their population tends to decrease.

Studies conducted on the changes between 1975 and 1982 (Aldeghi and Tabard, 1990) in the Paris region showed different results. The most frequent trend was the reinforcement of the initial characteristics of the areas. Except for an increase in the concentration of wealthy people in the towns that were the most wealthy initially, the general evolution between 1982 and 1990 shows a reduction of the social differences within areas. This is also the conclusion that Robson reaches, observing four indicators of poverty between 1981 and 1991 in the UK. The hierarchical opposition between South and North Britain is decreasing as a result of the worsening of the unemployment situation generally, but more markedly in the South, an area which was relatively less touched in 1981.

Conclusion

It may be noted that this method of describing France can be used for identifying areas that would justify active policies of development. Through this paper, it has been possible to observe that the start of the analysis is centred on the social position, although the results of other dimensions of life appear, such as the types of families, housing, nationality of inhabitants, age groups, etc. This confirms the link between different aspects of social differentiation and justifies the multi-dimensional approach to poverty.

This analysis does not claim to treat every aspect of local specificity; rather, it provides a reference framework that gives the possibility of situating each area in a larger structure. Locally, it can be interesting to take into consideration other criteria that are not treated in the Census, such as the level of income, the precariousness of situations, the dynamism of local associations, the habits of helping one another in certain communities, the possibilities of self-production to help to reduce the effects of low income, or the existence of a strong will to create a policy for integrating poor areas.

In order to establish points of comparisons between EU countries, it would be interesting to be able to make use of similar methodological research in other contexts than the French. One of the major spatial specificities of the French situation is the concentration of economic activity and intellectual elites in Paris and its southern and western suburbs. In general, the comfortably-off may be found in the centres of large towns across France. It is therefore unsurprising that the term 'inner city problems' has no equivalent in France, the 'problem neighbourhoods' being situated in outlying areas. With few exceptions, the renovation of large urban centres has been accompanied by the eviction of the working classes from the historical centres.

Table 9.1:   The 33 socioeconomic types of areas in France (1990 census)

No	Name of type	%
	Total households in France	100.0
A	*Agriculture pole*	13.1
A1	**Subgroup A1 – very agricultural, with crafts**	**5.6**
A11	The most agricultural, large farms, depopulation	1.8
A1212	Agriculture with crafts, trade and tertiary sector	1.7
A122	Very agricultural, small and medium-size farms	2.1
A2	**Subgroup A2 – agriculture – industry (wood and food-processing)**	**7.5**
A21	Agriculture and industries: textile-clothing	0.8
A2212	Agriculture and industries: various industries	3.0
A2222	Agriculture and industries: food-processing	2.1
A3	Agricultural workers: mainly in vineyards	1.8
I	*Working class pole*	*36.3*
I1	**Subgroup I1 – very working-class, mainly industry**	**27.9**
I11	Very working-class, textile-clothing, unskilled workers, depopulation	0.8
I1211	Various industries, mainly: building-trade, paper, printing and publishing	2.2
I1212	Skilled workers, technicians, large industrial complexes	1.4
I12211	Industrial: mines, nationalised industries, depopulation	0.5
I12212	Industrial, with skilled workers, metal-work, high depopulation	0.7
I12213	Very working-class, salaried craft workers, unemployment, priority districts, high depopulation	4.6
I12214	Very working-class, skilled workers, metal-work high depopulation	4.6
I12215	Workers, clerical staff, shopkeepers, textile industry, depopulation	2.5
I12221	Chemistry – pharmaceuticals – synthetic fibres	3.1
I12222	Production supervisory staff	7.2

I2	Subgroup I2 – Working-class areas with agriculture, high growth	8.4
I121	Agriculture/workers/tertiary activities, conversion zones, South of France	3.7
I122	Outer suburban working-class areas, West of France	4.8
M	*'Tertiary and technical middle-class' pole*	*41.0*
M1	Subgroup M1 – Tertiary middle-class, provincial towns	23.4
M111	Civil servants and local authority middle-class, large provincial towns	6.1
M1121	Trade, catering, tourism, high growth, retirement areas	2.6
M11221	Clerical staff, salaried craftsmen, Paris conurbation (except Paris)	2.5
M11222	Local authorities middle class, provincial towns	7.6
M12	Middle-class, traces of agriculture, outer suburbs, high growth	4.6
M2	Subgroup M2 – Middle-class production staff, outer suburban, growth	17.6
M211	Highly qualified production staff, growing outer suburbs of large towns	5.9
M212	Transport: airport and railway zones	4.5
M221	Teaching, research technicians	1.3
M222	Skilled technology, outer suburban, high growth, large conurbations, Ile-de-France	5.9
S	*'High-level tertiary sector – advanced technology pole'*	*9.6*
S1	Subgroup S1 – Company management, high technology, Paris conurbation	2.8
S11	High technology, industrial research, Paris conurbation	1.6
S12	Owner-managers, senior executive, banking, business services, Paris conurbation	1.2
S2	Subgroup S2 – Education, media – communication, personal services	6.8
S211	High-level tertiary sector, technology, South of Paris and Paris conurbation	2.1
S212	Personal services, wealthy provincial centres	2.3
S22	Trade, catering, artists, tertiary unemployment, Paris and tourist areas	2.4

Figure 9.1:   A visual representation of the main oppositions among areas in France

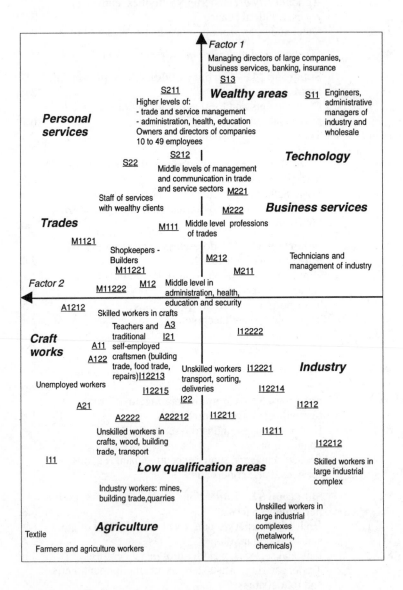

Underscore: the 33 socioeconomic types of areas in France
Source: 1990 Census – analysis by Nicole Tabard

MEASURING SOCIOECONOMIC DISINTEGRATION AT THE LOCAL LEVEL IN EUROPE: AN ANALYTICAL FRAMEWORK

Frank Moulaert[1]

Introduction

The purpose of this paper is to present some reflections on the measurement of social deprivation in localities within the European Union (EU). The stress is on 'socioeconomically disintegrated' localities, that is, those with severe problems of social and economic restructuring (Moulaert et al, 1992; 1993; 1994). Several considerations have inspired this paper.

First of all, since the last oil crisis at the end of the 1980s, social inequalities between regions and localities have increased in Europe and their study has become urgent (European Commission, 1991; Suarez-Villa and Roura, 1992). However, while we have systematic data illustrating this unevenness at the level of the regions, for localities this statistical measurement is extremely difficult to accomplish. Until now, we have to satisfy our curiosity by looking at some sparse data on unemployment, pockets of poverty and welfare incomes and by looking at aggregate information on socio-economic structure, etc. This brings us to the second reason for this paper, namely, the strong need to improve data on social deprivation at the local level. A third reason is of a more methodological order. There exists a tendency to study social exclusion in a strictly empiricist way (using statistical analysis and descriptive monographs), without looking at the qualitative aspects of the mechanisms underlying the generation of poverty at the local or the supralocal level. The viewpoint that will be defended here is that it is impossible to build a good statistical basis for studying local socioeconomic exclusion without a good theoretical analysis of the mechanisms leading to the exclusion of parts of the local populations.

The paper will address the following issues. First, it will provide some elements for building an analytical framework for studying socioeconomic exclusion at the local level. These elements are directly based on a study made for the European Commission's (DGV) Poverty 3 research programme 'Local Economic Development: a Pro-Active Strategy to Combat Poverty in the European Community'. The second section is devoted to the empirical consequences of this theoretical framework. It is argued that purely quantitative data are insufficient to evaluate the state of socioeconomic disintegration or integration of a locality, that different types of qualitative information are necessary and that the links between the two types of information must be established. The third section picks up the methodological implications and puts them into a coherent analytical framework.

An analytical framework for local analysis

The objective of the above mentioned Poverty 3 study on local socioeconomic development was to analyse the socioeconomic, sociopolitical and sociocultural structure and agency of socioeconomically disintegrated areas or localities (see below); to identify their main socioeconomic problems, their vulnerable and excluded groups; to gain insights into local development strategies; and to assess the potential for establishing strategies that better fit local needs.

To realise such broad objectives, the analytical perspective must be sufficiently wide, but at the same time coherent. It must offer explanations for various aspects of different development trajectories among localities. Depending on which locality we are talking about, some theories will be more relevant than others. In any case, the selected theories must fit a coherent analytical structure consisting of a view of society, a theoretical framework and appropriate empirical methods (Storper and Walker, 1983; Moulaert, 1987).

One implication is to accept only theories that establish links between the socioeconomic well-being of different groups in local areas and that explicitly or implicitly seek to understand or contribute to the improvement of the situation of the socio-economically most exposed groups (Leontidou, 1993; Moulaert, 1996). This is a logical consequence of the research agenda, that is, to establish development strategies *which are beneficial to local communities and their most vulnerable groups.* Moreover, among theories that deal with the processes of emancipation of localities and their specific target groups, only those are retained that deal with the interaction between the economic, social, political and cultural levels of society (Mingione, 1991; Leontidou, 1990; Moulaert and Delvainquière, 1994). Finally, the theories that are utilised, as well as rejecting economic and technological determinism, must not fall into the trap of non-economic functional determination, by proposing purely political or sociocultural solutions for anomalies in local communities that face severe economic problems. Rather, for the study of the social dynamics of localities, only theories with clear-cut human and social emancipatory thrust are considered, capable of illuminating a society with different types of social regulation and with an explicit role reserved to human agency. These theoretical choices also have consequences for the empirical methods used in the research. These must combine a double agenda: the discovery of the common trends in socioeconomic development on the one hand, the recognition of the specificity of the dynamics in each locality on the other.

The difficulty of drawing boundaries between types of regulatory logics, between functional rationales, or even between pertinent spatial levels is typical of a multifunctional and structure-agency approach (Moulaert and Swyngedouw, 1992). This difficulty is certainly quite acute when talking about local communities, where the local level cannot be properly examined without taking into account the links with 'meso' regional and 'macro' national or international dynamics. However, this should not discourage us from drawing some categorical boundaries for the study of local development. As can be seen in Table 10.1, we distinguish different subsystems in local communities and their broader spatial context (see Peck and Tickell, 1992; Mingione, 1991; Moulaert, 1987; 1996):

- production system and labour process

- labour market

- reproduction of labour: households and educational system

- households, housing and living environment

- political system and institutions

- planning agencies and strategies

- social movements.

Although a little artificial, it is helpful in providing a sufficiently complete list of the different elements of the subsystems, as well as the different forms of regulation intervening in their dynamics.

When, as is the case in this research, 'socioeconomically disintegrated areas' are at the core of the analysis, further analytical precautions must be taken. For theories belonging to different disciplines in social science, explaining growth and prosperity, well-being and good governance in regions and localities, usually offer only limited possibilities for explaining economic decline, socioeconomic disintegration and social exclusion. The explanation of bad fortune cannot simply be stated as the obverse of the mechanisms generating fortune and prosperity.

In our work, a 'socioeconomically disintegrated area' has been defined as an area partly or entirely cut off from the major economic development processes, and from the areas that these processes have benefited (Moulaert et al, 1990; Moulaert et al, 1992; Moulaert and Leontidou, 1995). For socioeconomically disintegrated areas, therefore, it is necessary to ask what are the mechanisms divorcing a locality from processes of prosperity and well-being. These mechanisms can be presented in a general way, as in Table 10.2. The contrast with what happens in the case of virtuous development processes can be illustrated for most subsystems of a local community.

Table 10.1:   **Possible subsystems of a locality community and their different levels of existence or interactivity**

Spatial scale Subsystem	Local	Regional/ national	Supranational
Production system: - labour process - technology - sectoral/ market - structure	- Small/medium sized enterprises - Branch plant - Independent worker - Family business - Production/ trade/ technology networks	National enterprise? Transfer technology? Regional/ national market? Intermediate trade flows	Transnational corporation Intra-firm trade Alliances Subcontractor networks
Labour market: - skills - jobs - labour time	Local labour market mechanisms: - - formal and informal - self-employ-ment - self-sufficiency	Integration in larger regional market: - division of labour, migration and commuting	Integration in firm's international division of labour International migration
Reproduction of labour: - households and education	Household economy: - structure and skills - gender relationships Local school system	Migration and commuting household members (workers, students) Transfer of income	Migration and commuting household members (workers, students) Transfer of income

Spatial scale Subsystem	Local	Regional/ national	Supranational
Reproduction of labour: - housing and living environment	Housing stock, renovation processes, social quality of neighbour- hood	Imitation and learning effects Development of regional life-style profiles	International- isation and homogen- isation of life and living styles
Political agencies and institutions	Local authorities and admini- strations	Regional/ national authorities and admini- strations	Supranational authorities and admini- strations
Planning agencies and strategies	Private/public/ mix	Idem	Idem
Issue movements: - political - ecological	Mobilisation on local or common issues	Idem regional issues Regional mobilisation on local issues	Idem international issues International mobilisation on issues of regions, localities

Source: Moulaert (1996)

Not only do the positive mechanisms that are analysed in growth and development based theories disappear, stagnate or go into reverse, but other mechanisms based on parallel initiatives, destruction, escape behaviour and disillusionment at the collective and individual level develop as well. Thus, for example, none of the contemporary leading theories on local production systems explain the decline of leading sectors and their drop in investment. Theories of local development based on high technology strategies, theories of industrial and technology districts all point out how success can and has been achieved, but not how decline could occur or how the need for alternative redevelopment strategies may emerge (Bingham and Mier, 1993; Moulaert and Delvainquière, 1994). The latter are covered by 'parallel' or 'informal' theories of decline and socioeconomic disintegration and redevelopment (Moulaert, 1996).

The ideal empirical agenda

The theoretical analysis in the previous section requires a detailed empirical follow-up. Such a follow-up may consist of two parts: a detailed analysis of each locality following a 'model for locality studies'; and a comparative analysis of development experiences, possibly leading to a typology.

A model for the locality studies

Although general mechanisms of disintegration can be identified (see Table 10.2), these may vary quite strongly among localities. The 'structured diversity' of localities must, therefore, be studied in great detail. This means that in order to learn about the different dimensions of their socioeconomic disintegration, their problems and development, for each locality we ask a number of common questions, without imposing strict rules on the rationale underlying the answers to these questions. Questions refer to different dimensions of the subsystems of localities (see again Table 10.1): to their socioeconomic geography, their physical infrastructure, transportation and communication system, their production structure (sector mix, labour market), their reproduction and collective consumption system (housing, education, social services, movements in different spheres of existence), socioeconomic, sociopolitical and sociocultural institutions, as well as the embeddedness of all these dynamics in broader spatial settings. But the questions also refer to the mechanisms of socioeconomic disintegration and the possible redevelopment strategies, as suggested in Table 10.2. The main headings of this detailed empirical research appear in Figure 10.1.

Table 10.2: Mechanisms of socioeconomic disintegration at the local level and processes of reemergence

Subsystem	Production system	Labour market	Reproduction of labour: households and education	Reproduction of labour: housing and environment	Political agencies and institutions	Planning agencies and institutions	Issue movements: social, political, ecological
Production system	- Decline of leading sectors - Drop in investment	- Job redundancies - No job creation	- Possible closure of schools - Decline in educational level	- General decline of urban environment	- Loss of political impact/image	- Loss of effectiveness - New planning priorities	- Establishment of parallel production circuits
Labour market	- Loss of dynamism in labour supply	- Rising unemployment - Mismatch S/D	- Low motivation of students - Orientation problems	- Loss of income: housing, education - Motivation problems	- Pressure for replacement income and jobs	- Job creation priorities/ new planning priorities	- Movements aiming at job creation - Alternative work circuits
Reproduction of labour: - households - education	- Distrust vis-à-vis employment possibilities in salaried labour relation	- Bifurcation in labour market strategies: - multi-jobs - training - liberal professions or indpt. labour	- Intra-family tensions - Demotivation - Decline in standard of living	- Migration	- Pressure on youth and education policy	- Call for training programmes - On the job training	

	- Declining investment environment	- Declining labour market environment	- Segmentation in living environments for families	- Demand for social housing - Demand for security policy	- Demand for improvement of social housing programmes	Housing movements, squattering
Reproduction of labour: - housing - living environment						
Political agencies and institutions	- Sectoral policy: restructuring versus innovation?	etc	etc			
Planning agencies and strategies						
Issue movements: social, political, ecological						

Figure 10.1:   Main headings of a locality file

---

1. Brief socioeconomic and sociocultural history of community

2. Political and administrative system

3. Local authorities: organisation, competencies

4. Socioeconomic regulation

5. Leading economic activities

6. Social reproduction: community, demography, class, family, gender

7. Social reproduction: educational system

8. Local planning/allocation in development initiatives/agencies

9. Prospects for future development

International comparison – the usefulness of typologies

In the setting of the research for Poverty 3, 29 localities were screened in this way (see Figure 10.2). This made it possible to identify the specificity of each locality, following a general logic, which, in the next stage of the analysis, would permit comparisons among localities to be made. More specifically, such an approach highlights the main mechanisms that are responsible for the socioeconomic disintegration of each locality and points at the domains where proactive strategies to counter the disintegration processes must be designed. Of course, economic disintegration plays a major role in the explanation of the socioeconomic problems of each locality. But the capacity of the local communities to solve their problems is dependant on the development of many other processes, such as the social cohesiveness of the local production systems, their embeddedness in the regional and national societies, the quality of their institutional system, the innovativeness of their development strategies, etc (Moulaert et al, 1994).

Figure 10.2: **Map of the localities involved in the research programme on 'Local Economic Development Strategies in Economically Disintegrated Areas'**

Source: Moulaert et al (1994)

Table 10.3 illustrates the value of comparing a socioeconomic structure and production model with development resources. Virtually none of the localities combines all the types of resources necessary to lead a coherent development strategy (Moulaert et al, 1994, ch 2). A large proportion of the largest industrial cities and ports bring together the various types of skills that are required; but Bremen, Dortmund and (south)

Cardiff do not use an integrated planning approach. Among the smaller traditional coal and metal manufacturing cities, none has a uniformly positive 'skills agenda'. Localities of the semi-rural type with miscellaneous light industry or metal and textile industries that score relatively well are Vigevano, Urbania and Mazamet. Note that quite a number of localities have developed integrated planning perspectives, but lack some of the skills to realise them: Comarca Montes de Oca, Agueda, Lavrion, Elgoibar, Perama. A locality that scores well for all skills and planning criteria is Gerona.

The role of quantitative data

It is obvious that in such an approach quantitative data play only a limited role. On the basis of the theories of development and underdevelopment used in the analysis, quantitative data can illustrate or can help to verify some hypotheses. But they can never replace a detailed qualitative analysis of structures, institutions and behavioural patterns that are at the basis of development in the localities. Moreover, their availability is limited.

In reality, only very straightforward data are available for each locality: sectoral structure, employment and unemployment, age structure, and population density. The data are the most complete in the UK, but for a number of countries it was not possible to provide local data for even the most basic variables. In Spain, land-use data are produced at the local level and are not systematically available. In Belgium, data at the sub-municipal level exist only sporadically. For Greek localities, no recent local migration data, income levels and land-use information are available. Statistical data at the level of the provinces exist for some areas, especially the most urban. In France, full data on land use and income per capita were unavailable to the research team. Germany provides an uneven picture according to the localities: Bremen and Hamburg produce data for all variables, while Dortmund and Rostock do not. For Portuguese localities, evidence on migration, land use and income is missing at the municipal level; the same holds for Italy as far as migration and land use are concerned.

In some countries there are also detailed data on local migration and on social well-being. However, these are usually produced on the initiative of the regional or local authorities. Therefore, data availability on more precise variables is very uneven among localities and definitions of variables vary. Only a country such as France (and the INSEE databank FIDEL, which combines different sources, domains and zones), manages to provide for the population census years a fairly exhaustive approach to the variables needed for satisfactory statistical analysis at the local level. (For the UK see Robson's chapter.)

Conclusion

The measurement of socioeconomic disintegration at the local level can only be done in the setting of a comprehensive understanding of the mechanisms that have produced this disintegration and of the processes that will eventually allow the localities to find new ways of redevelopment. Such a comprehensive understanding requires the development of an appropriate framework of analysis, including a value judgement about the goals of local development, the theories explaining development and redevelopment and the appropriate empirical methods to pursue the analysis.

Quantitative data play an important but partial role in the improvement of the analytical work. For the introduction of the planning perspective into the analytical work or to make analysis more useful for planning purposes, quantitative data are of relative use. They help to illustrate and test some of the mechanisms of development and disintegration; at the same time, they contribute to the evaluation of the extent of problems and possibilities. However, by themselves, they remain powerless in understanding the character of the socioeconomic processes at the level of the localities.

Table 10.3: Economic structure of localities and the resources of the local authorities

Type of locality / Type of resources	Rural communities	Semirural communities with miscellaneous light industry	Semirural communities with metal and textile	1. Coal mining communities 2. Metallurgy communities 3. Harbours	Special cases
Organisational capacity	Spatha -	Maniago-Vigevano +	Roanne+ Castres-Mazamet +/- Agueda-Urbania+	Rhondda-Dortmund+ Hamburg+ N-E Antwerp+ Valenciennes-	Gerona+ Sykies+ Bairro da Meira-Mar +/-
Technical skills		Arganil+ Comarca Montes de Oca-Ostiglia+	Agueda-	Charleroi+ Elgoibar+/- Barakaldo-Valenciennes+ NE Antwerp+	Fishguard+ Perama-Bairro da Beira-Mar +/-
Financial resources	Spatha-			Rostock-	Perama-

Type of locality / Type of resources	Rural communities	Semirural communities with miscellaneous light industry	Semirural communities with metal and textile	1. Coal mining communities 2. Metallurgy communities 3.. Harbours	Special cases
Planning perspective: integrated planning approach	Spatha-Almeida-	Vigevano +/- Ostiglia +/- Comarca Montes de Oca +	Urbania + Castres-Mazamet +/- Agueda +	Bremen - Rhondda +/- Charleroi + Dortmund-south Cardiff +/- Lavrion + Elgoibar + Calais-Hamburg + NE Antwerp + Valenciennes-Rostock?	Fishguard +/- Sykies +/- Beira-Mar +/- Perama + Gerona +

Key:

+ = available resources

- = non-existent or poor quality

neither + nor - = no particular problem

Source: Moulaert et al (1994)

The quantitative data that are of importance for effecting an appropriate analysis of local development, are insufficiently and incoherently available in the different nation states. The national statistical offices and Eurostat can certainly contribute to the production and publication of comparable and sufficient data for all municipalities of the EU. But another ambitious goal of many national and transnational statistical institutes, that is, to construct a uniform indicator of social stress or of disintegration at the local level, is misleading for social policy. The real-life social stress in a locality can only be measured whenever the socioeconomic structures, the institutions and the behavioural rules of different types of local agents are well understood.

Notes

1. This research was made possible by a research grant of the European Commission's 'Poverty 3' programme. I wish to thank Dr Lila Leontidou from King's College, Department of Geography, Jean-Cédric Delvainquière from Institut Fédératif de Recherche sur les Economies et Sociétés Industrielles (IFRESI), as well as an anonymous referee for their comments on earlier versions of this paper, and Jean-Bernard Boyabe for his research assistance.

eleven

THE DEVELOPMENT OF THE 1991 LOCAL DEPRIVATION INDEX

Brian Robson, Michael Bradford, Rachel Tye

Introduction

Measuring the socioeconomic deprivation of areas is an important preliminary to any understanding of social exclusion, of its genesis and of appropriate ways in which to tackle it. For governments, the measurement of deprivation has also been a widely-used way of determining priorities in resource allocation – not least because spatial targeting has been a central plank for many of the policy instruments used in the United Kingdom to tackle 'inner-city' problems. For example, a social index is used as an important element in calculating 'Standard Spending Assessments' through which central government grants to local authorities are determined; and the Department of the Environment's (DoE) ranking of local authorities, based on z-score analysis of 1981 data, was extensively used in the 1980s to guide decisions about which places qualified for targeted assistance (DoE, 1983).

This chapter provides an outline of the approach adopted in calculating an updated urban deprivation index based on 1991 data for use by the government (DoE, 1995). It discusses some of the technical issues raised by the solutions used in constructing the index and looks briefly at some of the results.

The task of developing an index of deprivation is not trivial. Governments use such indices for various purposes and the eventual applications are not always clear when an index is being developed. Since, ideally, the composition of any index should be guided by the purpose for which it will be used, this clearly presents an immediate difficulty. Furthermore, the basic concept of deprivation remains highly contested and its relationship to a series of similarly difficult concepts – such as disadvantage, poverty and need – is ambiguous (see Townsend, 1987). In our work the concept was given as wide a meaning as possible so that the index would be flexible enough to be used for the varied future purposes of government. We defined deprivation in an inclusive way, by exploring variables from a range of socioeconomic 'domains' (Table 11.1). We explored a wide array of indicators for a variety of entities, some of which referred to individuals, some to households and some to the environment in which people live. Many of the potential individual indicators can be interpreted in a number of ways in this respect; for example, the number of unemployed people in an area is both a measure of the job status of economically-active individuals and a reflection of the socio-economic environment in which people live.

One important decision was to focus on *outcome* measures and to avoid the use of indicators of vulnerable groups, such as non-white ethnic groups, single parents and lone pensioners. The index therefore includes measures of 'actual' deprivation rather than of people or households with a high propensity to being deprived. This is a contentious issue, but the decision to exclude measures of vulnerable groups is justified both because many within the particular vulnerable groups will not, in practice, be deprived and because there is an obvious danger of stereotyping such groups. In reality, comparison between the selected indicators and the measures of vulnerable groups showed high correlations, thereby suggesting that the use of 'outcome' measures does capture the expected overlap with vulnerable groups.

There are, of course, problems associated with outcome measures; for example, unemployment or receipt of social benefits may be temporary states for some people but longer term for others. Indeed, for every indicator that was finally selected there are caveats; for example, the proportion of households without a car is generally a good proxy for income as well as being a measure of accessibility to services and amenities, but it has a different meaning for rural areas than for central parts of large cities. In central London, in particular, it includes some rich households who choose not to have a car.

Interestingly, of all the indicators used, this was the indicator with the highest aggregate correlation with the three vulnerable groups mentioned above.

Table 11.1: Indicators used in the 1991 index

	Enumeration district	Ward	District
Environment Health			Standardised mortality
Shelter	- Overcrowding - Lacking amenities - Children in unsuitable accom-modation		
Security			Insurance premiums
Physical environment			Derelict land
Skills/ socialisation Education		Low education participation	
Family			Low attainment
Resource base Income	No car Children in low earner households		Income support
Jobs	Unemployment		Long-term unemployed

Note: All variables at lower scales are included in higher scales, ie, enumeration district (ED) indicators are used at ward scale and ward indicators at district scale.

From a large range of potential indicators, a small subset was eventually selected. The selection procedure involved a variety of considerations:

- the degree to which each potential indicator reflected a dimension of deprivation;

- its availability;

- the variation and level of the indicator;

- the avoidance of double-counting where one indicator included an element that was also included in another measure;

- the ease with which it could be comprehended.

Correlation analysis and various forms of factor analysis were also carried out to determine the spatial coincidence of indicators and the degree to which the measures reflected particular dimensions. Even in this task a degree of judgement was involved, since a high correlation could mean two indicators that reflect somewhat different dimensions but have very similar spatial patterns, or it could mean that the two were measuring the same aspect of a dimension and the inclusion of both would effectively double the weight of that aspect.

The need for flexibility

Given the variety of potential uses of the index, it was clearly important to develop an index that could be used in a flexible way. On some occasions the index would be used for rather general purposes, as in the bidding process for the Single Regeneration Budget (SRB); on others, it might be used for a specific policy area, such as housing or social services. It was therefore necessary to be able to disaggregate the index for particular purposes. Secondly, although the index was principally related to local authority districts, it was important to recognise that deprivation has very different patterns at different geographical scales and that the index may be used for policies targeted at different scales, such as whole authorities, inner areas, housing estates or other specific local areas. Not only do spatial patterns vary – with some areas having extensive deprivation spread thinly throughout the area and others having intense concentrations within small areas – but the geometry of administrative boundaries can affect the measurement of deprivation scores. As Figure 11.1 (p 199) demonstrates, because all the measures are based on spatial aggregates, both the over- and underbounding of district boundaries and the detailed configuration of boundaries can independently produce different deprivation scores even where the spatial patterns are identical.

We tackled this need for flexibility by developing a *matrix* approach rather than the more commonly-used vector of deprivation scores. Our use of a matrix rather than a single one-dimensional array of deprivation scores reflects the complexity of deprivation patterns on the ground and the need for flexibility and coverage of spatial scales. The matrix (a sample of which is shown in Table 11.2 for 100 of the 366 authorities in England) therefore includes three indices, one for each scale of district, ward and ED. Any temptation to create an overall single index from these three was avoided.

This matrix formulation is justified on two grounds. First, the complex geography of deprivation is highly dependant on the scale at which it is viewed (Holterman, 1975); while a district as a whole may appear not to suffer from high levels of deprivation, it can nevertheless contain in parts of its area levels of deprivation that are as severe as, if not more severe than those of another district with higher overall levels. The matrix formulation provides a more sensitive description of this complex geography of deprivation. Second, many public policies and the funding associated with them are targeted at one or more of these three scales and the use of a matrix enables the most appropriate scale to be used.

Inevitably, more measures were available at coarser spatial scales than at finer scales. For EDs and wards, Census data are virtually the only robust source. At coarser scales, particularly the district, there are many non-Census variables available. This means that, for the districts, a much more representative array of indicators was feasible, covering aspects of health, income and family circumstances.

Figure 11.1: Administrative geometrics

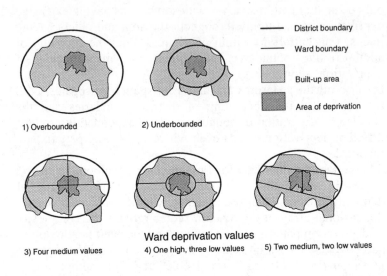

	District boundary
	Ward boundary
	Built-up area
	Area of deprivation

1) Overbounded   2) Underbounded

Ward deprivation values

3) Four medium values   4) One high, three low values   5) Two medium, two low values

In all cases, the pattern of deprivation is identical, but the configuration of administrative boundaries produce different values for deprivation scores, because they deal with spatial aggregates.

In the first two cases, over- and underbounding produces, respectively, a lower and a higher value at ED level. In cases (3)-(4), the pattern of ward boundaries produces a variety of scores at ward level.

Table 11.2: Deprivation Index for 100 ranked by district score

Authority	Degree		Spatial extent Ward level		ED level		Intensity	
	Overall score	Rank	% pop. in DEP wards	Rank	% EDs DEP	Rank	Mean of worst 3 wards	Rank
	(1)	(2)	(3)	(4)	(5)	(6)	(7)	(8)
Newham	39.3	1	100.0	1	56.0	5	17.6	9
Southwark	37.7	2	92.0	6	62.2	3	17.9	5
Hackney	37.1	3	100.0	1	82.1	1	18.5	4
Islington	36.7	4	100.0	1	60.8	4	17.4	11
Birmingham	36.5	5	64.4	14	19.5	19	18.7	2
Liverpool	36.0	6	68.0	13	21.0	17	16.3	19
Tower Hamlets	35.4	7	100.0	1	78.0	2	19.1	1
Lambeth	35.0	8	95.5	5	49.8	6	18.7	3
Sandwell	34.3	9	54.5	21	11.3	31	14.1	34
Haringey	32.3	10	79.5	10	44.4	7	16.6	16
Lewisham	32.3	11	71.0	12	31.0	12	17.6	8
Knowsley	32.3	12	58.9	18	26.4	14	14.7	28
Manchester	31.5	13	58.4	19	13.8	25	15.5	23
Greenwich	31.1	14	58.0	20	21.9	15	15.7	20
Camden	30.4	15	87.9	8	40.4	8	17.0	13
Hammersmith/Ful	30.0	16	86.6	7	39.7	9	17.4	10
Newcastle-on-T	26.7	17	37.7	26	15.4	22	15.1	26
Barking/Dag	25.8	18	36.6	28	11.4	30	13.8	36
Kensington/Chel	25.7	19	61.0	16	29.7	13	16.8	15

Authority	Degree		Spatial extent				Intensity	
	Overall score	Rank	Ward level % pop. in DEP wards	Rank	ED level % EDs DEP	Rank	Mean of worst 3 wards	Rank
	(1)	(2)	(3)	(4)	(5)	(6)	(7)	(8)
Waltham Forest	25.3	20	71.7	11	21.5	16	17.8	6
Wandsworth	25.3	21	61.0	17	20.4	18	15.6	21
South Tyneside	24.2	22	23.9	53	9.4	36	12.1	54
Bradford	23.6	23	27.8	44	13.2	26	15.3	25
Middlesbrough	23.2	24	30.9	40	4.9	79	10.5	79
Nottingham	23.0	25	34.1	33	8.0	44	14.5	30
Westminster	23.0	26	84.2	9	34.4	10	17.2	12
Wolverhampton	22.7	27	35.0	30	7.8	45	13.4	38
Salford	22.6	28	25.8	49	8.7	41	15.6	22
Brent	22.5	29	53.6	22	34.3	11	17.8	7
Blackpool	22.3	30	34.0	35	15.2	23	16.6	17
Blackburn	21.8	31	37.6	27	9.2	37	12.1	55
Gateshead	21.6	32	25.3	51	6.2	61	13.0	44
Sunderland	21.2	33	21.2	62	6.0	64	12.9	47
Hartlepool	20.6	34	17.5	73	2.3	130	9.4	91
Sheffield	20.6	35	36.1	29	10.2	35	16.5	18
Leicester	20.4	36	28.7	43	5.5	70	13.4	41
Ealing	20.1	37	40.5	25	14.0	24	14.4	31
Oldham	19.9	38	25.4	50	6.6	58	12.5	48
Brighton	19.7	39	62.4	15	15.9	21	14.3	33
Doncaster	19.7	40	22.8	57	5.8	68	11.2	66

Bristol	19.7	41	27.3	46	7.1	55	13.9	35
Southampton	19.7	42	44.8	23	12.9	27	14.4	32
Walsall	19.5	43	34.1	34	6.6	59	11.4	64
Portsmouth	19.3	44	30.2	41	12.4	28	14.9	27
Coventry	19.1	45	34.6	31	10.5	33	13.1	43
Preston	18.6	46	31.4	39	5.4	71	13.8	37
Lincoln	18.4	47	15.4	76	4.7	89	7.9	124
Bolton	17.9	48	19.0	66	4.7	88	11.5	62
Rochdale	16.9	49	20.4	64	5.0	78	11.6	60
Halton	16.8	50	11.6	100	4.3	93	8.0	117
N. Tyneside	16.3	51	18.3	70	6.1	62	10.7	73
Plymouth	16.0	52	32.8	36	12.4	29	16.8	14
Barnsley	15.7	53	0.0	206	0.5	244	7.0	142
St Helens	15.7	54	4.9	146	2.2	134	8.1	116
Leeds	15.5	55	22.7	58	5.9	67	15.4	24
Kingston-o-Hull	14.8	56	40.5	24	6.7	57	13.1	42
Burnley	13.6	57	14.6	82	6.0	65	9.6	86
Easington	13.3	58	0.0	206	0.5	235	6.4	152
Norwich	13.3	59	18.8	67	5.2	75	10.3	81
Rotheram	13.0	60	7.3	123	2.9	109	9.5	90
Wirral	12.7	61	21.5	60	4.7	87	11.8	59
Langbaurgh	12.2	62	10.2	108	2.0	141	9.4	93
Wansbeck	12.1	63	6.8	131	4.7	86	7.3	139
Stoke-on-Trent	12.0	64	13.6	86	2.0	138	8.9	103
Tameside	11.9	65	4.9	147	2.7	112	7.7	128
Derwentside	11.7	66	0.0	206	0.0	320	5.4	174
Great Grimsby	11.5	67	18.1	71	5.0	77	10.1	82
Hove	11.0	68	29.2	42	16.4	20	13.0	45

Authority	Degree		Spatial extent				Intensity	
			Ward level		ED level			
	Overall score	Rank	% pop. in DEP wards	Rank	% EDs DEP	Rank	Mean of worst 3 wards	Rank
	(1)	(2)	(3)	(4)	(5)	(6)	(7)	(8)
Stockton-on-T	10.5	69	6.8	130	3.8	98	11.0	69
Hastings	10.1	70	34.4	32	10.6	32	12.3	51
Wakefield	10.0	71	4.8	148	0.5	239	6.9	143
Oxford	9.0	72	32.1	38	8.5	43	11.9	57
Sefton	9.0	73	24.3	52	7.5	52	11.5	63
Wigan	8.9	74	3.3	155	1.5	161	7.4	135
Derby	8.7	75	23.7	55	3.6	99	10.7	75
Wear Valley	8.7	76	7.7	120	1.4	168	8.0	118
Scunthorpe	8.4	77	14.7	81	3.4	101	8.8	107
Corby	7.1	78	0.0	206	1.9	146	5.4	172
Bournemouth	6.5	79	23.1	56	10.2	34	14.7	29
Blyth Valley	6.3	80	0.0	206	0.0	320	5.6	170
Thanet	6.1	81	23.9	54	8.8	39	12.1	53
Harlow	5.1	82	0.0	206	0.0	320	6.6	150
Darlington	5.1	83	6.8	132	2.3	126	8.1	115
Mansfield	4.7	84	0.0	206	1.9	147	5.9	163
Sedgefield	4.2	85	0.0	206	0.6	224	5.7	166
Great Yarmouth	4.0	86	16.2	75	8.8	40	13.4	39
York	3.6	87	0.0	206	1.5	163	6.8	145
Kirklees	3.4	88	11.4	103	2.7	113	8.3	112
Hyndburn	3.1	89	5.9	140	1.8	151	7.2	141

City of London	3.0	90	0.0	206	0.0	320	3.8	196
Reading	2.0	91	18.7	69	7.3	53	12.2	52
Chesterfield	1.9	92	0.0	206	1.6	158	5.6	167
Thurrock	1.4	93	14.9	78	4.8	83	8.3	111
Barrow-in-F	1.4	94	12.4	93	2.7	112	7.8	126
Slough	1.1	95	10.7	105	4.8	85	7.8	125
Hereford	1.0	96	12.0	96	4.2	94	7.4	136
Enfield	0.5	97	26.9	48	8.9	38	13.0	46
Calderdale	0.4	98	11.7	99	5.1	76	9.2	100
Copeland	0.0	99	4.2	151	0.6	219	6.1	160
Bolsover	0.0	100	0.0	206	0.0	320	5.1	180

Note: Authorities are ranked by their overall district score. Different rankings would appear if they were ranked by one of the other three measures and different authorities would appear in the list of 100.

Eventually, six Census-based indicators were selected at the ED level, a seventh was added at the ward level and a further six non-Census indicators were added at the district level (Table 11.1). There are obvious difficulties in having different numbers of indicators at the three levels, which will be discussed later, but by including the non-Census sources it was possible to include indicators of dimensions such as health and security at the district level that were not available at the other scales.

At all three scales, the structure of the data was represented by two factors: one related to socioeconomic circumstances and one related to housing. Oblique rotations suggested that these factors were independent of one another. Split-half tests showed that the structure was stable, especially at the ED and ward levels. These analyses were carried out for background and clarification purposes and were not used to weight the indicators in any way. They were useful, however, for suggesting ways in which combinations of the indicators could subsequently be put together to produce a special index for a particular policy.

Measurement of the indicators

There are technical issues about how best to measure and standardise the indicators. The widely used z-score based on transformed data was used for the equivalent index for 1981. However, this is inappropriate for ED data where the denominator is small and variable, and where the numerator will be affected by Barnardisation and imputation that are used in reporting Census results in order to ensure anonymity (Cole, 1993). In place of z-scores, we decided to use signed chi-square value as a more appropriately robust measure (Jones and Kirby, 1980; Visvalingham, 1983; Morphet, 1992). Signed chi-square measures the extent to which the value for a specific place deviates from the national value. It uses absolute values for the numerator and denominator, rather than ratio values (Visvalingham, 1983). Hence, at the scale of EDs, for example, it lends more weight to those EDs with larger denominators. It has the merit that the value of zero reflects the value for the nation as a whole; places with positive scores are therefore, by definition, worse than the national value and places with negative scores are better. By contrast, in the case of z-scores, a value of zero reflects the mean of all EDs, a figure that will vary with different geometries of ED boundaries. The arguments for using signed chi-square for EDs are clearly strong.

We decided to use the technique at all three scales. This was obviously justified at the ED scale where denominators for many EDs are extremely small and hence lack robustness. Even at the ward level, however, some indicators have considerable variability in the size of their denominators, the lowest of which can also be quite small. This justifies the use of signed chi-square for wards. At the district level it was used partly for consistency, but mainly because it reflects absolute as well as relative amounts of deprivation, something that a single statistic rarely does. A 30% unemployment rate or a 10% rate of inadequate housing, for example, may be more difficult to tackle and have greater negative effects if they represent twice as many unemployed people or twice the number of poorly-housed households. For two areas with identical percentages on an indicator, the chi-square statistic gives a greater value to that place with the larger denominator, thereby reflecting the greater absolute extent of the problem. This logic is, of course, reversed for places with negative chi-square values. However, the index aims to measure deprivation rather than well-being and the focus of our attention is therefore on places with positive (deprived) rather than negative (non-deprived) scores.

The question of whether to transform indicators is a difficult one. We decided to use a logarithmic transformation because the data would be used in correlation analysis but, more importantly, because the indicators would be combined to form a composite index for each geographical level. The transformation has the effect of differentially depressing extreme scores around the value of zero. If the data had not been transformed, an extreme value for one indicator would have had a disproportionate effect on the composite index. Transformation reduces the effects of extremes without losing their importance to the indicator. In short, it narrows the variation among the maximum values of all the indicators. As with other forms of measurement, the maximum values are highest where the median percentage is very low and where the highest percentage is close to 100%. Indicators with such distributions have a slightly extra weight within an index for their extreme values. The transformation also means that the contribution through the signed chi-square of the absolute as against the relative value of deprivation is dampened down, especially at the district level. Thus, while the absolute values of deprivation were represented in the index, transformation meant that the varying size of districts did not unduly dominate the deprivation values.

The overall index for each level was then simply taken as the addition of the transformed signed chi-squared values for the relevant number of indicators.   Unlike the earlier 1981 index, it was not thought to be appropriate to weight any of the indicators.   Weights could have been based on policy considerations (such as double-weighting unemployment) or on the coefficients associated with multivariate analysis.   Neither approach seemed justifiable: the first would have presupposed that particular policy domains would be addressed in using the index and this was not the case; the second would have given undue credence to the particular set of indicators used in the index and would, in any case, have made the index less transparent and interpretable.   It was therefore decided not to use any weightings.   Although the addition of unweighted indicators is a superficially simple solution, the decision not to weight is a compromise between, on the one hand, multiplying (rather than adding) measures in order to reflect the amount of area multiple deprivation and, on the other hand, weighting measures at less than 1.0 in order to reflect their intercorrelation.

The structure of the deprivation matrix

The matrix therefore consists of three definitions of deprivation drawn from the spatial scales of district, ward and ED and based on the unweighted signed chi-square values:

*   **Degree**. At the district scale, we use the unweighted sum of the 13 indicators. This can be considered as measuring the overall degree of deprivation within a district.

- **Spatial extent**. The ED and ward-level indices were used to measure the spatial extent of deprivation within a district. This is based on the proportion of a district's EDs or wards that are included within the worst 7% and 10% respectively of the country's EDs and wards. These selected cut-off points were determined on the basis of the correlations between the rankings for the top 2% to 12% (at 1% intervals), which showed that 7% was the point for EDs at which the correlations became more stable and high, and 10% for wards. For wards the matrix shows the proportion of a district's population living in the top 10% of the country's deprived wards. This allows for the different size of wards. Given the small number of wards in a district, it is inevitably very sensitive to a slight variation in the cut-off point; hence the use of population provides a more sensitive measure.

- **Intensity**. The third measure in the matrix captures the intensity of deprivation. One district may have a number of EDs or wards lying just above the 7% and 10% cut-off points, whereas in another they could lie within the worst 1% of the country. Such differences in the levels of intensity of deprivation are not captured in the measure of spatial extent. The measure of intensity is therefore used at the ward scale as the mean of the three most deprived wards. The figure of three was chosen as a compromise number, being more than 10% of the wards of all districts. Averaging is a quick and rather crude measure, but the chi-square method does take some account of the variation in size of wards and any aggregation of households into a combined new unit with its own index value would have given a misleading impression that the three wards were necessarily contiguous.

The matrix therefore contains three different definitions of deprivation that embody the different scales at which measurement can be made. It is this approach that gives some novelty to the index and allows it to be used in a highly flexible fashion so that the ED scores will reveal those 'non-deprived' districts that nevertheless contain small pockets of concentrated deprivation.

Patterns of results

Inspection of the results within the matrix shows that there is some variability in the ranking of some authorities on each of the three types of measure. Some show little variation. For example, on the basis of the degree and extent measures alone, many districts are ranked high on both measures (eg, Hackney is 3rd on the district index, joint-1st on the ward-based extent measure and 1st on the ED-based extent measure; while Knowsley is 12th and 14th; and Newcastle is 17th and 22nd).

Other districts show major changes in their ranking. This can, of course, result from the spatial patterning of deprivation, or from the inclusion of more indicators in the district level index, or indeed a combination of the two effects. The effect of including more indicators at the district level was explored by comparing the district level index with one based on only the indicators used at the ED level. This showed that the inclusion of seven more measures at the district scale has the general effect of increasing the degree of deprivation measured in the Midlands and the North, while reducing the degree in the South. There are exceptions to this among the districts: for example, Southwark and Barking and Dagenham in the South, and Leicester and Hull in the Midlands and North. There are also a number of districts that rank similarly on both indices (Islington, Hackney, Newham, Tower Hamlets, Haringey, Lewisham and Bristol in the South, and Lincoln, Blackpool, Coventry, Rochdale, Stoke, Great Grimsby and Scunthorpe in the Midlands and the North). Nevertheless, there is a predominant geographical pattern that suggests that the Census-based indicators at ED and ward level (which largely relate to housing and unemployment) reflect problems in those fields in southern authorities; whereas, by including the wider range of domains reflected in the non-Census indicators on health and education, the greater degree of general deprivation in northern areas emerges.

In addition to the differences arising from the different sets of indicators at the three scales, the comparison of the spatial extent and degree of deprivation also shows interesting variations as a result of the spatial geometry of the patterns of local deprivation. Stoke and Sefton form an interesting contrast in this respect. Sefton lies in the low 50s for the spatial extent ranking, but only in the 70s for the district index. Clearly the deprivation around Bootle and the south of the district is revealed in the measure of spatial extent, while the better-off, more northerly areas of Crosby and Southport offset this by showing lower levels for the measure of degree of deprivation at the district scale. Stoke, on the other hand, ranks in the 60s at the district level but only 138th and 80th at the ED and ward scales. Stoke, a non-Urban Programme Authority, has long argued for financial support on the grounds that it does not have the concentrations of deprivation found in other districts – that its deprived households and individuals are more evenly spread over the district even though its degree of overall deprivation is quite high. This argument is borne out by the matrix of deprivation. Middlesbrough and Hove are two more good examples of districts where there is a difference between the spatial extent and the index ranking. Middlesbrough is ranked 24th on the district index, but it is only 79th at the ED scale. Obviously its deprivation is more widespread and less concentrated than in Hove, which appears as 20th at the ED scale but 66th at the district level.

Comparison of the rankings on intensity with those on spatial extent provides another example of the use of the matrix to interpret the complexity of deprivation, since it can pinpoint authorities whose overall score conceals the existence of areas of localised severe deprivation and also those that are 'overbounded'. For example, Leeds ranks 24th on intensity, much higher than for the other three measures (55th, 56th, 67th). This reflects the district's overbounded nature. Given that it is the central district within its conurbation, the boundaries of Leeds are generously drawn and contain extensive semirural areas and outer suburbs. Its large area masks the deprivation to be found in many of its areas. Certainly the intensity would have been concealed if only the degree and extent measures had been used. Plymouth's and Sheffield's intensities are even higher, 14th and 18th respectively, even though their other rankings are much lower (52nd, 33rd, 29th; and 35th, 26th, 35th). In contrast – given their rankings on the other measures – Blackburn and Middlesbrough, for example, and South Tyneside, Lincoln and Halton, all have relatively low intensities.

Such comparisons suggest ways in which the matrix can be used to reveal the variations in deprivation across sets of authorities. While many authorities show consistently high (or low) deprivation rankings regardless of which measure is used, there are many cases where the rankings differ on one or other of the measures. This provides a powerful justification for using the matrix rather than a vector of scores as a measure. Were one to use the matrix as a descriptor of overall deprivation, we would argue that it is inappropriate to use any single measure or indeed to succumb to the temptation to average the rankings across all of the measures. Instead, the matrix can be used to isolate sets of 'worst' authorities by using simple operational rules to combine the different measures. For example, in reporting to the DoE, use was made of two approaches: use of natural breaks in the sequence of values in the district, ward and ED values; and the use of a selected rank (such as 50) in order to select places that rank less than the cut-off on any two of the three matrix measures (see DoE, 1995, p 118).

Changes in deprivation between 1981 and 1991

Comparisons between 1981 and 1991 are not simple. Direct comparisons between the results of the 1981 index and the 1991 index are not possible since they use different indicators and different methods. There are also technical difficulties: the boundaries of wards and EDs have changed over the decade; some variables in the 1991 Census were not collected in the 1981 Census and some from 1981 were collected in a different way in 1991; there are differences in the population base of the two Censuses and variations in the degree of undercount.

In order to make comparisons, the data were all converted to the common geographical base of 1981-based wards. Use was made of four near-identical indicators that could be measured both for 1981 and 1991:

- unemployment

- households without a car

- households with more than one person per room

- households (1981) or residents (1991) with poor amenities (the discrepancy arising from the fact that this indicator was not recorded in 1981 for residents).

Two analyses were explored. First was a cross-sectional analysis using chi-square calculations for 1981 and for 1991. This allowed comparison between the relative position and values of districts for each year compared to the national values for those years. In 1991 there were slightly more districts worse than the national value. Of these, many more had chi-square scores of between 0 and 5, while fewer had scores of over 5. These differences suggest a wider spread of deprivation across authorities associated with the North–South changes over the period. The most marked change was the *relative* improvement in many northern areas, resulting mainly from the spread of unemployment elsewhere. The North-West and the North-East in particular both show such relative improvement. Most of the relative deterioration was in the South and was marked in Outer London. Across the districts, the number that contained at least one deprived ward increased somewhat over the decade. At the same time, the number of districts containing a large area of deprivation declined; in other words, relative deprivation spread to other districts. Likewise, on the intensity measure, there were far fewer districts with intensities of over 10; thereby indicating that more districts had evidence of deprivation, while there were fewer with high levels of spatial extent and of intensity. Overall, it seems clear that deprivation was less concentrated in 1991 than was the case 10 years earlier. Much of this spreading-out is connected with North–South shifts in deprivation that resulted from the impact of the late-1980s' recession on service jobs and hence on the employment and housing markets of the South.

The second approach was to look at the dynamics of change, using chi-square analysis to examine the actual dynamics of 1981-91 change (as opposed to cross-sectional comparison of 1981 results with 1991 results). This approach identifies areas in which change was greater or less than the nationally-expected change. The expected value of an indicator for each district was defined as the 1991 denominator value for the indicator, multiplied by the 1981 proportion of the indicator for the district and the difference between 1981 and 1991 in the national proportions for the indicator. The measure therefore takes into account the absolute change in the national values of the indicators and compares every district to that national change.

Of the districts showing relative improvement, almost three quarters were in the North and the Midlands. Again, it was in Outer London where the most marked relative deterioration occurred. Outside Greater London, the greatest relative deterioration was found in Norwich, Reading, Bristol, Southampton and Torbay. Most of the northern districts experienced relative improvement, particularly in the North-West, North-East and West Yorkshire. The Midlands showed a more mixed pattern. South Yorkshire tended to have relatively deteriorated; its links to coalfields may well partly explain this. Many of the northern areas that show relative deterioration are also associated with coalfields.

Within the conurbations, there are some interesting differences that tend to support the view that some polarisation occurred in the 1980s between the inner and outer areas of the conurbations. For example, while Manchester showed relative improvement compared to the nation as a whole, it improved much less than surrounding districts within its conurbation. This is also the case for Newcastle and Birmingham, both of which deteriorated relatively, whereas a large number of the rest of their conurbation districts improved.

Comparison between the results of, on the one hand, the cross-sectional change in 1981 and 1991 and, on the other, the analysis of direct 1981-91 change shows very similar general patterns of *relative* deterioration in the South and improvement in the North. It must be remembered that both measures are relative rather than absolute: the cross-sectional analysis compares the relative distribution of deprivation at the two dates, while the change analysis examines change relative to national change over the decade. This combination of cross-sectional comparison and change relative to national change captures both the relative change in position and the relative dynamics of change. Taken together, the two analyses usefully complement each other. For example, according to the former, much of Inner London has experienced little change; it remains relatively very deprived compared with the nation as a whole. Yet the dynamics analysis shows that many of the authorities deteriorated more than would be expected given national change over the decade. This is, for example, especially true of Tower Hamlets and Southwark. Similarly, parts of the North-East, such as Newcastle, Sunderland and Langbaurgh, show a much improved position in 1991 given their relative position in 1981; but the change analysis shows that this apparent improvement is exaggerated given their change relative to the national change.

Overall, it is clear that the 1980s saw a diffusion of relative deprivation to areas that had not suffered at the start of the decade. Many of the areas that showed relative improvement between 1981 and 1991 (for example, those in northern authorities such as Newcastle or Manchester) changed little relative to national change; their apparent 'improvement' was therefore a reflection of the wider national spread of relative deprivation. The set of places at the top of the rankings of deprivation appears to have remained relatively constant between 1981 and 1991. This suggests that those places that were most deprived at the start of the decade remained deprived at its close and, indeed, many of the very worst areas, such as the inner cores of conurbations, showed a continuing decline relative to the peripheral parts of their areas.

Conclusion

The matrix developed for – and now being used by – government, therefore contains measures of the degree of deprivation, its spatial extent at two scales, and its intensity. These measures capture much more of the complex geography of deprivation than can any one index. It is hoped that the deprivation matrix based on the overall index at each scale, and backed up by various disaggregations of the indices at each scale, will be an advance on the old 1981 index and might more appropriately inform government's allocational and policy decisions in the future.

twelve

PUBLIC ATTITUDES TO SOCIAL EXCLUSION: SOME PROBLEMS OF MEASUREMENT AND ANALYSIS[1]

Professor Peter Golding

Introduction

In the June 1994 European Parliamentary elections there was widespread dismay at the signs, across the continent, of growing apathy or disenchantment with the elections and the whole apparatus of European politics and policies. In recent years such growing evidence of both hostility and disdain for the European ideal and its institutional manifestations has continued to frustrate and disturb the more involved and committed. Yet the fact remains that public opinion and preferences matter in European policy. Policy does not evolve in a vacuum. Public opinion sets the limits within which legitimate politics can act. This is as true in poverty policy as in any other area. Policy that has as its core the task of persuading some sections of the community to forego privilege in order to improve the circumstances of others is, of all policy areas, bound to face opposition. Indeed, many would argue that the key to understanding the history of redistribution and social security policies is to investigate the clash of ideology and political power between the more and less comfortable groups in society.

That is not my task here. In this chapter I wish to review recent evidence on public attitudes to poverty in Europe as a backdrop to discussions about the feasibility and attractiveness of various policy options. I will be drawing on the evidence provided by the 1993 Eurobarometer 40 Survey conducted for the European Commission. Central among the questions we must pose is how the European people conceive poverty. Throughout history, claims that poverty is only sensibly understood as a thoroughgoing inability to survive, a lack of the basic essentials of food and shelter, have been contested by arguments that poverty is inescapably social in essence, and can only be understood as a lack of the necessary resources to take part in the life of society. It is this latter view that has underpinned the shift from 'poverty' to 'social exclusion' as the terminology buttressing European policy in this area (for a general discussion see Golding, 1986). The Poverty 3 programme, we have often been reminded, is about "much more than money" (see the chapter by Berghman). Social exclusion refers to "multi-dimensional disadvantage which is of substantial duration and which involves dissociation from the major social and occupational milieux of society" (Room et al, 1992). For the European Commission, people are in poverty when their resources are "so limited as to exclude them from the minimum acceptable way of life in the states in which they live" (Hansen, 1994).

The niceties of this definition are not my concern here. Certainly such a shift poses enormous problems for measurement and conceptualisation, since it necessarily imposes a subjective assessment of social conditions onto a calibration of material resources. However, many social scientists would argue that that is the epistemological status of all social measures; it is simply more explicit in this formulation. The importance of this shift in emphasis, however (and I readily confirm that it is a shift I heartily welcome as both conceptually necessary and politically desirable), is that it makes research into public attitudes all the more crucial in addressing the development of policy. Firstly, it suggests that poverty is itself experienced as a reflection of attitudes and beliefs held both by those enduring deprivation and by those in the wider society (remembering that over time these are not continuously and mutually exclusive groups). Secondly, it invites an investigation of the likely support for and opposition to various policy initiatives. In part this will relate to how people define poverty (the threshold of tolerability and the acceptability of differing indicators of poverty), in part to their willingness to accede to policies with zero-sum resource implications.   These issues require a more substantial elaboration than is possible for present circumstances. In this chapter I simply wish to review some of the findings of the recent Eurobarometer research. I shall do so by looking, first, at the extent to which people recognise that poverty exists; secondly, at what people believe constitutes poverty; thirdly, at what they believe to be its causes; and fourthly, at attitudes to policy to address poverty. Finally I suggest some concerns about the methodology and approach of this research.

The survey conducted for the European Commission in 1993 is the third in a series of studies of perceptions of poverty in Europe. The first was undertaken in 1976 (European Commission, 1977), the second in 1989 (European Commission, 1990a). In looking at the most recent data I shall, where appropriate and possible, be drawing comparisons with the data from the earlier surveys.

Does poverty exist?

The most basic question must be whether people believe that poverty is an issue in the societies in which they live. Table 12.1 shows that across Europe over a third of the population believes that poverty exists. However, a third also say that nobody lives in poverty, and in Denmark and Luxembourg a majority take this view. Even in the United Kingdom, where the numbers in poverty have been growing the fastest, the largest proportion of respondents deny that there is poverty. The question relates specifically to 'the area where you live', it should be noted. In 1989 over half the respondents across the countries claimed there was no poverty in their area, especially in Germany, Spain, Luxembourg, and the UK.

People were also asked about their likelihood of coming across poverty. What is striking about these figures (Table 12.2) is the increasing proportion who deny coming across poverty. Over three times as many say they never encounter poverty as those who say they often see such conditions. When the term 'social exclusion' is substituted for 'poverty', an even higher proportion suggest that nobody where they live could be defined as living in this way.

Table 12.1: In the area where you live, are there people who live in one or other of the following situations? (1993)

	Belg	Denm	Ger	Grec	Spain	Fra	Ire	Italy	Lux'	N'lands	Portu	UK	EC12+
Extreme poverty	9.3	3.2	8.7	32.9	14.2	18.3	11.8	10.3	4.3	3.9	27.1	10.8	12.5
Poverty	31.4	19.6	27.9	62.0	27.4	42.2	30.8	27.2	10.7	21.2	50.9	27.0	31.3
Risk of poverty	38.6	21.8	39.2	47.4	30.1	43.4	34.1	34.3	21.2	32.7	25.5	39.5	37.4
Nobody	24.4	59.6	33.8	16.2	41.9	24.0	30.3	38.9	54.4	45.5	16.3	35.2	33.7

Table 12.2: Do you ever happen to see for yourself the conditions in which these people [in poverty] really live? (If yes, do you see these conditions often, sometimes or rarely?) (1993)

	Belg	Denm	Ger	Grec	Spain	Fra	Ire	Italy	Lux'	N'lands	Portu	UK	EC12+
Yes often	6.3	8.9	8.5	18.9	11.4	15.4	9.2	8.4	6.3	6.9	12.3	8.8	10.3
Yes sometimes	22.9	24.1	25.1	31.2	34.5	36.1	24.5	28.7	21.4	27.2	27.6	22.3	28.3
Yes rarely	22.5	25.9	25.4	21.5	20.2	19.0	18.3	17.7	27.5	14.3	17.4	18.1	20.3
No never	41.4	40.6	35.3	26.5	32.2	28.3	44.9	40.0	41.1	49.5	39.4	47.6	37.5

Table 12.3 shows the extent to which people thought the gap between rich and poor to be increasing. With the possible exception of Denmark, an overwhelming majority in most countries see the gap widening. This has increased since the earlier surveys, with a growing sense among Europeans of both increasing poverty and increasing gaps between the advantaged and the disadvantaged. Between 1989 and 1993 the proportion across the Community who believed that the gap had increased grew from 70% to 80%. Whether people believe this gap as just or avoidable is to some extent tackled elsewhere in the survey, though without any clear articulation to these questions.

What constitutes poverty?

The very fact that we have moved the policy concern to a wider target than poverty makes it all the more important that we understand the vocabulary and conceptual language of the general population. Table 12.4 shows what people believe to contribute to a definition of poverty. I have given the findings in rank order rather than raw percentages to emphasise the results, though this was not the format of the question in the Eurobarometer survey. Homelessness takes pride of place among the life-styles that people recognise as poverty. Quite what people might mean by some of the other categories cannot be interrogated here. However, it may be that this finding suggests that people have a fairly basic notion of destitution in mind when asked to flesh out the concept of poverty.

Table 12.5 shows what people believe to be the absolute necessities of life. Extended exploration of these data and their correlates would allow us to disinter the social consensus level of acceptable living standards that has become a key element of approaches to poverty research in recent years (see Mack and Lansley, 1985). Notable here is the split between 'subsistence' elements and 'life-style' elements. At one extreme few dissent from the view that water is an essential. But what are we to make of some of the other categories? For example, on the surface it is a surprise to see 'being able to benefit from social welfare' receiving almost as much support. But, in fact, the questionnaire item actually reads 'being able to benefit from social welfare when in need, such as, in the case of

Table 12.3: Which of these opinions about our society comes closest to your own? (%) (1993)

	Belg	Denm	Ger	Grec	Spain	Fra	Ire	Italy	Lux'	N'lands	Portu	UK	EC12+
Rich get richer/poor get poorer	83.5	57.3	82.6	77.7	68.3	81.5	79.9	77.5	68.6	68.0	76.5	84.1	78.9
Less and less difference in income between rich and poor	7.9	35.8	9.0	15.3	23.0	8.9	12.4	15.1	19.2	22.2	18.0	10.5	13.2

Table 12.4: Rank order of responses to the following question: For each one of the following situations, would you define it as poverty or not? (%) (1993)

	Belg	Denm	Ger	Grec	Spain	Fra	Ire	Italy	Lux'	N'lands	Portu	UK	EC12+
Living on street because no home	1	1	1	1	1	1	1	1	1	1	1	1	1
Drug-dependent	4	4	4	10	8	6	5	10	5	3	7	6	6
Living in social exclusion	2	2	2	4	3	2	3	3	2	2	3	5	2
1 year unemployed	5	5	7	3	2	4	6	5	7	6	5	2	4
Being an input in psychiatry	10	10	8	9	10	9	8	9	8	8	11	7	11
Living in home for elderly	12	12	12	11	12	12	12	11	12	11	12	12	12

	Belg	Denm	Ger	Grec	Spain	Fra	Ire	Italy	Lux'	N'lands	Portu	UK	EC12+
Living on fringe of society by choice	8	8	9	12	7	11	10	6	9	7	4	9	9
Living in poor area	3	3	5	8	4	3	4	2	4	4	2	3	3
Living on the road	11	11	3	2	11	10	2	7	3	12	9	4	6
Asylum seekers	7	7	10	5	5	8	7	8	6	5	7	8	8
Physical handicap	9	9	6	7	9	7	11	12	11	9	10	7	10
Immigrant in modest circumstances	6	6	11	6	6	5	9	4	10	10	6	11	7

Table 12.5: What proportion of respondents believe these items to be absolute necessities? (1993)

	Belg	Denm	Ger	Grec	Spain	Fra	Ire	Italy	Lux'	N'lands	Portu	UK	EC12+
Water/electricity	97	84	95	100	96	17	94	97	99	94	99	95	97
Welfare	96	94	94	97	95	97	95	95	98	92	98	94	95
Indoor toilet	90	62	76	94	89	79	86	96	94	78	98	75	83
Own living space	78	39	79	63	69	86	76	84	89	67	90	72	77
Good education	81	61	85	82	83	83	87	77	89	65	84	91	83
Car	22	13	25	44	18	38	32	29	50	12	40	15	26
Leisure time	43	53	45	71	53	42	58	38	61	52	64	56	48
Healthy diet	84	80	84	88	83	86	92	75	92	97	97	88	84
Good job	78	67	86	94	86	72	79	78	85	79	85	70	79
Annual holiday	24	59	29	79	62	40	29	34	34	30	72	35	39

	Belg	Denm	Ger	Grec	Spain	Fra	Ire	Italy	Lux'	N'lands	Portu	UK	EC12+
Health care	94	96	94	97	34	96	94	90	97	97	98	95	94
Friendly neighbours	52	49	55	82	54	51	66	52	71	51	86	50	54
Go out with family and friends	48	61	53	81	66	66	75	61	61	46	95	65	62
Useful to others	63	75	64	93	73	71	76	70	69	61	87	74	70
Feeling recognised by society	63	81	61	86	75	66	68	67	68	89	74	56	65
Social life	29	49	42	57	29	37	46	33	49	52	50	60	42

unemployment, sickness or invalidity, or old age'. Which of these are people responding to? It is impossible to tell, and therefore impossible to rank this item among the other 'essentials'. It would be interesting to know why holidays feature so prominently in the views of Iberian Europeans. Is this the tourist trade or southern European life-style conventions being tapped?

The causes of poverty

Table 12.6 uses an item that has been employed in each of the three surveys. The findings would seem to suggest a secular decline in victim blaming during the last two decades. Much more than previously, Europeans attribute poverty to social injustice. It is not possible to tell, however, from the survey question, whether they define poverty as social injustice or merely see a causal link between them. Distinctly fewer explain poverty by reference to individual inadequacy or culpability. Or so it would appear.

Table 12.6:   Aggregate answers to causes of 'poverty'

	1976 EC9	1989 EC9	1993 EC9	1993 EC12+
There are people in need because:				
a) It is an inevitable part of modern life	14	20	27	25
b) Injustice in our society	26	33	39	40
c) Laziness or lack of willpower	25	17	11	11
d) They have been unlucky	16	17	13	13

What, then, do we make of findings elsewhere suggesting that, after prolonged unemployment, the cause of poverty nominated most frequently is alcoholism, and not far behind, drug abuse?

The four explanations are selected in different rank orders in the different countries (Table 12.7). Denmark, the UK and Holland seem more convinced by the inevitability of poverty than its emanation from injustice. In Table 12.8 we can see that laziness is more often seen as a cause of poverty than welfare cuts in Italy, and is seen as more than a deprived upbringing in Germany. The subtleties of these perceptions warrant more investigation than this tabulation allows, a point I return to in the final section.

Although not presented here, this question reveals unexpected variances when the phrase social exclusion is substituted for poverty. In Italy the previously mentioned priorities are reversed: 4.8% believe laziness causes social exclusion while 11.2% attribute it to welfare cuts. Again, the different mind set prompted by social exclusion in the context of this survey may not be what the formulators of the Poverty 3 and 4 programmes have in mind.

Anti-poverty policy

What, then, do Europeans think can be done about the problem of poverty and social exclusion? Table 12.9 shows their relative unfamiliarity with the role of the European Community. Only in Portugal do more respondents seem to know and approve of Community action than profess ignorance of it.

Table 12.10 shows, not surprisingly, that roughly three quarters of respondents (with, again, a much higher proportion in Portugal) think the issue should become a priority for the European Union (EU).

However, one is bound to ask 'a priority compared with what?' It is difficult to extrapolate from this question, without some sense of just how Europeans would prioritise such policies against other competing demands. Offered a choice of two approaches to the problem (Table 12.11) it would seem that respondents prefer general action across populations rather than policies targeted at priority areas.

Table 12.7: Rank order of why there are people who live in need (1993)

Reason	Belg	Denm	Ger	Grec*	Spain	Fra	Ire	Italy	Lux'	N'lands	Portu	UK
a) Unlucky	3	2	4	2	3	3	3	2	3	2	2	4
b) Laziness/ willpower	4	4	3	3	4	4	4	3	2	4	3	3
c) Injustice	1	3	1	1	1	1	1	1	1	3	1	2
d) Inevitable	2	1	2	3	2	2	2	4	4	1	4	1

* b and d scores equal

Table 12.8: Here are some reasons that might explain why people are poor. Which three do you think are most common (1993 selected countries)

	Belg	Denm	Ger	Fra	Ire	Italy	N'lands	UK	EC12+
Long-term unemployed	64.3	34.4	51.8	81.1	69.1	59.2	49.3	74.7	62.1
Sickness	30.5	24.4	37.3	25.0	18.1	26.2	20.1	12.3	24.8
Broken family	20.2	34.7	38.0	13.9	32.3	21.9	29.5	32.1	25.3
Deprived upbringing	6.5	12.4	6.1	6.5	10.4	17.3	8.1	16.9	11.1
Welfare cuts	21.5	18.0	20.2	21.2	19.6	9.6	38.3	30.1	20.4
Laziness	7.2	5.1	15.1	3.0	6.7	11.0	7.5	8.8	10.1

Table 12.9: Have you heard of the European Community taking action to combat poverty and social exclusion? (If yes, do you think it is a good or bad thing?) (1993)

	Belg	Denm	Ger	Grec	Spain	Fra	Ire	Italy	Lux'	N'lands	Portu	UK	EC12+
Yes, good	18.3	34.8	21.9	43.4	22.5	22.5	22.5	23.9	29.4	15.5	47.7	19.2	23.0
Yes, bad	0.9	1.8	0.6	0.8	0.6	1.6	0.5	0.3	1.3	0.8	0.4	1.5	0.9
Yes, neither good nor bad	3.6	2.5	1.6	1.4	3.3	2.3	1.6	1.4	5.9	2.9	5.9	1.5	2.1
No, not heard of it	70.0	57.4	68.6	48.8	68.1	69.9	64.5	66.4	53.2	78.6	43.7	73.7	68.2

Table 12.10: Do you think that the fight against poverty and social exclusion should become a priority objective for the European Union or not? (1993)

	Belg	Denm	Ger	Grec	Spain	Fra	Ire	Italy	Lux'	N'lands	Portu	UK	EC12+
Yes	70.7	82.9	76.7	84.1	85.9	75.5	84.4	79.9	63.9	69.9	91.5	73.3	77.8
No	12.6	12.3	10.5	7.9	5.9	14.0	4.9	8.2	17.8	22.2	3.8	15.3	11.3
Okay	16.2	4.8	12.6	7.9	8.2	10.4	10.7	11.9	18.3	8.2	4.7	10.3	10.7

Table 12.11: What do you think would be the best way to combat poverty and social exclusion and to allow everyone to find their place in society? (1993)

Two possible answers for respondents:
a) 'Concentrate action on priority areas'
b) 'Take general action in all areas that have an impact on poverty and social exclusion'.

	Belg	Denm	Ger	Grec	Spain	Fra	Ire	Italy	Lux'	N'lands	Portu	UK	EC12+
(a)	29.3	31.0	23.2	31.2	18.2	37.5	29.1	18.8	39.1	40.3	26.6	24.2	25.8
(b)	53.2	60.3	65.5	53.1	50.3	52.1	53.5	55.0	42.4	50.7	52.5	65.3	58.0

Some questions of method

My main concern in this chapter is not to review the findings of the survey but to stress the absolute necessity of investigating public opinion as a backdrop to the development of EU policy on poverty and social exclusion. We have moved to the practice of defining the problem as a matter of belief and opinion rather than simply a calculation of income. This makes it vital that we have some sensitive measure of how people in the EU perceive necessary social participation standards, and that we work towards a clear and scientifically reliable calibration of the links between those standards and objective living conditions. In that regard it continues to be inadequate, in my view, to invest such faith in the inevitably superficial and partial findings of the occasional Eurobarometer survey. I have previously noted a number of technical and conceptual difficulties with earlier surveys (Golding, 1980). Here I merely wish to note a few further reservations about how far this work takes us in the vital task of understanding the nature of public opinion and ideology on this crucial topic. I should stress, once more, that this is not a reflection on the design, implementation, or analysis of the survey, nor a critique of its analysts, but a questioning of the adequacy of this approach to the complexity of the problem.

The survey method

It must be recognised that beliefs about poverty and social exclusion are complex, contradictory, and extensive. A battery of questions in a cross-national survey can only ever be a crude approximation to the intricacy of belief systems in this area. We need a far more extended array of methodologies, including qualitative approaches, such as the techniques developed by ethnographic, discourse and rhetoric research, in order adequately to understand what Europeans are thinking, and thinking about, when we ask them to talk about social exclusion. The problems arise both from the intrinsic limitations of survey methodology, and from the particular formulations of the Eurobarometer surveys.

The limits to surveys as a method for interrogating attitudes are familiar, and need no rehearsal here. However, when amplified by the particular limitations of this survey (see Golding, 1980) they place very major constraints on the adaptation of these findings for policy formulation. The variation in sampling methods across countries, the difficulties of translation, the use of hypothetical questions, the complexity of the issues addressed, the subtleties of local conditions and linguistic nuances, and so on, all raise considerable doubts about these findings.

The words we use

A cross-national survey is the most difficult of instruments to employ, not least because of the intractable problem of vocabulary. Subtleties of nuance and interpretation pose enormous problems when questions are translated across cultures and languages. As we move from *misère*, to *pauvreté*, to *exclusion sociale* we are quite obviously drawing on a multi-coloured palette of concepts and ideas. Yet our picture is essentially monochrome, quite unable to reveal the diversity of attitudes beneath the surface answers the survey generates.

One problem is the wording of the questions. For example one (Qn 76) asks in English, 'Still thinking of these people, are there those who seem to you to be beyond help: no assistance or policy will get them out of it?' What is being tapped here – attitudes to the folly or inadequacy of policy, to the pathetic inadequacy of a resolutely self-excluding under-class, to the shortcomings of our charitable efforts? It is impossible to tell. Another asks 'Are there people in your country who do not have access to necessary health care?' But what do they think is necessary, what do we mean by access? Of course it is simple to nit-pick at the vocabulary of questions in this way. In the earlier paper I have drawn attention to the odd vocabulary that arises from translated questionnaires. But the fact is that this matters, because we are addressing attitudes of necessary complexity that are all too sensitive to these variations and uncertainties.

The central issue of social exclusion is an obvious example. If we ask people whether there are people who live in their area in poverty (Qn 68) and in social exclusion the aggregate answers across the respondent population to these questions are not greatly varied (see Tables 12.1 and 12.2). Whereas 43.8% believe there are people in extreme poverty or poverty, 39.5% think there are people in total or some social exclusion. But within countries the variation is much greater. In Portugal, for example, the figure for poverty is 78%, for social exclusion 49.4%. In Holland more people see social exclusion (38.7%) than poverty (25.1%). What are we to make of these findings? Are these people describing the same thing? Are their mental referents at all comparable? A closer look at the questions using social exclusion reveals a more interesting pattern. When we ask people what constitutes poverty or social exclusion the gap between the answers to the two seems largest when dealing with such questions as homelessness and institutionalisation. There is some indication, in other words, that respondents are attuned to physical and social isolation when talking about social exclusion. This is not, perhaps, the same thing as the subtle and well-honed conception in the minds of the formulators of Poverty 3 and 4.

The range of questions

One of the strengths of the Eurobarometer series has been the continuity afforded by the repetition of some of the questions. However, this also acts as a trap, imposing assumptions about the questions that can be asked and that will be meaningful and relevant to respondents. One example of this is the interesting attempt in Eurobarometer 40 to ask people about charity and voluntary organisations as means for tackling poverty. My own research in the UK, however, reveals just how complex an area this is in people's ideological and belief systems (Fenton et al, 1993; and forthcoming). Using discussion groups and a very extensive questionnaire to address this single issue we discovered that attitudes to charity were embedded in a complex, but patterned array of beliefs about the nature of giving, the welfare state, and social and personal relationships. Reducing this to just one or two questions cannot adequately capture this complexity.

Conclusion

Policy does not develop in a vacuum. Politicians must appeal to their electorates in terms that are meaningful, and in turn will respond with measures designed to elicit support. This is nowhere more crucial than in an area that in most countries is the core of social policy, and in terms of social security one of the largest, if not the largest, element in public expenditure. My argument here, and it can only be very preliminarily illustrated in this chapter, is that we currently do not have an adequate instrument to investigate this question. Without a sensitive, reliable, and extensive measure of public opinion about poverty and social exclusion it will be as impossible to develop adequate policies as if we had not addressed the difficult problem of measuring income levels and poverty itself. Yet the energy and attention given to the latter is immensely greater than that given to investigating the culture and ideology within which these policies have to operate.

Poverty may be understood as partial and truncated citizenship. To investigate how people understand the inequalities around them, the complex links between living standards and life-styles requires far more than is possible within the confines of the Eurobarometer survey, conducted three times in 18 years. Major developments in theory and methodology have been largely bypassed because of the relegation of this question to a minor and marginal place in the firmament of poverty research. This chapter is a plea to rectify this. The major changes that have taken place in demographic and social structures have generated substantial debates around concepts of citizenship, difference, sectoral cleavage, post-industrialism, and so on. These need to be digested and applied to our investigation of social exclusion far more extensively than hitherto. Among other urgent tasks we need to:

- Employ complementary methodologies to investigate the language, vocabulary, and structure of people's attitudes and beliefs in this area. This means a far greater use of qualitative techniques, ethnographic research, and discourse and rhetorical analysis.

- Investigate the cultural environment within which these beliefs are generated. We have no comparative study of the appearance and consumption of ideas about poverty in the public sphere, for example. One necessary, and relatively inexpensive study would be a proper comparative investigation of the way in which poverty and social exclusion appear and are reported in the media. People spend a far greater proportion of their time, and disposable income, on media consumption in the 1990s than they did in the 1970s. What are the links between mediated and situated sources of information and imagery about poverty, and what is the nature of that imagery? Without such a study we can say little about the significance of the Eurobarometer surveys, let alone draw policy conclusions about matters where we may feel the public is misinformed.

This is not the place to set out an alternative research agenda. But any attempt to measure social exclusion must recognise that it is a cultural as well as a material process. To develop sensitive and sophisticated measures of people's incomes while only partially to investigate the state of the public mind is to impoverish poverty research. No other research task is more urgent or more overdue.

Notes

1. I wish to acknowledge the assistance of Simon Cross in the preparation of data for this paper. I am grateful to the European Commission for making data from the most recent Eurobarometer survey available to me to facilitate preparation of this chapter. I should stress that data presented here are my own summations from the simple cross-tabulations available to me. No additional analysis from original data has been possible, nor consultation with the survey's authors (see Rigaux, 1994).

thirteen

CONCLUSIONS

Graham Room

Introduction

The seminar at which the papers brought together in this book were originally presented had three principal concerns. It is around these three concerns that this concluding chapter is organised:

- the conceptualisation of social exclusion;

- the measurement of social exclusion (in particular, using already available data sources);

- the definition of indicators for monitoring the effectiveness of policies for combating social exclusion.

The measurement of social exclusion

Until recent years it was commonplace in poverty research – in particular, cross-national studies within Europe – to focus on the disposable income (or expenditure) of an individual or household at a moment in time. This was the basis for the various estimates of the overall poverty rate in the European Union (EU) that have appeared during the last decade and a half. The papers gathered here serve, however, to consolidate a three-fold broadening of perspective:

- from income/expenditure to multi-dimensional disadvantage

- from a moment in time to a dynamic analysis

- from the individual or household to the local community in its spatial dimension.

This does not mean that there is no merit in continuing the sorts of cross-national comparison of poverty rates that the European Commission has orchestrated in recent years (not overlooking, however, the technical problems that must continue to be addressed within these comparisons), if the aim is to offer some very broad-brush overview of the EU's experience of disadvantage among its citizens. What it does mean, however, is that for many purposes no simple measures can suffice; a more differentiated range of analytical tools and indicators is required.

Much information is already being collected at national and EU level. However, not all of the data that are relevant to the analysis and monitoring of social exclusion are yet being sufficiently exploited. The first step should be to remedy this. The gaps that remain should then be filled, something which could require the collection of new data. As well as the data sources for which Eurostat is itself responsible, it is important to make full use of data sources available at national level. It is necessary, moreover, to distinguish between what might be possible in the short, medium and long term: using existing data sources, extending them, and creating new ones.

Eurostat could play a key role in ensuring improved data availability: in part, through the surveys for which it is at present responsible; in part, perhaps, through eventual new surveys; in part, by negotiation and discussion with national statistical institutes as to the data which they should collect; and in part, by its more general role in setting standards for statistical work. The implementation of an eventual gap-filling statistical programme could therefore be through a variety of approaches: deeper analysis of existing data; inclusion of additional questions or modules to existing Eurostat household surveys; and agreements with national statistical institutes for the incorporation of harmonised indicators in their household surveys.

Extension from financial to multidimensional disadvantage

The papers brought together in this book confirm the concern of researchers and policy makers with multidimensional disadvantage, rather than with financial indicators alone. Two points are at issue here: first, that financial indicators, such as low income, are insufficiently reliable as proxies for general hardship; second, that it is important for policy and for explanatory purposes to disentangle different elements of hardship and to identify their interrelationships. Nevertheless, the key importance of financial resources in triggering and perpetuating social exclusion should be recognised, since a whole range of deprivations and hardships are associated with lack of such resources. Even with regard to financial disadvantage, therefore, efforts to improve the statistical data are required.

As yet there appear to be no unique, formal definitions of social exclusion that would command general assent. This should not, however, delay attempts at operationalisation in terms of a subset of characteristic domains and indicators on which there is consensus (including, for example, education, employment, working environment, health, housing, social participation, as well as command over goods and services). The general approach should be to proceed from these *domains* (eg, command over goods and services) to *subdomains* (eg, income), to *indicators* (eg, 50% of average equivalised disposable income), to an examination of *data availability* and then to the development of a *statistical programme* to fill gaps. The *data availability* criterion would not be satisfied unless the statistics on each indicator were such as to allow thresholds or norms (eg, overcrowded accommodation, chronic ill-health) to be distinguished (even if the determination of norms had to be based on subjective, arbitrary value-judgements). At each stage in this approach, account should, of course, be taken of the domains, subdomains and indicators that are already being used by the statistical communities in the individual member states, in order as far as possible to build upon what is already being done. It would be important to ensure some cross-referencing between the various domains, lest they be investigated in isolation from each other. The outcome could be an articulated conceptual system of indicators to meet a variety of needs. However, there is no presumption that this would lead to the elaboration of composite or synthetic indicators of social exclusion.

The European Community Household Panel Survey is likely to prove a key source for the measurement of social exclusion. It will, of course, have limitations (eg, in terms of sample size, response rate, accuracy of respondents' recollections and the range of questions that the survey poses). Nevertheless, it has some major potential strengths (eg, in exploring correlations between different sorts of disadvantage and in suggesting possible causal relationships).

Household surveys may nevertheless still not adequately cover the responsiveness of institutions to the alleviation of social exclusion. Thus, the role and validity of administrative data in shedding light on the interaction between the government agency and the citizen should receive the fullest possible consideration. However, because of the inherent limitation of administrative information in fully capturing the complete pool of needy, their full potential might only be realisable through micro-linkage with household survey data. Even so, some of the most seriously socially-excluded populations are excluded also from the administrative and survey statistical network (although the population censuses may not be too defective in their coverage). Thus, novel supplementary statistical instruments, including the possible exploitation of non-official sources, may require further consideration.

For some users it may be possible to give priority to a few indicators in particular, depending on their specific policy purpose. And of course, in the short term, before some of the present data gaps can be remedied, different users will find themselves having to make pragmatic use of such indicators as are available for their purposes.

Extension from a static to a dynamic analysis

The collection of papers brought together here (in particular, those by Walker and by Buhr and Leibfried) confirm the shift of emphasis from a static to a dynamic analysis. As Walker writes, "far from time simply being the medium in which poverty occurs, it helps to forge different experiences". It is not enough to count the numbers and describe the characteristics of the socially excluded; it is also necessary to understand and monitor the *process* of social exclusion and to identify the factors that can trigger entry or exit from situations of exclusion. Yet, as Walker again writes, "there is growing evidence that the events which trigger poverty are widespread but that poverty is a comparatively rare outcome". To explain the circumstances under which particular trigger events do result in poverty is an important research priority.

There are a number of national panel surveys that provide insights into these dynamics. They are, however, somewhat heterogeneous. Currently, whatever the limitations, there is no alternative to the European Community Household Panel Survey for obtaining comparable data on such dynamics, including those events (eg, changes in labour market status), in family structures and hence generally in incomes, which trigger a downward spiral into the abyss of social exclusion or which enable ascent and social reinsertion. Information of this sort would be of interest not only to the EU institutions, but also to national policy makers, as they seek to interpret their own policies and social trends in relation to developments in other EU countries; and it would represent a specific added value of the European Community Household Panel Survey as far as those national policy makers are concerned. This suggests that a priority should be to nurture, and even enhance, the Household Panel over a long period of time in order to be able to generate, inter alia, unambiguous profiles of social exclusion probabilities and trajectories. This work will also act as a catalyst in promoting greater homogeneity and com-parability among the various national panels that the Household Panel will complement but not replace. Indeed, this convergence under the influence of the Household Panel is already, to some extent, apparent.

Among the factors that can trigger entry or exit from situations of exclusion are, of course, the welfare benefits and services provided by the public authorities. Again, therefore, administrative data that shed light on the interaction between the government agency and the citizen should receive the fullest possible consideration if these dynamics of social exclusion are

to be monitored. A statistical programme might include supplementary longitudinal administrative files for studying the
financial dependancy of those who are trapped on one benefit or
another; or for providing a sampling frame for surveys into their
behaviour and other aspects of their living conditions.

Extension from the individual or household to the local community in its spatial dimension

The papers gathered here confirm a shift of emphasis from the
individual and household to the local community in its spatial
dimension. This has two implications as far as the measurement
of social exclusion is concerned. First, the vulnerability of an
individual or household to social exclusion depends in part on
the local community resources on which that individual or
household can draw. Deprivation is caused not only by lack of
personal resources but also by insufficient or unsatisfactory
community facilities, such as dilapidated schools, remotely-
sited shops, poor public transport networks and so on; indeed,
such an environment tends to reinforce and perpetuate
household poverty (see, for example, the chapter by
Kristensen).   Household surveys and panel studies need to
include questions on the availability or non-availability of these
local community resources, if we are to understand the
differential vulnerability of different individuals and households
to social exclusion and disadvantage. No less important are
local traditions of mutual aid, self-help organisations and other
elements of development potential, as highlighted by Moulaert's
contribution to this volume.

Second, in combating social exclusion, policy makers must
consider what actions they will take to invest in these local
community resources, complementing action targeted on
particular individuals and households.   In many countries,
poverty alleviation measures include pinpointed resource
allocation to particularly run-down localities, such as derelict
inner urban city centres or areas of industrial decline. Both the
Regional Fund and the Social Fund have a geographical
dimension. As far as a statistical programme is concerned, the
need is to ensure that policy makers have the indicators that

they need in order to identify those local communities where investments of this sort may be particularly effective.

One model of such spatial analysis is provided by Robson's contribution to this collection. He demonstrates, first, how Census and other data can be used to identify local communities that have high concentrations of disadvantaged households. Second, by making comparisons with the 1981 Census data, Robson is able to show the changes that have taken place in the national map of local disadvantage. A second model is that offered by Aldeghi. Aldeghi and Tabard, again using Census data, investigate the extent to which, in France, different neighbourhoods are socioeconomically segregated (in terms of their residents) and enjoy corresponding variations in housing conditions, overcrowding, networks of community support, etc. Both of these analyses, for the UK and France respectively, could be extended to other EU countries, using a common methodology.

Robson and Aldeghi primarily use data drawn from household responses to the Census. They consequently do not include data about the unsatisfactory community facilities (dilapidated schools, remotely-sited shops, poor public transport networks, and so on) that were referred to above, nor about the forms of collective action and development potential to which Moulaert refers. For these additional and independent data would be required. But, unless some form of common geo-referencing is available, Census enumeration districts (EDs) would have to be aggregated to conform to suitable administrative boundaries to permit merging or matching with independent data of this sort. This involves the danger of committing the ecological fallacy (ie, assuming any simple relationship between indicators of disadvantaged areas and disadvantaged persons). This danger can be tested by proceeding from the smallest spatial unit and progressively aggregating. Robson himself examines some of the meth-odological strategies that could be employed for this aggregation.

For more general improvements in the quality of the data that are available for analysing these spatial aspects of social exclusion, further specific studies would be required. These would need to deal, for example, with the choice of relevant Census indicators, their robustness, the appropriate spatial level

for both statistical analysis and policy interventions, carto-
graphic aspects and the key types of community resources that
characterise social exclusion. They would also need to explore
the kinds of questions that could be added to the Household
Panel Survey without overburdening it or compromising its
longitudinal value, and the techniques by which data on
community resources could be grafted on to a Census-based
poverty map. The initial approach might best be through small-
scale, exploratory pilots on one or two countries.

Indicators for monitoring the effectiveness of policies

The policy interest in indicators for monitoring policies on
social exclusion comes, at EU level, from both Directorate-
General V (DGV), including the Social Fund, and Directorate-
General XII (DGXII) (Framework IV). For example, they may
be relevant to the monitoring of Social Fund activities and the
allocation of EU resources.   In addition, it is evident that
national governments have a strong interest in developing more
coherent and policy-relevant indicators in this area. However, a
number of the papers in this book challenge the assumptions on
which current indicators are based and therefore also the
policies with which these indicators are associated.   These
challenges are informed by the three-fold shift in perspective
with which this chapter began.

Several papers, by their analysis of the multidimensionality
of disadvantage, challenge conventional indicators and policies
targeted on separate aspects of disadvantage. The Whelans seek
to disentangle the causes, constituents and consequences of
social disadvantage and exclusion, in part, because of the
obvious importance of these distinctions for policy. Simply
identifying different dimensions is insufficient. Similarly, a
principal concern of Paugam's paper is to analyse the process or
'spiral' of precariousness in such a way as to disentangle the
causal chains that are involved and the relative importance of
different dimensions of disadvantage in precipitating 'social
disqualification'.   Paugam is especially interested in the
relationships between labour market situation and family and
community networks: his approach could be highly relevant,

inter alia, to indicators of need in relation to the personal social services, with their support to fractured social networks.

Two of the papers confront directly and critically the notions of time that are embodied in official indicators of disadvantage or exclusion. In the final section of his paper, Walker indicates some of the ways in which an appreciation of the temporal aspects of poverty could hold implications for policy. Focusing more narrowly on social assistance, Buhr and Leibfried argue that at least in Germany, existing policies – and the use of data on social assistance receipt to monitor the volume and movement of social assistance recipients – rest on quite specific accounting periods. The paper demonstrates that a more differentiated approach to the definition of accounting periods will allow a more refined mapping of both volume and movement. It also renders problematic the distinction between long-term and short-term dependance: a distinction that in some social assistance systems is important for triggering additional measures of support to the person in question. One simple and obvious measure of social exclusion – the long-term receipt of social assistance – is thus shown to be less straightforward than might have been expected. It may benefit from better identification of the events that trigger long-term poverty.

Finally, Robson offers an analogous critique of the notions of space that underlie traditional indicators of spatial deprivation, at least in the UK. Just as Buhr and Leibfried demonstrate that different notions of time can generate different maps of the social assistance population, so Robson demonstrates that different notions of space (in particular, the way in which the geographical boundaries of local communities are drawn) can generate different rankings of these local communities in terms of the deprivation they suffer. He shows that indicators of spatial deprivation will, moreover, generate different rankings of local communities, depending not only on the boundaries that are taken to these communities, but also on whether it is the *average* degree of deprivation within each community that is considered, or the degree of deprivation within the *worst-affected* sections of each community – the *intensity* of deprivation. Here Robson's argument is analogous to that of Walker. For what both Robson and Walker highlight is the relationship between the extent and the intensity of poverty and disadvantage; or, to restate the issue, the degree to which, within the poor population, poverty and deprivation are evenly or unevenly distributed.

Aldeghi assesses the criteria being used in the priority programmes that have been undertaken in France during recent years, targeted on disadvantaged neighbourhoods. No system of national indicators analogous to that offered by Robson (itself standing in a tradition of such indicators within the UK) has been developed for this purpose in France. Aldeghi is able to evaluate the extent to which those neighbourhoods, whose municipalities have been identified for priority treatment, are consistent with her own indicators. One of her findings is that in municipalities suffering general disadvantage the contrast between the priority areas and the rest of the town is slight; in more prosperous cities, the contrast tends to be much greater, and the designation of specific priority neighbourhoods correspondingly more plausible.

To expose the assumptions that underlie conventional policies and indicators is extremely important in a political context. These papers demonstrate that simple unidimensional indicators are too crude for guiding and monitoring policy and that policy makers need a range of more differentiated tools. On the other hand, at least in the short term, there are major gaps in the data that are required for these tools and policy makers find themselves having to make pragmatic use of such indicators as are available. For example, Kristensen, in his contribution to this book, gives details of the indicators of social exclusion that are being utilised in Denmark using readily available administrative data, for the purpose of identifying housing estates in the greatest difficulties. This pragmatism can be risky, however. Thus, among the indicators of spatial disadvantage that Kristensen commends to policy makers are the types of car to be found parked in different neighbourhoods and photographic images of such neighbourhoods. These forms of evidence are likely to be unreliable guides to action, unless treated as strictly subsidiary to more conventional types of indicator.

The conceptualisation of social exclusion

Throughout this book, there have been a variety of attempts to reexamine the concepts of poverty and social exclusion and to apply these concepts empirically. Thus, for example, in chapter 1 I suggested that the modern notion of poverty is primarily focused upon distributional issues: the lack of resources at the disposal of an individual or a household and the resulting low level of consumption. Much of the recent methodological debate has been concerned with whether this poverty should be measured 'directly' in terms of the level of consumption (or, more precisely, the failure to consume certain 'essentials') or 'indirectly' in terms of the lack of financial resources with which to obtain such a level of consumption (Ringen, 1988; Callan et al, 1993; Holleröd, 1995).

In contrast, notions such as social exclusion, suggested in chapter 1, focus primarily on relational issues: in other words, inadequate social participation, lack of social integration and lack of power. Social exclusion is the process of becoming detached from the organisations and communities of which the society is composed and from the rights and obligations that they embody. These communities may, on the one hand, involve particularistic loyalties – to fellow workers in a trade union, to a local neighbourhood, to a professional organisation; or they may, on the other hand, involve membership of a national community, as expressed, for example, in the egalitarian social rights of modern welfare systems (Marshall, 1950).

As recalled in chapter 1, one recent attempt to synthesise these two conceptual traditions has been the European Observatory on Policies to Combat Social Exclusion, established in 1990, which roots its analysis of social exclusion in these social rights of citizenship (Room et al, 1991; 1992). The Observatory has thus sought to investigate social exclusion in both relational and distributional terms: to evaluate, on the one hand, the extent to which some groups of the population are denied access to the principal social and occupational milieux and to the welfare institutions that embody modern notions of social citizenship; to examine, on the other hand, the patterns of multidimensional disadvantage to which these groups are then vulnerable, especially insofar as these persist over time.

It is now, however, possible to take this conceptual reappraisal further. The main tradition of poverty research, with its focus on low levels of consumption and/or the lack of financial resources by which this is caused, offers a static perspective. Some researchers have adopted a more dynamic approach, monitoring how the resources and consumption of particular households change over time; it is, however, with current consumption that they have been primarily concerned. In contrast, as several of the contributions to this book reveal, the inclusion of an intertemporal dimension draws particular attention to processes of investment and disinvestment. Assets (not just financial) representing past investments are crucial to understanding vulnerability to exclusion. So are the processes by which such resources are eroded.

Walker refers to the capacity – or incapacity – of a family, to build up a stock of household goods in times of (relative) plenty, as being crucial to its ability to survive in harder times. On the other hand, Paugam's paper refers to the erosion of the conjugal relationship and of wider networks of kinship support that tends to accompany marginalisation from the labour market; and the Whelans refer to the erosion of physical health itself that such marginalisation may induce. Public policies – in terms of health care, training, fiscal incentives, etc – can play a crucial role in determining the extent to which households can maintain and enlarge their investments in these personal resources.

However, this concern with the renewal and erosion of investments is not limited to those papers that focus on the individual or household. Several of the papers that are concerned with spatial aspects of disadvantage highlight the importance of local community resources for patterns of social exclusion. These resources (the public transport system, local authority services, etc) will crucially affect the exclusion and disadvantage that individuals and households experience. As Kristensen emphasises, these resources will, in turn, be shaped by public policies: not only those focused on individual households, but also those that represent investments in our urban infrastructure. If these investments are inadequate, local communities may find that not only are high proportions of their residents suffering high unemployment, poor health and other forms of individual disadvantage, but that in addition, local community resources are threatened with collapse. In these circumstances, the chances of individual persons avoiding generalised social exclusion may become catastrophically low. The investments that we, as a society, make in our urban infrastructure are therefore fateful for the patterns of life that can be lived in local neighbourhoods. Only very restricted ways of life are possible within housing estates that lack services, including those built as dormitories for industrial cities whose employment base has now disappeared.

These collective 'investments' and assets also include the traditions of collective action, the networks of mutual aid and the other aspects of local development potential to which Moulaert points (see also Room et al, 1993, ch 4, for an analysis of the development potential of local communities as revealed by the action-research projects in the second European Commission poverty programme). These traditions and potentialities are also shaped by public policies: for example, by housing policies that replace neighbourhoods embodying the disorderly incremental modifications of many years, with well-planned housing estates inhospitable to social identities defined in relation to earlier generations. What Moulaert seeks to investigate are the conditions under which these assets are renewed or deteriorate.

These collective investments and disinvestments play a crucial role in determining the levels of consumption that individuals and households are able to enjoy, the levels of poverty that they experience and the social relationships to which they can contribute and on which they are able to call. But upon what factors do these investments themselves depend?

First, as already noted, public policies in a wide variety of domains are of the greatest importance. In seeking to combat social exclusion, policy makers are faced with the question as to the form and extent of the investment that they are ready to make in local community resources, complementing their efforts to ensure that individuals and households are able to make the personal investments that will help them to survive times of hardship. Hence the importance of the indicators for guiding and monitoring such policies, as discussed in the previous section of this chapter.

However, these policies operate within the larger processes of stratification and competition of an urban-industrial society.

The papers by the Whelans and by Paugam include class analysis of the labour market position of those who are at high risk of social exclusion, opening the way to closer links with some of the mainstream sociological analyses of class and social mobility (see, for example, Erikson and Goldthorpe, 1993). The paper by Moulaert includes consideration of the political economy of urban competition, as cities compete to attract investment and employment, albeit with major negative consequences for less advantaged local communities, reshaping or consolidating the map of spatial deprivation.

It is through its public policies, and in response to these processes of stratification and competition, that our societies define and redefine the moral obligations that should exist among its citizens and the rights that different sections of the community should enjoy. It is with these moral solidarities and their changing contours that Golding, for example, deals. His contribution to this volume is, of course, as much methodological as substantive, concerned as it is with some of the pitfalls involved in measuring public attitudes towards social exclusion. However, his critique does not imply that to monitor such attitudes is unimportant: quite the contrary, because, as Golding insists, "public opinion sets the limits within which legitimate politics can act".

Some researchers have suggested that during recent years the principal lines of moral solidarity that had been established in our west European societies during the preceding decades have been fragmenting (Jordan, 1994). From the side of the non-poor, the fragmentation means that the poor have been abandoned; for the poor, the result is that there are few incentives for participating in the wider society – a society in which they now have little stake. Moulaert's paper can be read as a similar analysis of the disintegration of moral solidarity between poor and non-poor communities and of the changing patterns of incentives, opportunities and threats that these poor communities confront. Alongside this narrowing of moral solidarity, there is some evidence of widening disadvantage between poor and non-poor communities. The empirical results produced by Aldeghi and her colleagues indicate that for France, at least, the 1980s saw some reinforcement of the social segregation within large and more prosperous urban centres (except for the Paris region, where social differences were falling). Robson finds that in the UK during the 1980s, "many of the very worst areas such as the inner cores of conurbations showed a continuing decline relative to the peripheral parts of their areas". Polarisation of this sort, if indeed accompanied by the narrowing of public concern, would on any definition represent a worsening of social exclusion.

Conclusion

Berghman, in his contribution to this book, highlighted the central role that European programmes of research and action-research have played over recent years in refocusing discussion around the notion of social exclusion rather than poverty. What has been no less evident, however, is that this notion of social exclusion has until now been used in a rather loose and incoherent manner, rendering it of little value as a guide for research or policy.

This book, bringing together contributions from researchers in a number of different EU countries, has demonstrated the extent to which some greater coherence can be brought to the discussion, even if much dissension remains, rooted in part in different national traditions of analysis. It has also highlighted some of the new priorities for data collection, if forms and processes of social exclusion are to be investigated on a systematically comparative basis.

REFERENCES

Aldeghi, I. and Tabard, N. (1987) *Espace et modes de vie-synthèse*, Paris: CREDOC, rapport n° 4969.

Aldeghi, I. and Tabard, N. (1988a) *Développement social des quartiers: les sites concernés et leurs caractéristiques socioéconomiques par rapport aux autres communes françaises ou aux autres quartiers de l'Ile-de-France*, Paris: CREDOC, rapport n° 5010.

Aldeghi, I. and Tabard, N. (1988b) *L'emploi des femmes dans la dynamique spatiale,* Paris: CREDOC.

Aldeghi, I. and Tabard, N. (1990) *Transformation socio-professionnelle des communes de l'Ile de France entre 1975 et 1982*, Paris: CREDOC, rapport n° 80.

Ashworth, K., Walker, R., Trinder, P. and Jenkins, S. (1995) *British benefit dynamics,* Loughborough: Centre for Research in Social Policy.

Atkinson, A. (1984) *The economics of inequality*, Oxford: Oxford University Press.

Barthe, M-A. (1987) 'Les formes de la pauvreté dans la societé francaise', *Revue française des Affaires Sociales,* vol 2, pp 113-25.

Bingham, R.D. and Mier, R. (eds) (1993) *Theories of local economic development. Perspectives from across the disciplines*, Newbury Park: Sage.

Blane, D., Davey-Smith, G. and Bartley, M. (1993) 'Social selection: what does it contribute to social class differences in health?', *Sociology of Health and Illness,* vol 15, pp 2-5.

Blaxter, M. (1989) 'A comparison of measures of inequality in mobility', in A.J. Fox (ed), *Health inequalities in European countries,* Aldershot: Gower.

Blaxter, M. (1990) *Health and lifestyle,* London: Tavistock-Routledge.

Booth, C. (1903), *Life and labour of the people of London*, London: Macmillan.

Bouget, D. and Nogues, H. (1993) 'L'évaluation des politiques de lutte contre les exclusions sociales', in M. Ferrera, 'The evaluation of social policies: experiences and perspectives', *Quaderni della Revista 'Il Politico'*, no 38, p 74 ff.

Bradshaw, J. (1993) *Technology, employment and income distribution*, mimeo, Manchester: School of Management, UMIST.

Brückner, H. (1995) *Times of poverty: lessons from the Bremen Longitudinal Social Assistance Sample*, Munich: Universität.

Brueck, G. (1976) *Allgemeine Sozialpolitik*, Köln: Bund.

Bruto da Costa, A., Anderson, J., Chigot, C., Duffy, K., Mancho, S. and Mernagh, M. (1994) *Contribution of the 'Poverty 3' programme to the understanding of poverty, exclusion and integration*, Lille: Animation et Recherche (EEIG).

Buhr, P. (1995) *Dynamik von Armut. Dauer und biographische Bedeutung von Sozialhilfe-bezug*, Opladen: Westdeutscher Verlag.

Buhr, P. and Leisering, L. (1995) 'Armut im Lebenslauf. Armut und Armutspolitik aus der Sicht der dynamischen Armutsforschung', *Nachrichtendienst des Deutschen Vereins für öffentliche und private Fürsorge*, vol 75, no 2, pp 73-77.

Buhr, P. and Ludwig, M. (1991) *Armutsdynamiken. Zeitanalysen in der Armutsforschung der USA und der Bundesrepublik Deutschland*, Bremen: Sonderfor-schungsbereich 186 (Sfb 186 Arbeitspapier Nr. 8).

Buhr, P. and Voges, W. (1991) 'Eine Ursache kommt selten allein. Ursachen und Ursachenwechsel in der Sozialhilfe', *Sozialer Fortschritt*, vol 40, no 11, pp 261-70.

Buhr, P., Leibfried, S., Ludwig, M. and Voges, W. (1990a) 'Wege durch die Sozialhilfe. Der Bremer Ansatz zur Untersuchung "bekämpfter Armut" im zeitlichen Verlauf', in W. Dressel, W.R. Heinz, G. Peters und K. Schober (eds), *Lebenslauf, Arbeitsmarkt und Sozialpolitik*, Nürnberg: Institut für Arbeitsmarkt-und Berufsforschung der Bundesanstalt für Arbeit (Beiträge zur Arbeitsmarkt-und Berufsforschung 133).

Buhr, P., Leisering, L., Ludwig, M. and Zwick, M. (1991) 'Armutspolitik und Sozialhilfe in vier Jahrzehnten', in B. Blanke und H. Wollmann (eds), *Die alte Bundesrepublik. Kontinuität und Wandel*, Opladen: Westdeutscher Verlag, (Leviathan Sonderheft 12).

Buhr, P., Ludwig, M. and Leibfried, S. (1992) 'Sind wir auf dem Weg zu einer verbesserten Armutsberichterstattung? Anmerkungen zur geplanten Reform der Sozialhilfe-statistik', *Nachrichtendienst des Deutschen Vereins für öffentliche und private Fürsorge*, vol 72, no 7, pp 215-21.

Buhr, P., Ludwig, M. and Priester, T. (1990b) *Die Bremer 10%-Stichprobe von Sozialhilfeakten. Konstruktion und Auswertungsperspektiven*, Bremen: Zentrum für Sozial-politik (ZeS Arbeitspapier Nr. 1).

Burkhauser, R., Holden, K. and Feaster, D. (1988) 'Incidence, timing and events associated with poverty', *Journal of Gerontology*, vol 43, pp 846-52.

Busch-Geertsema, V. and Ruhstrat, E-U. (1992) 'Kein Schattendasein für Langzeitarme! Wider die Verharmlosung von Langzeitarmut im Zusammenhang mit der "dynamischen" Armutsforschung', *Nachrichtendienst des deutschen Vereins für öffentliche und private Fürsorge*, vol 72, no 11, pp 366-70.

Byudvalget (1994) *Rapport Fra Byudvalget 1-2*, Copenhagen: Udgivet Af Indenrigsministeriet et al.

Callan, T. and Nolan, B. (1991) 'Concepts of poverty and the poverty line: a critical survey of approaches to measuring poverty', *Journal of Economic Surveys*, vol 5, no 3, pp 243-62.

Callan, T., Nolan, B. and Whelan, C.T. (1993) 'Resources, deprivation and the measurement of poverty', *Journal of Social Policy*, vol 22, no 2, pp 141-72.

Carbonaro, G. (1993) 'La povertà: definizioni e misure', in Tutela, numero monografico su *Povertà ed escluzione sociale: le cifre, le politiche*, anno VIII-n.2/3, giu-sett.

Castellan, M., Marpsat, M. and Goldberger, M. (1992) 'Les quartiers prioritaires de la politique de la ville', Paris: INSEE.

Castels, R. (1990) 'Extreme cases of marginalisation: from vulnerability to deaffiliation', paper presented to a conference 'Poverty, Marginalisation and Social Exclusion in the Europe of the 1990s', organised under the auspices of the European Commission, Alghero, Sardinia.

Chenu, A. and Tabard, N. (1993) 'Les transformations socioprofessionnelles du territoire français entre 1982 et 1990', *Population*, n° 6, INED, pp 1735-70.

Choffel, P. (1993) 'La Mission "Villes"', *Courrier des statistiques*, n° 67-68, INSEE, Paris.

Christiansen, U., Kjær Jensen, M., Kristensen, H., Lindhardtsen, H., Varming, M. and Og Vestergaard, H. (1993) *Bedre Bebyggelser – Bedre Liv?*, Hørsholm: Statens Byggeforskningsinstitut (Sbi-Byplanlægning 65).

Commissione d'indagine sulla povertà e l'emarginazione (1985) *La povertà in Italia*, Roma.

Commissione d'indagine sulla povertà e l'emarginazione (1992) *Secondo rapporto sulla povertà in Italia*, Milan: Franco Angeli.

Citro, C. and Michael, R. (1995) *Measuring poverty: a new approach*, Washington: National Academy Press.

Cole, K. (1993) 'Coping with data modification, small populations and other features of the 1991 small area statistics', in S. Simpson (ed), *Census indicators of local poverty and deprivation: methodological issues*, London: Local Authorities Research and Intelligence Association.

Commins, P. (ed) (1993) *Combating exclusion in Ireland 1990-1994, A Midway Report*, Brussels: European Commission.

Cosimo, R (1991) 'Approccio soggettivo allo studio della povertà in termini di benessere: alcune note metodologiche', in *Rivista milanese di economia*, anno X – no 37, gennaio-marzo.

Council of the European Communities (1989) 'Resolution on combating social exclusion', 89/C277/01, *Official Journal of the European Communities*, C277/1, Brussels.

Council of the European Communities (1992a) 'Recommendation on the convergence of social protection objectives and policies' 92/442/CEE, *Official Journal of the European Communities*, L245/49, Brussels.

Council of the European Communities (1992b) *Treaty on European Union*, Brussels.

Daly, M. (1994) 'The Syracuse University PSID and GSEP Equivalent Data File', paper presented at a conference on 'Use of the PSID for international comparative research', Cologne, June.

Davey-Smith, G., Bartley, M. and Blane, D. (1990) 'The Black Report on socio-economic inequalities in health 10 years on', *British Medical Journal,* vol 301, pp 373-77.

Dawes, L. (1993) *Long-term unemployment and labour market flexibility,* Leicester: University Centre for Labour Market Studies.

de Tombeur, C. and Ladewig, N. (1994) *LIS information guide,* LIS Working Papers, Walferdange, Luxembourg: CEPS/INSTEAD.

Deleeck, H. et al (1989) 'The adequacy of the social security system in Belgium 1976-1985', *Journal of Social Policy,* vol 18, part 1, pp 91-117.

Deleeck, H., Van Den Bosch, K. and De Lathouwer, L. (1992) *Poverty and the adequacy of social security in Europe,* Aldershot: Avebury.

Desai, M. (1986) 'Drawing the line: on defining the poverty threshold', in P. Golding (ed), *Excluding the poor,* London: Child Poverty Action Group.

Desai, M. and Shah, A. (1988) 'An econometric approach to the measurement of poverty', *Oxford Economic Papers,* vol 40, no 3.

de Singly, F. (1993) *Sociologie de la famille contemporaine,* Paris: Nathan, coll. '128'.

Desplanques, G. and Tabard, N. (1991) 'La localisation de la population étrangère', *Economie et Statistique,* n° 242, pp 51-62, Paris: INSEE.

Desrosieres, A., Goy, A. and Thevenot, L. (1983) 'L'identité sociale dans le travail statistique, la nouvelle nomenclature des professions et catégories sociales', *Economie et Statistique,* n° 152, pp 55-81, Paris: INSEE.

Dickes, P. (1982) 'Pauvrete et conditions d'existence; Theories, modeles et mesures', *Document PSELL No 8,* Luxembourg: CEPS.

Dirven, H. and Berghman, J. (1991) *Poverty, insecurity of subsistence and relative deprivation in the Netherlands – Report 1991,* Social Security Series, Report 16, Tilburg: KUB.

Dobson, B., Beardsworth, A., Keil, T. and Walker, R. (1994) *Diet, choice and poverty: social, cultural and nutritional aspects of food consumption among low income families,* London: Family Policy Studies Centre.

Department of the Environment (1983) *'Urban deprivation',* *Information Note,* 2, Inner Cities Directorate, London: DoE.

Department of the Environment (1995) *1991 deprivation index: a review of approaches and a matrix of results*, London: DoE.

Duffy, K. (1995) *Social exclusion and human dignity in Europe*, Strasbourg: Council of Europe.

Elias, P. and Steiner, V. (1993) *The causes and consequences of recurrent spells of unemployment in Britain and Germany*, London: Anglo-German Foundation and European Commission.

Erikson, R. and Goldthorpe, J.H. (1993) *The constant flux: a study of class mobility in industrial societies*, Oxford: Clarendon.

Esping-Andersen, G. (1990) *Three worlds of welfare capitalism*, London: Polity Press.

Esping-Andersen, G. and Korpi, K. (1984) 'Social policy as class politics in post-war capitalism: Scandinavia, Austria and Germany', in J.H. Goldthorpe (ed), *Order and conflict in contemporary capitalism*, Oxford: Oxford University Press.

European Commission (1977) *The perception of poverty in Europe* (V/171/77-E), Brussels.

European Commission (1981) *Final report from the Commission to the Council on the first programme of pilot schemes and studies to combat poverty*, COM(81)769, Brussels.

European Commission (1990a) *The perception of poverty in Europe*, V/467/90-EN, Brussels.

European Commission (1990b) *Community charter of the fundamental rights of workers*, Brussels.

European Commission (1991) *The regions in the 1990s*, Directorate-General for Regional Policy, Brussels.

European Commission (1993a) *Employment in Europe 1993*, Brussels.

European Commission (1993b) *Growth, competitiveness, employment – the challenges and ways forward into the 21st Century*, Bulletin of the European Communities, Supplement 6/93, Brussels.

European Commission (1994a) *European social policy – the way forward for the Union*, COM(94)333, Brussels.

European Commission (1994b) *Social protection in Europe*, Brussels.

Eurostat (1990) *Poverty in figures: Europe in the 1980s*, Luxembourg.

Eurostat (1991) *Régions, Nomenclature des unités territoriales statistiques*, Luxembourg.

Eurostat (1992) *Digest of statistics on social protection in Europe*, vol 1: Old age; vol 2: Invalidity/disability; vol 3: Survivors; vol 4: Family, Luxembourg.

Eurostat (1993) *European Community Household Panel: strategy and policy*, Luxembourg.

Falkingham, J. and Hills, J. (eds) (1994) *The dynamic of welfare*, Hemel Hempstead: Prentice Hall/Harvester Wheatsheaf.

Fenton, N., Golding, P. and Radley, A. (1993) *Charities, media and public opinion*, Loughborough: Communication Research Centre, Loughborough University.

Fenton, N., Golding, P. and Radley, A. (forthcoming) *Beyond the welfare state*, London: John Libbey.

Forsé, M. (1993) 'La fréquence des relations de sociabilité: typologie et évolution', *L'Annee sociologique*, vol 43.

Gailly, B. and Hausman, P. (1984) 'Désavantages relatifs à une mesure objective de la pauvreté', in G. Sarpellon (ed), *Understanding poverty*, Milan.

Galland, O. (1984) 'Précarité et entrées dans la vie', *Revue française de Sociologie*, XXV,1, pp 49-66.

George, V. and Howard, I. (1991) *Poverty amidst affluence: Britain and the United States*, Aldershot: Edward Elgar.

Goedhart, T., Halberstadt, V., Kapteyn, A. and Van Praag, B.M.S. (1977) 'The poverty line: concept and measurement', *The Journal of Human Resources*, vol 12, pp 503-20.

Goldberg, D. (1972) *The detection of psychiatric illness by questionnaire*, Oxford: Oxford University Press.

Golding, P. (1980) 'In the eye of the beholder', in *Europe against poverty, vol II: cross national studies*, Canterbury: Espoir, University of Kent.

Golding, P. (ed) (1986) *Excluding the poor*, London: Child Poverty Action Group.

Green, A.E. (1994) *The geography of poverty and wealth*, Coventry: Institute for Employment Research, University of Warwick.

Gregg, P. and Wadsworth, J. (1994) *Opportunity knocks? Job separations, engagements and claimant status*, London: National Institute of Economic and Social Research.

Hansen, F.K. (1994) 'Poverty and measurement', background paper presented at seminar on the 'Measurement and analysis of social exclusion', Centre for Research in European Social and Employment Policy, University of Bath, 17-18 June 1994.

Hausman, P. et al (1989) *National report for Luxembourg on the EURPOASS project*, Luxembourg: CEPS.

Headey, B., Habich, R., and Krause, P. (1990) *The duration and extent of poverty: is Germany a two-thirds society?*, Berlin: Wissenschaftszentrum, Working Paper.

Heady, P. and Smyth, M. (1989) *Living standards during unemployment*, London: Office of Population Censuses and Surveys, HMSO.

Héran, F. (1988) 'La sociabilité, une pratique culturelle', *Economie et statistique*, 216, novembre, pp 8-22.

Herpin, N. (1992) 'La famille à l'épreuve du chômage', *Economie et statistique*, 266, juillet-août, pp 43-57.

Hoggart, R. (1957) *The uses of literacy,* London: Chatto and Windus.

Holleröd, B. (1995) 'The truly poor: direct and indirect consensual measurement of poverty in Sweden', *Journal of European Social Policy*, vol 5, no 2, pp 111-30.

Holterman, S. (1975) *Areas of urban deprivation in Great Britain: an analysis of census data*, Social Trends, London: HMSO.

ISTAT (1993) *Rapporto annuale*, Roma.

Jehoel-Gijsbers, G. and Heinen, A. (1991) *Mentale incongruentie en arbeidsmarktgedrag*, Social Security Series, Report nr 13, Tilburg: KUB.

Jehoel-Gijsbers, G. and Vissers, A. (1995) *Sociale zekerheid en arbeidsparticipatie*, The Hague: OSA (Stichting Organisatie voor Strategisch Arbeidsmarktonderzoek).

Jones, K. and Kirby, A. (1980) *The use of chi-square maps in the analysis of census data*, Geoforum, 11, 409-17.

Jordan, B. (1994) Comment on Berghman's paper, presented at seminar on the 'Measurement and analysis of social exclusion', Centre for Research in European Social and Employment Policy, University of Bath, 17-18 June 1994.

Jordan, B. et al (1992) *Trapped in poverty?*, London: Routledge.
Kaufman, J-C. (1993) *Sociologie du couple*, Paris: Presses Universitaires de France, coll. 'Que sais-je?'
Kazepov, J. (1994) *Cittadinanza e Povertà: Istituzioni e trasformazioni nei percorsi di esclusione in Lombardia (Italia) e nel Baden-Wurttemberg (Germania)*, PhD thesis, Milan.
Kazepov, J., Mingione, E. and Zajczyk, F. (1995) *Povertà estrema: istituzioni e percorsi a Milano*, Franco Angeli, Milano.
Kempson, E. et al, (1994) *Hard times*, London: Policy Studies Institute.
Kristensen, H. (1995) 'Socialpolitisk Byfornyelse?', *Samfundsøkonomen*, no 1, pp 38-42.
Lavindkomstkommissionen (1982) *Lavindkomstkommissionens betænkning,* Copenhagen: Betænkning nr 946.
Lazarsfeld, P., Jahoda, M. and Zeisel, H. (1970) *Les chômeurs de Marienthal*, Paris: Editions de Minuit, coll. 'Le sens commun' (1ère édition en Emglish, 1957).
Leibfried, S., Leisering, L., Buhr, P., Ludwig, M., Mædje, E., Olk, T., Voges, W. and Zwick, M. (1995) *Zeit der Armut.Lebensläufe im Sozialstaat*, Frankfurt a.M.: Suhrkamp.
Leibfried, S. and Pierson, P. (1992) 'Prospects for social Europe', *Politics and Society*, vol 20, no 3, pp 333-66.
Leibfried, S. and Voges, W. (eds) (1992) *Armut im modernen Wohlfahrtsstaat*, Opladen: Westdeutscher Verlag (Kölner Zeitschrift für Soziologie und Sozialpsychologie, Sonderheft 32).
Leisering, L. (1993) 'Armut hat viele Gesichter. Vom Nutzen dynamischer Armutsforschung', in *Nachrichtendienst des deutschen Vereins für öffentliche und private Fürsorge*, vol 72, pp 297-305.
Leisering, L. and Voges, W. (1992) 'Erzeugt der Wohlfahrtstaat seine eigene Klientel? Eine theoretische und empirische Analyse von Armutsprozessen', in S. Leibfried and W. Voges (eds) *Armut im modernen Wohlfahrstaat*, Opladen: Westdeutscher Verlag.
Leisering, L. and Zwick, M. (1990) 'Heterogenisierung der Armut? Alte und neue Perspektiven zum Strukturwandel der

Armutsbevölkerung der Bundesrepublik Deutschland', in *Zeitschrift für Sozialreform*, vol 36, no 11/12, pp. 715-45.

Leontidou, L. (1990) *The mediterranean city in transition*, Cambridge: Cambridge University Press.

Ludwig, M. (1992) 'Sozialhilfekarrieren: Ein Teufelskreis der Armut?', in *Nachrichtendienst des deutschen Vereins für öffentliche und private Fürsorge*, vol 72, no 11, pp 359-65.

Ludwig, M. (1995) *Armutskarrieren zwischen sozialem Abstieg und Aufstieg*, Opladen: Westdeutscher Verlag.

Lundberg, O. (1991) 'Childhood living conditions, health status, and social mobility: a contribution to the health selection debate', *European Sociological Review*, vol 7, no 2, pp 149-62.

Lundberg, O. (1993) 'The impact of childhood living conditions on illness and mortality in adulthood', *Social Science and Medicine,* vol 36, pp 385-93.

Mack, J. and Lansley, S. (1985) *Poor Britain,* London: George Allen and Unwin.

Mansfield, M. (1986) 'The political arithmetic of poverty', *Social Policy and Administration,* vol 20, no 1, pp 45-47.

Mansuy, M. and Marpsat, M. (1991) 'Les quartiers des grandes villes: contrastes sociaux en milieu urbain', *Economie et Statistique*, n° 245, pp 33-47, Paris: INSEE.

Marpsat, M. (1986) 'Les agglomérations multicommunales: évolution des définitions et de leur mise en oeuvre', *Courrier des statistiques*, n° 39, pp 28-31, Paris: INSEE.

Marpsat, M. (1993) 'Déchiffrer la ville', *Courrier des statistiques*, n° 67-68, pp 27-35, Paris: INSEE.

Marshall, G., Roberts, S., Burgoyne, C. and Routh, D. (forthcoming), *Social class and underclass in Britain and the United* States, Oxford: Nuffield College.

Marshall, T.H. (1950) *Citizenship and social class*, Cambridge: Cambridge University Press.

Martin, C. (1994) 'Diversité des trajectoires post-désunion. Entre le risque de solitude, la défense de son autonomie et la recomposition familiale', *Population* 6, pp 1569-96.

Mauri, G., Micheli, G. and Zajczyk, F. (1993) *Vita di famiglia. Social Survey in Veneto*, Milan: Franco Angeli.

Micheli, G. and Laffi, S. (1994) *Derive: percorsi di povertà non estreme da una survey sociale in Veneto*, Milano: Franco Angeli.

Middleton, S. and Mitchell (1994) 'Budgeting for survival: strategies and support', in S. Middleton, K. Ashworth and R. Walker (eds) *Family fortunes*, London: CPAG, pp 119-32.

Middleton, S., Ashworth, K. and Walker, R. (eds) (1994) *Family fortunes*, London: CPAG.

Miller, G. (1993) *The future of social security in Europe in the context of economic and monetary union*, report to the European Commission, Brussels: Observatoire Social Européen.

Mingione, E. (1991) *Fragmented societies. A sociology of economic life beyond the market paradigm*, Oxford: Basil Blackwell.

Mitton, R., Willmott, P. and Willmott, P. (1983) *Unemployment, poverty and social policy in Europe*, London: Bedford Square Press.

Morgan, C. (1994) *Family resources survey, Great Britain 1993/94,* London: Government Statistical Service.

Morlicchio, E. and Spanò, A. (1992) 'La povertà a Napoli', in *Inchiesta*, anno XXII, no 97-98, luglio-dicembre 1992.

Morphet, C. (1992) 'The interpretation of small area census data', *Area*, vol 24, no 1, pp 63-72.

Morris, L.D. (1993) 'Is there a British underclass?', *International Journal of Urban and Regional Research,* vol 17, no 3, pp 404-12.

Morris, L.D. and Irwin, S. (1992) 'Employment histories and the concept of the underclass', *Sociology*, vol 28, no 3, pp 401-21.

Moulaert, F. (1987) 'An institutional revisitation of the Storper-Walker theory of labor'. *International Journal of Urban and Regional Research*, vol 11, pp 309-30.

Moulaert, F. and Delvainquière, J.C. (1994) 'The role of cultural specificity in local development strategies', in L. Bekemans (ed), *Europe of the regions*, Brussels: European University Press.

Moulaert, F. and Leontidou, L. (1995) 'Localités désintégrées et stratégies de lutte contre la pauvreté: une réflexion méthodologique postmoderne', *Espaces et Sociétés*, vol 78, pp 35-53.

Moulaert, F. and Swyngedouw, E. (1992) 'Accumulation and Organization in C&C industries: a regulationist approach', in P. Cooke, F. Moulaert, E. Swyngedouw, O. Weinstein and P. Wells, *Towards global localisation: the computing and communication industries in Britain and France,* London: University College London Press.

Moulaert, F., Aller, R., Cooke, P., Courlet, C., Häusserman, H. and da Rosa Pires, A. (1990) 'Integrated area development and efficacy of local action', in G. Abou Sada and N. Yeates (eds), *Research perspectives,* Lille: Animation et Recherche (EEIG).

Moulaert, F. (1996) 'Rediscovering spatial inequality in Europe. Building blocks for an appropriate "regulationist" framework', *Society and Space,* forthcoming.

Moulaert, F., Leontidou, L. et al (1992) *Local development strategies in economically disintegrated areas: a proactive strategy against poverty in the European Community report 1,* European Commission, Brussels.

Moulaert, F., Leontidou, L. et al (1993) *Local development strategies in economically disintegrated areas: a proactive strategy against poverty in the European Community, report 2,* European Commission, Brussels.

Moulaert, F., Leontidou, L. et al (1994) *Local development strategies in economically disintegrated areas: a proactive strategy against poverty in the European Community, report 3,* European Commission, Brussels.

Muffels, R. (1993a) 'Deprivation standards of living indicators', in J. Berghman and B. Cantillon, *The European face of social security,* Aldershot: Avebury.

Muffels, R. (1993b) *Welfare economic effects of social security – essays on poverty, social security and labour market: evidence from panel data,* Social Security Series, Report 21, Tilburg: KUB.

Muffels, R., Berghman, J. and Dirven, H. (1992) 'A multi-method approach to monitor the evolution of poverty', *Journal of European Social Policy,* vol 2, pp. 193-213.

Negri, N. (1993) 'L'analisi della rete dei disagi', in P. Guidicini e G. Pieretti, *La residualità come valore,* Milano: Franco Angeli.

Nolan, B. and Whelan, C.T. (forthcoming) *Resources, deprivation and the measurement of poverty,* Oxford: Oxford University Press.

Nussbaum, M.C. and Sen, A. (1993) *The quality of life*, Oxford: Clarendon Press.

O'Higgins, M. and Jenkins, S. (1989) 'Poverty in Europe', paper read to the EUROSTAT Conference on Poverty Statistics, Nordwijk, the Netherlands, October 1989.

Paugam, S. (1991) *La disqualification sociale. Essai sur la nouvelle pauvreté*, Paris: Presses Universitaires de France, coll. 'sociologies' (3rd edn, 1994).

Paugam, S. (1993) *La société française et ses pauvres. L'expérience du revenu minimum d'insertion*, Paris: Presses Universitaires de France, coll. 'recherches politiques' (2nd edn, forthcoming 1995).

Paugam, S. (1995) 'L'habitat socialement disqualifié', in F. Ascher (ed), *Le Logement en questions*, Paris: Ed. de l'Auvbe.

Paugam, S., Prélis, A. and Zoyem, J-P. (1994) *Apprehension de la pauvreté sous l'angle de la disqualification sociale*, Paris: CERC, report for Eurostat/DGV of the European Commission.

Paugam, S., Zoyem, J-P. and Charbonnel, J-M. (1993) *Précarité et risque d'exclusion en France,* Paris: La Documentation Française, coll. 'Documents du CERC', no 109.

Peck, J. and Tickell, A. (1992) *Local modes of social regulation? Regulation theory, Thatcherism and uneven development,* Manchester: School of Geography, SPA Working Paper 14.

Piachaud, D. (1981) 'Peter Townsend and the Holy Grail', *New Society*, 10 September, pp 419-21.

Piachaud, D. (1987) 'Problems in the definition and measurement of poverty', *Journal of Social Policy*, vol 16, no 2, pp 147-64.

Pissarides, C. (1986) 'Unemployment and vacancies in Britain', *Economic Policy*, vol 3, pp 500-59.

Poverty 3 (1992) *The dynamics of the Programme at half-way stage*, Lille: Animation et Recherche (EEIG).

Poverty Summit (1992) *The Edinburgh Declaration*, Edinburgh University: Department of Social Policy and Social Work.

Rasch, G. (1960) *A mathematical theory of objectivity and its consequences for model construction*, Copenhagen: Nielsen and Lydiche.

Rhein, C. (1991) 'Ségrégation et mobilité différentielle', *Les annales de la Recherche Urbaine*, n° 50, pp 65-72, Paris.

Rigaux, N. (1994) *La Perception de la Pauvrete et de l'exclusion sociale en Europe*, unpublished manuscript.

Ringen, S. (1988) 'Direct and indirect measures of poverty', *Journal of Social Policy*, vol 17, part 3, pp 351-65.

Robbins, D. (1990) *Marginalisation and social exclusion*, report to the European Commission, Brussels.

Robbins, D. (1993) *Towards a Europe of solidarity: combatting social exclusion*, V/6171/93, Brussels: European Commission.

Robbins, D. et al (1994) *National policies to combat social exclusion* (Third Annual Report of the European Observatory on Policies to Combat Social Exclusion), Brussels: European Commission.

Room, G. et al (1990) *'New poverty' in the European Community*, London: Macmillan.

Room, G. et al (1991) *National policies to combat social exclusion* (First Annual Report of the EC Observatory on Policies to Combat Social Exclusion), Brussels: European Commission.

Room, G. et al (1992) *National policies to combat social exclusion* (Second Annual Report of the EC Observatory on Policies to Combat Social Exclusion), Brussels: European Commission.

Room, G. et al (1993) *Anti-poverty action-research in Europe*, Bristol: SAUS Publications.

Room, G. (1995) 'Poverty in Europe: competing paradigms of analysis', *Policy and Politics*, vol 23, no 2, pp 103-13.

Rowntree, B.S. (1901) *Poverty: a study of town life*, London: Macmillan.

Runciman, W.G. (1990) 'How many classes are there in contemporary British society?', *Sociology*, vol 24, no 3, pp 377-96.

Salonen, T. (1993) *Margins of welfare*, Torna: Hällestad Press.

Sarpellon, G. (1992) *Secondo Rapporto sulla Povertà in Italia*, Milan: Franco Angeli.

Schnapper, D. (1981) L'*épreuve du chômage*, Paris: Gallimard (new edn, 1994).

Schwartz, O. (1990) *Le monde privé des ouvriers. Hommes et femmes du Nord,* Paris: Presses Universitaires de France, coll. 'pratiques théoriques'.

Schwarz, U. (1995) *Sozialhilfeverwaltung und Klientel – Zur Relevanz von Zeit- und Handlungsdimensionen in der Sozialhilfepraxis. Ergebnisse einer empirischen Analyse anhand von Experteninterviews,* Bremen: Sonderforschungsbereich 186 (unpublished).

Sen, A. (1982) 'Choice', *Welfare and Measurement,* Oxford: Blackwell.

Sen, A. (1993) *Il tenore di vita,* Venice: Marsilio.

Sen, A. (1992) *Inequality re-examined,* Oxford: Clarendon Press.

Sgritta, G.B. and Innocenzi, G.F. (1993) 'La povertà', in M. Paci, *Le dimensioni della disuguaglianza,* Bologna: Il Mulino.

Shaw, A. et al (1995) *Moving off income support? Obstacles, opportunities, choices,* Loughborough: Centre for Research in Social Policy, Working Paper 246.

Silver, H. (1994) 'Social exclusion and social solidarity: three paradigms', *International Labour Review,* vol 133, no 5-6, pp 531-78.

Smith, D.J. (1992) 'Defending the underclass', in D.J. Smith (ed), *Understanding the underclass,* London: Policy Studies Institute.

Storper, M. and Walker, R. (1983) 'A theory of labor and location', *International Journal of Urban and Regional Research,* vol 7, pp 1-43.

Suarez-Villa, L. and Roura, J.R.C. (1992) 'Regional economic integration and the evolution of disparities', *Papers in Regional Science,* 72(4), pp 369-87.

Tabard, N. (1993a) *Représentation socio-économique du territoire,* Paris: INSEE, document de travail n°F/9304.

Tabard, N. (1993b) *Quartiers pauvres, quartiers riches, position dans la hiérarchie spatiale,* Paris: INSEE, document de travail n°F/9311-2.

Tabard, N. (1993c) 'Des quartiers pauvres aux banlieues aisées: une représentation sociale du territoire', *Economie et Statistique,* n° 270, pp 5-22, Paris: INSEE.

Teekens, R. and Zaidi, A. (1989) 'Poverty estimates based on Expenditure Data', paper read to the EUROSTAT

Conference on Poverty Statistics, Nordwijk, The Netherlands, October 1989.

Townsend, P. (1979) *Poverty in the United Kingdom*, Harmondsworth: Penguin.

Townsend, P. (1987) 'Deprivation', *Journal of Social Policy*, vol 16, part 2, pp 125-46.

Townsend, P. (1993) *The international analysis of poverty*, London: Harvester Wheatsheaf.

Tricart, J-P. (1994) Contribution to the seminar on the 'Measurement and analysis of social exclusion', Centre for Research in European Social and Employment Policy, University of Bath, 17-18 June 1994.

Van Praag, B.M.S. (1984) 'A comparison of objective and subjective measures of poverty', in G. Sarpellon (ed), *Understanding poverty*, Milan: Franco Angeli.

Veit Wilson, J. (1994) *Dignity not poverty – A minimum income standard for the UK*, London: Institute for Public Policy Research.

Vinot, F. (1993) 'Informations infra-communales en Rhône-Alpes, le cas des CAF', *Courrier des statistiques*, n° 67-68, pp 41-44, Paris: INSEE.

Visvalingham, M. (1993) *Area-based social indicators: signed chi-square as an alternative to ratios*, Social Indicators Research, vol 13, pp 311-29.

Voges, W. and Leibfried, S. (1990) 'Keine Sonne fûr die Armut. Vom Sozialhilfebezug als Verlauf ("Karriere") – Ohne umfassendere Information keine wirksame Armutsbekämpfung', in: *Nachrichtendienst des Deutschen Vereins für öffentliche und private Fürsorge*, vol 70, no 5, pp 135-41.

Von Rosenbladt, B. (1990) *European Community Household Panel – feasibility study*, Munich: Infratest.

Vranken, J., Geldof, D. and Van Menxel, G. (1994) *Armoede en Sociale Uitsluiting – Jaarboek 1994* (Poverty and Social Exclusion – Yearbook 1994), Leuven: Acco.

Walker, R. et al (1995) 'Managing to eat on a low income', *Nutrition and Food Science*, no 3, May/June, pp 5-10.

Walker, R. (1991) *Poverty and poverty dynamics*, Loughborough: Centre for Research in Social Policy, Working Paper 135.

Walker, R. (1994) *Poverty dynamics: issues and examples*, Aldershot: Avebury.

Walker, R. et al (1994) 'Pretty, pretty please – just like a parrot', in S. Middleton, K. Ashworth and R. Walker (eds), *Family fortunes*, London: CPAG, pp 88-104.

Walker, R., Shaw, A. and Hull, L. (1995) 'Responding to the risk of unemployment', in *Risk, Insurance and Welfare*, London: Association of British Insurers, pp 37-52.

Webb, S. (1995) *Poverty dynamics in Great Britain*, London: Institute of Fiscal Studies.

Wenzel, G. and Leibfried, S. (1986) *Armut und Sozialhilferecht. Eine sozialwissenschaftlich orientierte Einführung für die Sozialhilfepraxis*, Weinheim und Basel: Beltz.

Whelan C.T. (1996) 'Marginalisation, deprivation and fatalism in the Republic of Ireland: class and underclass perspectives', *European Sociological Review*, 12:1.

Whelan, B. (1993) 'Non-monetary indicators of poverty', in J. Berghman and B. Cantillon, *The European face of social security*, Aldershot: Avebury.

Whelan, C.T. (1992) 'The role of income, life-style deprivation and financial strain in mediating the impact of unemployment on psychological distress: evidence from the Republic of Ireland', *Journal of Occupational and Organizational Psychology*, vol 65, pp 331-44.

Whelan, C.T. (1994) 'Social class, unemployment and psychological distress', *European Sociological Review,* vol 10, no 1, pp 49-61.

Whelan, C.T., Hannan, D.F. and Creighton, S. (1991) *Unemployment, poverty and psychological distress*, Dublin: ESRI (General Research Series Paper No 150).

Whelan, C.T., Breen, R. and Whelan, B.J. (1992) 'Industrialisation, class formation and social mobility in Ireland', in J.H. Goldthorpe and C.T. Whelan (eds), *The development of industrial society*, Oxford: Oxford University Press.

Wilkinson, R.G. (ed) (1986) *Class and health: research and longitudinal data*, Tavistock, London.

Yepez del Castillo, I. (1994) 'A comparative approach to social exclusion: lessons from France and Belgium', *International Labour Review*, vol 133, no 5-6, pp 613-34.

INDEX